International Centre for
Financial Regulation

Making Good Financial Regulation

Towards a Policy Response to Regulatory Capture

Edited by Stefano Pagliari

Grosvenor House
Publishing Limited

This book is published by
Grosvenor House Publishing Ltd
28-30 High Street, Guildford, Surrey, GU1 3EL.
www.grosvenorhousepublishing.co.uk

A CIP record for this book
is available from the British Library

ISBN 978-1-78148-548-4

About the International Centre for Financial Regulation

The International Centre for Financial Regulation is the only independent, non-partisan organisation to be exclusively focused on best practice in all aspects of financial regulation internationally. The ICFR believes in the promotion of efficient, orderly and fair markets which offer appropriate protection for investors and retail consumers alike. Financial centres of the future should be based upon sound principles of regulation, with supervisors, regulators and participants who act in the interest of all stakeholders.

The world's financial markets have never been under greater scrutiny. Individual governments are understandably focused on their own domestic priorities, but effective and sustainable regulation needs to be global. The role of the ICFR is to encourage dialogue that identifies best practice across the traditional financial centres in the US, Europe and Asia and embraces emerging and developing economies worldwide.

The ICFR is in the unique position of being able to bring together senior representatives of both the private and official sectors in an environment where open and valuable debate on the essential issues of financial regulation can take place. Whilst it is not a lobby organisation the ICFR is focused on promoting regulation that is proportionate to the risks involved and intends that its work will influence policy and practice across the global financial system.

Since its launch in 2009 the ICFR has, through the consistent quality of its work, developed a brand recognised globally. The ICFR delivers its work through research, events and training and additionally offers insights into current thinking on regulation through both its Website – icffr.org and the ICFR – Intuition Regulatory Portal.

Table of Contents

Foreword
Regulators, Financial Industry and the Problem of Regulatory Capture

Robert Jenkins[1]

Driven by hubris, greed and stupidity bankers led the charge off the cliff. But where were the regulators? Why did they not see it coming? Why did they not prevent it? Why did they trust bankers to know what was best for banking? In short, how could regulators have been so dumb as to believe that bankers were so smart? This publication supplies answers to these questions. It explores the ways in which regulators can sometimes be captivated, co-opted and conned by those they regulate. Best of all, it suggests a number of actionable policies to mitigate the problem.

Industry influence operates at all levels of the rule making ranks – from the peak of politics to the substrata of supervision. It need not be unhealthy. Indeed, interaction between regulators and the regulated is natural and normal. Yes, industry seeks to shape the rules under which it will operate. But rule-makers need industry input in order to craft sensible policy. Some degree of influence is therefore inevitable. Unfortunately, there are times and industries where special interest groups are able to bring disproportionate influence to bear – a condition called "regulatory capture." The financial sector is one such industry and the run-up to the crisis one such time. The obvious question which arises: is such influence still excessive and thus unduly shaping the needed regulatory response?

---

[1] Robert Jenkins is a practitioner, regulator and academic. He is an external member of the Financial Policy Committee of the Bank of England and Adjunct Professor, Finance at London Business School. Prior to his appointment to the BoE, Mr. Jenkins spent 16 years running bank trading rooms followed by 18 years managing investment management businesses. From 2007 to 2009 he Chaired the Investment Management Association, UK.

My first encounter with "capture" came at a moment of meltdown in 2008. At the time I chaired both a London-based investment firm and the trade association representing the UK investment industry. As financial panic spread I watched in disbelief as bankers trooped through the doors of Downing Street to advise Government on how best to address a problem which bankers themselves had largely created. Far from being discredited, the guidance of these "experts" was eagerly sought – and with virtually no counterbalancing input from other stakeholders groups. Over the succeeding months officials went on to tap a more appropriate range of expertise. But at that key moment in time - capture was complete.

"Political capture" can be fueled by campaign contributions but in the case above, it resulted from the pervasive beliefs of the day. The theology of the time maintained that: markets were efficient and would provide the necessary discipline to participants; the financial sector could be left largely to police itself; global banking and their host centers were engaged in fierce global competition; regulation should facilitate that competition and not get in its way; and therefore, when it came to regulation, less was more. This set of beliefs permeated the body politic, shaped the regulatory approach of "light touch" and, believe it or not, established a mindset amongst some supervisors that the regulated banks were to be seen as "clients." The technical term here is "cognitive or intellectual" capture. The non-technical term is brainwashed

Four years on, one might imagine that bankers' ability to bewitch and bamboozle would have ebbed. Alas not. Their formidable lobby has led and continues to lead an effective campaign to persuade pundits, public and politicians that calls for higher capital requirements are impeding the economic recovery. It is an argument framed so as to force the gullible and well intentioned to choose between public safety and economic growth. It is a false argument and a false choice. It ignores the facts - not the least of which is an entire half century of post-war expansion during which bankers operated profitably at lower levels of leverage. That such myths find favour with otherwise intelligent commentators shows that intellectual capture is alive and well. Other stakeholders in financial stability - such as the investment industry, should speak up to help counter the sway of the spurious but seductive. Indeed, a proposal to mobilize better the competing interests in the regulatory debate is one of the author's principal recommendations.

This publication is not a polemic. It did not begin with a particular point of view followed by a search for supporting facts. Its conclusions flow from a dispassionate review of the question. The objective of the author, as indeed that of its sponsoring publisher, is the making of better regulation. What therefore, could be more timely than an analysis of a key impediment to effective rule making and supervision?

The work contains a series of thoughtful reflections on the topic of capture in the regulation of the financial sector. It examines the issue through the eyes of both the regulator and regulated. It taps perspectives of both the practitioner and the academic. And it takes a useful look at other highly regulated but non-financial industries in a quest for relevant lessons and solutions. Finally, the publication proposes a series of specific policy responses designed to combat the worst aspects of capture. The recommendations in this volume are presented as actionable "low hanging fruit" – which they are, provided excessive industry influence does not prevent their adoption.

About the Authors

Lawrence Baxter is Professor of Practice of Law at Duke Law School

Clive Briault is a Senior Adviser on regulation at KPMG in London, and former Senior Regulator at the Financial Services Authority and Bank of England

Daniel Carpenter is the Allie S. Freed Professor of Government and Director of the Center for American Political Studies in the Faculty of Arts and Sciences at Harvard University

Gerry Cross is Managing Director for Advocacy at the Association for Financial Markets in Europe

David Currie is Chairman of the International Centre for Financial Regulation and former Chairman of Ofcom

Jane Diplock is a member of the Public Interest Oversight Board and former Chairman of the Executive Committee of the International Organisation of Securities Commissions

Christine Farnish is the Chair of Consumer Focus, and former Director of Consumer Affairs at the Financial Services Authority

David Green is a former Senior Regulator at the Bank of England and the Financial Services Authority, and Risk Advisor at the Central Bank of Ireland

John Mogg is Chairman of the Gas and Electricity Markets Authority and former Director General of the Internal Market and Financial Services at the European Commission

David Moss is the John G. McLean Professor of Business Administration at Harvard Business School and founder of The Tobin Project

Tony Porter is Professor in the Department of Political Science at McMaster University

Richard Raeburn is Chairman of the European Association of Corporate Treasurers

Adam Ridley is Chairman of Equitas Trust and former Director General of the London Investment Banking Association

Stefano Pagliari is a PhD Candidate at the University of Waterloo and a Research Associate at the International Centre for Financial Regulation

Andrew Sheng is Chief Adviser to the China Banking Regulatory Commission and former Chairman of the Hong Kong Securities and Futures Commission

David Strachan is Co-Head of the Deloitte Centre for Regulatory Strategy and former senior regulator at the Bank of England and the Financial Services Authority

Melanie Wachtell Stinnett is Director of Policy and Communications at The Tobin Project

Andrew Walter is Reader in International Political Economy at the London School of Economics and Political Science

Kevin Young is Assistant Professor in the Department of Political Science at the University of Massachusetts Amherst

1.0 How Can We Mitigate Capture in Financial Regulation?

Stefano Pagliari[1]

1.1 Introduction

The interaction between policymakers and market participants in the regulation of financial markets is marked by a paradox. In a dynamic and technically complex environment such as that of financial markets, regulatory authorities are required to develop a constant and close interaction with the market participants they regulate in order to stay abreast of rapidly changing financial markets, to monitor the build-up of risks, and to understand the impact of their regulatory policies. However, the same proximity between regulators and market participants that is required for regulators to effectively perform their responsibilities has also been described as opening the regulatory process to the risk of unduly favouring narrow industry interests at the expense of the public. This distortion in the regulatory process is commonly defined as "regulatory capture".

The problem of regulatory capture in financial regulation has attracted renewed attention in the aftermath of the global financial crisis. Different academic works, journalistic accounts, as well as official inquiries have all emphasized the impact which the undue influence of special interests has played in causing a relaxation of regulatory

[1] Stefano Pagliari is a PhD Candidate at the University of Waterloo and a Research Associate at the International Centre for Financial Regulation. His work focuses on the political economy of the regulatory response to the global financial crisis. His published work appears in International Organization, the Journal of European Integration, and the Journal of European Law and he is the Co-Editor (with Eric Helleiner and Hubert Zimmerman) of 'Global Finance in Crisis: The Politics of International Regulatory Change' (Routledge, 2009).

constraints in the period preceding the crisis.[2] The Governor of the Bank of England, Mervyn King, has branded regulatory capture as 'one of the major problems leading up to the crisis'.[3]

However, despite references to regulatory capture having permeated much of the discourse on financial regulation, and in spite of a significant body of academic studies and commentaries dissecting the regulatory process in finance and the relationship between policymakers and the financial industry, only a minority of these works has ventured into a systematic discussion of policy solutions to mitigate capture in financial regulation. As Carpenter and Moss have argued in an important recent contribution to the subject, 'all too often, observers of regulation are quicker to yelp about capture than to think hard about how it might be prevented or mitigated. Analyses stop at diagnosis without venturing to the matter of cure.'[4] This tendency also applies to the same regulators and regulated institutions that have been the targets of criticism. These have been reluctant to publicly discuss any deficiencies or conflicts which may emerge from their interaction, or indeed any measures which could strengthen the integrity of the policymaking process in finance. As a result, a debate regarding how to structure the interaction between the financial industry and regulatory agencies has struggled to emerge in the public policy sphere, and that of capture has remained a subject that 'generates more heat than light'.[5]

This publication aims to make a contribution towards addressing this gap in the academic literature and public policy debate by identifying a set of realistic policy measures which seek to mitigate the risk that the process through which financial rules are designed and

---

[2] See for instance FCIC (2011). The Financial Crisis Inquiry Report. *Final Report of the National Commission on the Causes of the Financial and Economic Crisis in the United States*. Washington, DC, The Financial Crisis Inquiry Commission; Johnson and Kwak (2010). *13 Bankers*. New York, Pantheon Books.

[3] Cited by Masters (2011). 'King calls for discretionary powers'. *Financial Times*. London. 3 November.

[4] Carpenter and Moss (forthcoming). Draft chapter of 'Introduction'. In: *Preventing Regulatory Capture: Special Interest Influence, and How to Limit It*, by Carpenter and Moss (forthcoming), Cambridge, Cambridge University Press, p.5.

[5] Strachan (this volume).

implemented may be captured by special interests. In order to achieve this objective, this publication departs from the existing analysis of regulatory capture in finance in two important ways. First, it draws on a variety of perspectives, combining the contribution of academics with the experience of regulators and former regulators, financial industry practitioners, as well as other stakeholders such as consumer groups and non-financial end users. Second, rather than looking at finance in isolation, this publication includes perspective from different academics and policymakers whose primary experience and research extends to sectors outside of the financial realm, such as regulation of the telecommunication industry, energy markets, and the automobile industry. Concerns regarding the undue influence of special interests are not unique to financial policymaking, and a closer look at the experience of these sectors outside of finance offers important insights into possible policy responses to the problem of capture in the financial regulatory arena.

This introductory chapter will summarize the main findings of the different contributions. The first part of this chapter will discuss four aspects of the policymaking process that have been identified by different authors as conducive to diverting the content of regulatory policies away from public interest and towards favouring special interests: 1) the asymmetrical participation of the financial industry and other stakeholders in the formulation of regulatory policies; 2) the institutional context within which financial regulatory policies are designed and implemented; 3) the ideas, beliefs and mind-sets guiding the work of regulators; and 4) the broader political context in which the financial regulatory process takes place.

The acknowledgement of multiple channels and mechanisms that may lead regulation to unduly favour narrow interests has led different commentators in the past to discount the possibility of effectively countering this phenomenon. Contrary to this perspective, this publication argues that the risk that regulatory policies will divert from the public interest to favour special interests can be mitigated through different strategies to balance the impact of factors driving regulatory capture. The wide range of mitigating strategies discussed by the different contributors to this publication and the broader literature will be divided into three broad agendas, based on the respective points of intervention in the regulatory policymaking process.

A first set of proposals focuses on the engagement of different stakeholders in the regulatory process and seeks to mitigate capture by promoting greater balance and diversity among the groups competing to influence the content of regulatory policies. Some of the different solutions discussed to achieve this objective include the creation of participatory mechanisms that favour the engagement of a broader range of groups, measures to strengthen the position of consumer groups and other groups with a diffuse membership in the policymaking process, and approaches to foster the emergence of countervailing forces against the risk of capture within the financial industry.

A second set of proposals focuses on the institutional context within which regulatory policies are designed and implemented and seeks to mitigate the risk of capture by reforming those elements that may bias the action of regulators in favour of certain stakeholders. These measures include reforms to the mandates of regulatory agencies, changes in internal decision making procedures, reforms in staffing and recruitment practices, as well as changes in the level and sources of funding.

Finally, a third set of proposals seeks to mitigate the risk of capture by subjecting the regulatory process to greater external scrutiny. These recommendations include measures to increase the transparency of the regulatory process, increasing the legal system's scrutiny of the regulatory process, the creation of expert review bodies to monitor the integrity of the regulatory process, and measures which seek to strengthen reciprocal oversight against the risk of capture from other regulatory agencies within the same country and at the international level.

1.2 What is regulatory capture?

The concept of regulatory capture is often traced back to the work of Nobel Laureate George Stigler four decades before the outbreak of the crisis. Stigler argued that concentrated producer groups are able to systematically exercise a disproportionate influence over the conduct of their regulators to the point of shaping regulation to suit their interests rather than their mandate to maximize social welfare.[6] Since Stigler's pioneering work, an important scholarly tradition known as the "special interest" theory of regulation has analysed the dynamics which may lead regulatory agencies to unduly favour the industry they had responsibility for regulating and thus to deviate from the public interest.[7]

While the analysis of regulatory capture has developed primarily to shed light on distortions in the regulation of other industries outside of finance, this 'theory of private distortion of public purpose'[8] has become a privileged lens through which to interpret financial regulatory policymaking. Most attempts to theorize and analyse the process of capture in financial regulation have emerged from the US experience.[9] However, references to the undue influence of special interests have also informed different analyses of financial policymaking in other industrialized countries,[10] at the European level,[11] in emerging market countries,[12] as well as within international bodies such as the Basel Committee and the International Organization of Securities Commissions, where the influence of financial industry groups over the international regulatory initiatives has led different authors to develop the concept of "transnational

---

[6] Stigler (1971). 'The Theory of Economic Regulation.' *Bell Journal of Economics and Management Science*, 2: 3-21.

[7] See Peltzman (1976). 'Towards a More General Theory of Regulation.' *Journal of Law and Economics*, 19: 211-48; Laffont and Tirole (1991). 'The politics of government decision making. A theory of regulatory capture.' *Quarterly Journal of Economics*, 106: 4. For a review of the literature see Dal Bó (2006). 'Regulatory Capture: A Review.' *Oxford Review of Economic Policy*, 22(2): 203-25.

[8] Baxter (this volume).

[9] Johnson and Kwak (2010), *op. cit. in footnote 1.*

[10] See Ridley (this volume) for the UK experience

[11] Mügge (2010). *Widen the Market, Narrow the Competition.* Colchester, ECPR Press.

[12] Walter (2008). *Governing Finance: East Asia's Adoption of International Standards.* Ithaca, Cornell University Press

regulatory capture".[13] Indeed, the fact that the analysis of regulatory capture has developed primarily from the US experience has often meant analysts have overlooked how the nature and the extent of regulatory capture may vary considerably across these contexts.

The concept of regulatory capture has also been associated with different phases of the financial regulatory policymaking process. Most attention has been paid to the rulemaking phase. In this area, undue influence of the regulated sector is most commonly associated either with the absence of regulatory measures that would impose costs on the regulated entity or with the introduction of rules that fail to adequately defend broader societal preferences. However, regulatory capture could also manifest itself in the development of more stringent regulations that allow market leaders to eliminate present and future competition.[14] Furthermore, the concept of capture has also been used as an analytical lens to explain failures in other phases of the regulatory policymaking process in finance, such as in the supervision of financial firms,[15] or in the enforcement[16] and implementation phases of financial regulation[17]. In these phases, pressures from the regulated institutions have been presented as conducive to a lack of tough enforcement and investigation, or conducive to episodes of regulatory forbearance where regulation is not fully enforced. As Walter suggests in this volume, the more 'opaque, extended, and complex' nature of the implementation phase provides a more fertile terrain for the influence of organized interests

---

[13] Underhill and Zhang (2008). 'Setting the rules: private power, political underpinnings, and legitimacy in global monetary and financial governance.' *International Affairs* 84(3): 535-54; Lall (2011). 'From failure to failure: The politics of international banking regulation.' *Review of International Political Economy*; for a critique see Young (2012). 'Transnational regulatory capture? An empirical examination of the transnational lobbying of the Basel Committee on Banking Supervision.' *Review of International Political Economy*.

[14] Mattli and Woods (2009). 'In Whose Benefit? Explaining Regulatory Change in Global Politics.' In: *The Politics of Global Regulation*, by Mattli and Woods, eds (2009), Princeton, NJ, Princeton University Press.

[15] Baxter (2011). 'Capture in Financial Regulation: Can We Channel It Toward the Common Good?' *Cornell Journal of Law and Public Policy* 21(1): 175-200, p. 187.

[16] Sheng (this volume).

[17] Walter (2008), *op. cit. in footnote* 11.

than does the rulemaking process, since a trade-off may exist between the intensity of the pressures exercised by these interests during the rulemaking and implementation phases.[18]

The popularity of regulatory capture as one of the main analytical lenses through which to explore failures in financial regulatory policymaking also reflects some of the limitations of this concept, starting from its ambiguity. Different works have frequently refrained from seeking to define regulatory capture or provided very different definitions of this phenomenon. A more analytically precise definition of regulatory capture comes from Carpenter and Moss, who have described this concept as 'the result or process by which regulation (in law or application) is, at least partially, by intent and action of the industry regulated, consistently or repeatedly directed away from the public interest and towards the interests of the regulated industry'.[19] However, the application of this definition to the financial policy realm relies on the capacity to clearly define where the "public interest" resides in a given regulatory issue and to identify when a policy shift away from this solution is the result of the action of special interests with clearly delineated and divergent interests. The uncertainty surrounding the impact of financial regulatory policies and the presence of at times competing objectives, such as ensuring stability and a stable flow of credit to the economy, make the task of identifying the public interest ex-ante often challenging. The definition of capture presented by Baxter bypasses the problem of identifying what is in the public interest, since he argues that regulatory capture is present 'whenever a particular sector to the regulatory regime has acquired influence disproportionate to the balance of interests envisaged when the regulatory system was established'.[20]

A second limitation of the concept derives from the fact that, as Baxter argues, regulatory capture is 'at once a theory of legislative and regulatory motivation and a vituperative accusation levelled at results

---

[18] Walter (this volume).

[19] Carpenter and Moss (forthcoming), *op. cit. in footnote* 3; Carpenter, Moss, Wachtell Stinnett (this volume).

[20] Baxter (2011), p. 176, *op. cit. in footnote* 14.

unfavourable to one of the contesting groups'.[21] As a result, this allegation is likely to be raised even if the regulation strikes the right balance among competing interests. However, claims regarding the extent of this phenomenon are frequently supported by only weak empirical evidence. Carpenter and Moss argue that analysts have often inferred capture from episodes in which regulators partially rely upon firms, from patterns of regulatory advantage granted to certain groups, or simply 'on the basis of observations of undesired regulatory outcomes, even though those outcomes might be caused by a number of things besides capture such as 'regulators' incompetence, inefficiency, or randomness'.[22]

Given the difficulties in defining and assessing capture, it comes as no surprise that disagreements persist among different commentators regarding the extent of this phenomenon, including among the contributors to this volume. For some authors, undue influence exercised by financial industry groups remains a structural distortion in the regulatory process in finance, which limits the possibility of achieving effective policies.[23] In their review of the broader literature, Carpenter and Moss find little support among empirical researchers for this kind of extensive influence by special interests leading to regulation detrimental to the broader public. Instead, they argue that capture seems to manifest itself in degrees, in some cases having no discernible effects on regulation, and more commonly limiting a regulator's efforts to serve the public interest, but not to the point of compromising the regulatory policy.[24] For others, capture remains more an issue of "perception" than reality, which could still undermine the confidence in the rulemaking process if left unchecked.[25] Furthermore, various authors in this publication argue that undue or inappropriate influence over the financial regulatory process could

---

[21] Baxter (this volume).

[22] Carpenter and Moss (forthcoming) op. cit. in footnote 3. See also Carpenter (2004). 'Protection without Capture: Product Approval by a politically Responsive, Learning Regulator.' *American Political Science Review* 98(4); Baxter (2011), *op. cit. in footnote* 14; Young (2012), op. cit. in footnote 12.

[23] Johnson and Kwak (2010), *op. cit. in footnote* 1.

[24] Carpenter, Moss, and Wachtell Stinnett (this volume).

[25] Strachan (this volume).

come from a plurality of stakeholders besides the largest financial services firms or the financial sector targeted by the regulation in question. From this perspective, capture by the industry which is directly targeted by the regulation is only a subset of different captures, and a multitude of participants within or outside finance are capable of exercising 'an influence that knocks the regulator off its original balance', which may include large consumers,[26] NGOs,[27] or politicians following their own electoral considerations.[28]

However, the most important source of disagreement among the different scholars and commentators in this publication concerns the mechanisms through which regulatory policies come to diverge from the public interest towards unduly favouring narrow interests. Building upon the taxonomy introduced by Baker,[29] it is possible to identify four aspects of the financial policymaking process that make financial regulatory policymaking particularly prone to be captured.

1.2.1 The asymmetrical nature of stakeholders' participation in the regulatory process

The first element identified by the literature as influencing capture is to be found in the asymmetric participation of different stakeholders in the financial regulatory process. The central premise underlying theories of regulatory capture is the notion that the actions of regulators are significantly influenced by the mobilization of different organized interests and stakeholders deploying an array of financial

---

[26] Mogg (this volume) argues that in the world of gas and electricity, the risk of undue influence on the regulatory process comes not only from the producers such as power generators and suppliers, but also from the same group that regulators are duty-bound to protect, that is, consumers, in particular large corporate consumers.

[27] The US Environmental Protection Agency (EPA) has sometimes been criticized for being captured by environmental groups rather than the industries it regulates. See Kwak (forthcoming). 'Cultural Capture and the Financial Crisis.' In: *Preventing Regulatory Capture: Special Interest Influence, and How to Limit It*, by Carpenter and Moss (forthcoming). Cambridge, Cambridge University Press.

[28] See Mogg, Briault, Ridley, Green, and Strachan (this volume).

[29] This taxonomy draws upon Baker (2010). 'Restraining regulatory capture? Anglo-America, crisis politics and trajectories of change in global financial governance.' *International Affairs*, 86(3): 647-663

and technical resources in the attempt to influence the content of regulatory policies. However, different commentators have argued that in financial regulatory policymaking this competition among stakeholders, to influence the content of financial regulatory policies, is characterized by a concentration of resources in the hands of a restricted range of financial firms.

Much attention has been directed towards the financial resources that these groups are capable of harnessing in the policymaking process.[30] This is particularly the case in the US context: in the period from 1999 to 2008 the financial sector spent US $2.7 billion in reported federal lobbying expenses,[31] and during the financial crisis the same sector incurred daily expenses of US $1.4 million to lobby Congress.[32] However, the greater imbalance among stakeholders is not in terms of financial resources, but rather in terms of technical information, which Mogg describes as the 'fuel' that regulators require to regulate complex policy environments.[33] Theorists of regulatory capture have highlighted how "capture" is more likely when regulation is highly complex, and when information asymmetries between the regulated industry and the regulators are greater. The complexity inherent in financial regulatory policies and the built-in advantage that the financial firms targeted by specific regulation have in terms of knowledge and information vis-à-vis other stakeholders are factors that increase the dependence on industry for expertise.

Moreover, many analysts have lamented the lack of engagement with financial regulatory debates from stakeholders such as deposit holders, investors, and consumers of financial services. Besides being disadvantaged vis-à-vis financial industry groups in terms of financial resources and technical expertise, these groups' voices remain hindered by their diffuse nature and the resulting 'collective action

---

[30] Igan, Mishra and Tressel (2009). A Fistful of Dollars: Lobbying and the Financial Crisis. IMF Working Paper, WP/09/287. Washington, DC; Johnson (2009). "The Quiet Coup." *The Atlantic*, May 2009.

[31] FCIC (2011), p. xviii, *op. cit. in footnote 1*.

[32] Americans for Financial Reform (2010). *Wall Street Influence, By the Numbers*.

[33] Mogg (this volume).

problems'.[34] While the financial groups who are the primary target of regulation will have strong incentives to constantly monitor and seek to steer the action of regulators, other stakeholders face greater challenges in coordinating and in mobilizing the organizational and informational resources required to compete with the financial industry groups in the marketplace for influencing regulation.[35] Indeed, the survey of respondents to financial consultations conducted by Pagliari and Young finds that less than 10% of the stakeholders who respond to financial regulatory consultations belong to trade unions, consumer protection groups, non-governmental organizations, or research institutions.[36]

However, the tendency to aggregate figures regarding the participation of different financial interest groups and the money spent by these groups to lobby policymakers often masks the fact that the interests and demands of different financial groups frequently diverge and in some cases counteract each other. In addition, the presence of "consumers" of financial regulatory services in financial regulatory debates is more diverse than most regulatory capture theorists assume. For instance, Mogg suggests that, in the case of energy, regulation is important to differentiate between the millions of households who pay the bills but do not engage in regulatory debates over the energy markets and the large corporate energy consumers who are instead better positioned to solve collective action problems, engage with regulators and resist decisions going against their interests.[37] This insight also applies to the case of financial regulation. Pagliari and Young argue that while NGOs and consumer organizations are proportionally less active in response to financial regulatory policies than in other sectors, non-financial

---

[34] Olson (1965). *The Logic of Collective Action: Public Goods and the Theory of Groups*. Harvard University Press

[35] Stigler (1971), *op. cit. in footnote* 5; Wilson (1980). *The Politics of Regulation*. Wilson. New York, Basic Books; and Mattli and Woods (2009), *op. cit. in footnote* 13. See Farnish (this volume) for the experience of consumers groups.

[36] Pagliari and Young (this volume). See also Pagliari and Young (2012). 'Leveraged Interests: Financial Industry Power and the Role of Private Sector Coalitions'. Available at www.stefanopagliari.net

[37] Mogg (this volume).

business groups that represent the large end users of financial services are instead active participants and their impact over the design of regulatory policies has indeed increased in the aftermath of the crisis.[38] In other words, debates surrounding financial regulatory policies do not always present the sort of frontal and asymmetrical clash between competing producers' and consumers' interests described by some regulatory capture theorists, but rather they often involve a greater plurality of stakeholders and heterogeneous coalitions comprising both financial and non-financial stakeholders.

1.2.2 The institutional context

A second factor identified by the literature as influencing the possibility that regulatory policies will be captured is the institutional context within which the societal participation discussed above is channelled. Unlike other areas analysed by theories of regulatory capture, financial regulatory policies are seldom designed and implemented by politicians themselves. Instead, this task is delegated in normal times to independent regulatory agencies that are not part of the executive branch of government.[39] While the delegation of regulatory functions to independent agencies has been an attempt to protect the regulatory process from short-term pressures of politically influential stakeholders, the institutional design of independent regulatory agencies may still tilt the playing field in favour of certain stakeholders.

Despite the statutory autonomy of independent regulatory agencies, financial industry groups continue to maintain preferential access

---

[38] Pagliari and Young (this volume); see also Raeburn (this volume) on the experience of corporate end users in the regulatory response to the crisis.

[39] Masciandaro, Quintyn and Taylor (2008). Financial Supervisory Independence and Accountability – Exploring the Determinants. IMF Working Paper, WP/08/147. Washington, DC, International Monetary Fund.. For a theory of capture accounting for the delegation of regulatory power, see Spiller (1990). 'Politicians, Interest Groups, and Regulators: A Multiple-Principals Agency Theory of Regulation, or "Let Them be Bribed".' *Journal of Law & Economics*, 33(1): 65-101.

to regulators and to interact with them in an often opaque and discretionary environment, with many discussions occurring behind closed doors. Other institutional features of environments in which this interaction takes place may lead regulators to unduly favour the financial industry groups under their surveillance.

One of these is the formal mandate of regulatory agencies. In some cases, regulatory agencies have often been granted an explicit mandate to promote the interests of certain groups over others.[40] For instance, certain regulatory agencies such as the US Office of the Comptroller of the Currency are statutorily directed to promote the interests of the banks under their oversight.[41] Similarly, the mandate of the UK Financial Services Authority (FSA) includes a clause to "have regard to" the competitiveness of the financial services industry, an element which has been described as skewing the incentives of regulators, and increasing the risk they will prioritize the role of the City of London over other statutory duties.[42]

Others incentives to favour financial industry groups may be embedded in the governance of regulatory agencies. In particular, different regulatory agencies rely on levies applied to the financial industry as the primary source of funding. In some cases, financial industry representatives have a direct representation on the boards of regulatory agencies and thus potentially influence key decisions and the selection of executives.[43] In particular, the governance of the Federal Reserve System has come under the spotlight in recent years, since executives of banks that are regulated by the Fed and that have

---

[40] Hardy (2006). 'Regulatory Capture in Banking.' IMF Working Paper, WP/06/34, January 2006.

[41] Baxter (this volume).

[42] Warwick Commission on International Financial Reform (2009). *In Praise of Unlevel Playing Fields. The Report of the Second Warwick Commission*. Coventry, University of Warwick; Baker (2010), *op. cit. in footnote* 28.

[43] For the governance of central banks with regulatory responsibilities, see Frisell, Roszbach and Spagnolo (2008). 'Governing the Governors: A Clinical Study of Central Banks.' Sveriges Rikbank Working Paper, Series 221.

received emergency loans during the crisis often serve on its board of directors.[44]

Moreover, much attention has been paid to the hiring practices in regulatory agencies and in particular to the "revolving doors" that exist between the financial industry and regulatory agencies. This term points to the fact that regulators often find their best career opportunities within the firms they regulate, but the reverse trend is also true, that is, the flow of individuals from the industry to the regulatory positions.[45] Debates regarding the relationship between revolving doors and regulatory capture have primarily emerged in the US context, where the flow of people between regulators and the financial industry has remained a defining feature of the main regulatory institutions since their creations. European regulatory bodies have instead been characterized by career silos with bureaucrats spending most of their career in the state sector under various restrictions discouraging the transition. However, a shift towards a more US-style flow of individuals between regulatory agencies and the financial industry is noticeable in many jurisdictions such as in the UK, where the FSA in recent years has deliberately sought to hire lawyers from the private sector in order to strengthen its enforcement division.[46]

Theories of regulatory capture have held that revolving doors may distort regulatory policies in favour of the financial industry. Firms that

---

[44] GAO (2011a). *Federal Reserve Bank Governance. Opportunities Exist to Broaden Director Recruitment Efforts and Increase Transparency.* United States Government Accountability Office. GAO-12-18. The notion that these banks may benefit from the appointment of their representative on the Federal Reserve Boards is supported by the tendency of their stock price to rise in the aftermath of this announcement, while recent research has provided evidence that banks with Fed directorships were more likely to receive public funding during the financial crisis. See Adams (2011). 'Who Directs the Fed?' ECGI - Finance Working Paper, No. 293/2011; Duchin and Sosyura (2010). 'TARP Investments: Financial and Politics.' Ross School of Business Working Papers.

[45] Woodward (2001). 'Regulatory Capture at the U.S. Securities and Exchange Commission.' In Barth, Brumbaugh and Yago, eds (2000). *Restructuring Regulation and Financial Institutions.* Milken Institute Press

[46] Masters (2012). Enter the revolving regulators. *Financial Times.* London. 23 April 2012. For the case of Japan, see Walter (this volume).

hire former regulators have been described as having an unfair advantage over other groups owing to insider knowledge and preferential access to the regulatory agency.[47] Most importantly, given that regulatory authorities often find in the firms they regulate and supervise the most common source of future employment, this could create incentives to be lenient towards prospective future employers. The academic literature has presented only mixed evidence of this sort of inter-temporal conflict of interest, and some authors have argued that those regulators more likely to be hired by industry are often those that are tougher in their supervisory activity.[48]

1.2.3 Intellectual capture

While the traditional concept of regulatory capture in the academic literature has focused on material incentives between regulators and different stakeholders, the recent financial crisis has led a number of authors to broaden this concept and to investigate how the possibility that regulatory policies will favour a narrow set of special interests could be influenced by the regulators' ideas, beliefs and mind-sets. Terms such as "intellectual capture", "cognitive capture", and "cultural capture" have been used to signal instances where, as Kwak argues, special interests are able to 'shape policy outcomes through influences other than material incentives and rational debate'[49].

For instance, Buiter has argued that in the period before the crisis the Federal Reserve displayed 'excess sensitivity ... not just to asset prices but also to the concerns and fears of Wall Street more generally'.[50] For

---

[47] Lall (2012), *op. cit. in footnote* 12.

[48] DeHaan, Koh, Kedia and Rajgopal (2011). 'Does the Revolving Door Affect the SEC's Enforcement Outcomes?' Unpublished manuscript. GAO (2011b). 'Securities and Exchange Commission. Existing Post-Employment Controls Could be Further Strengthened', United States Government Accountability Office. Report to Congressional Committees. POGO (2011). 'Revolving Regulators: SEC Faces Ethics Challenges with Revolving Door', Project on Government Oversight. Currie (this volume).

[49] Kwak (forthcoming), *op. cit. in footnote* 26.

[50] Buiter (2009). Central Banks and Financial Crises. *Maintaining Stability in a Changing Financial System*, Federal Reserve Bank of Kansas City.

Dorn, in the period preceding the crisis, 'regulators found it "natural" to utilize models and datasets developed by private interests, so sidelining questions of systemic risk and public interest'.[51] This diagnosis of pre-crisis regulatory failures has been acknowledged by regulators and former regulators. The Chairman of the FSA, Lord Adair Turner, has argued that before the crisis regulatory authorities were prone to 'regulatory capture through the intellectual zeitgeist', which enabled the influence of banking lobbies to hold sway.[52]

However, different views remain regarding which factors determine this form of capture. Several analyses have acknowledged the importance of the broader intellectual climate of the period, in particular the ascendancy within the academic community and many regulatory authorities of ideas highlighting the efficiency of financial markets at understanding and allocating risks, their self-stabilizing nature, and the benefits of financial innovations for the real economy.[53] This change in the dominant paradigm provided the intellectual basis for several important pieces of legislation in the period before the crisis, from Basel II to a greater reliance on disclosure and market discipline, as well as a broader reassessment of the purpose of regulation and a scaling down in the ambitions of regulatory action.[54]

Other authors have identified sources of intellectual capture inside the regulatory process, and discussed how the repeated interaction between regulators and the financial industry could contribute to align the way in which regulators think about problems with the view of the industry they regulate. Building upon the insights coming from

---

[51] Dorn (2010). 'The Governance of Securities. Ponzi Finance, Regulatory Convergence, Credit Crunch.' *British Journal of Criminology*, 50(1): 23-45.

[52] Turner (2009). 'Roundtable: How to tame global finance.' *Prospect*, 162, August 27. See also Briault (this volume).

[53] Sheng (this volume); Baker (2010), *op. cit. in footnote* 28.

[54] Warwick Commission on International Financial Reform (2009), *op. cit. in footnote* 41. FSA (2009). *Turner Review: A regulatory response to the global banking crisis.* London, Financial Services Authority

psychological studies on the importance of group identities, Barth, Caprio, and Levine have argued that 'even well-intentioned, incorruptible officials might be subject to the same human psychological factors that induce referees and umpires in sport to conform to the interests of the home crowd'.[55] In the case of financial regulators, the home crowd is represented by the financial services firms with whom they interact on a daily basis in order to perform their regulatory and supervisory duties.

Kwak has further broken down the sources of this bias in favour of the financial services industry and argued that regulators are more likely to trust and to adopt positions advanced by 1) 'people whom they perceive as being in their in-group', 2) 'people whom they perceive to be of higher status in social, economic, intellectual, or other terms', and 3) 'people who are in their social networks'.[56] According to Kwak, financial regulators often identify themselves as 'economically sophisticated steward[s] of efficient financial markets' and are more likely to side with the financial institutions which enjoy a higher prestige because of their technical knowledge and with whom they share more social networks than with consumer groups and other stakeholders. According to Kwak, the potential for this sort of capture increases with the complexity of the problem: 'faced with uncertainty deciding between competing theories of the world and the public interest, people are more likely to fall back on the signals communicated by identity, status, or relationships'.[57]

From a similar perspective, different scholars have argued that the major impact of the revolving doors phenomenon and the repeated interaction between regulators and regulated firms as described above is not the conflict of interests which may result, but rather the nurturing of a kind of 'consanguinity'[58] in the policymaking process,

---

[55] Barth, Caprio and Levine (2012), p. 38, *op. cit. in footnote 1*.
[56] Kwak (forthcoming), *op. cit. in footnote 26*.
[57] Ibid.
[58] Baxter (2011), p. 184, *op. cit. in footnote 14*.

supporting a process of intellectual convergence between like-minded individuals across the public and private sector, socialization, and, ultimately, "intellectual capture".[59]

1.2.4 Capture through the political process

Finally, while the different faces of capture described above pertain to the interaction between regulators and the regulated firms, different commentators have broadened this analysis to account for the role of the politicians, governments and legislative bodies who define the responsibilities that independent regulatory agencies need to follow and grant them the resources and powers to perform these tasks. The relationship between regulators and their political masters creates additional venues for regulatory capture, as different stakeholders will often seek to change regulators' course of action of regulators indirectly through the political process.[60]

The literature has identified different factors which influence the potential that elected politicians will heed the demands of certain special interests and interfere in regulators' actions. First, in countries such as the United States, the financial industry remains one of the major contributors to politicians' electoral campaigns across the political spectrum; consequently it is able to exercise a significant influence over the voting behaviour of Congress on certain regulatory issues. Second, given the significant externalities that certain financial regulatory issues may have on the rest of the economy, politicians may interfere in the actions of regulators in order to achieve key political objectives such as economic growth, employment, social and economic stability. Different authors have therefore highlighted the

---

[59] Tsingou (2008). Transnational private governance and the Basel process: banking regulation, private interests and Basel II. *Transnational Private Governance and its Limits*. Nolke and Graz. London, Routledge. Seabrooke and Tsingou (2009). 'Revolving Doors and Linked Ecologies in the World Economy: Policy Locations and the Practice of International Financial Reform.' CSGR Working Paper, 260/09; Warwick Commission on International Financial Reform (2009), *op. cit. in footnote* 41.

[60] Fullenkamp and Sharma (2012). 'Good Financial Regulation: Changing the Process is Crucial.' *ICFR-Financial Times Research Prize*. Green (this volume). Sheng (this volume).

risk that politicians may pressure regulators in order to achieve short-term political objectives by pleasing powerful electoral constituencies or special interest groups, regardless of changes in the legislation.[61]

This sort of interference is particularly likely in the context of booms. The critical role that the supply of credit plays in ensuring the growth of the economy creates strong incentives for politicians to avoid regulatory policies that may interfere with 'the (apparently) successful prevailing machinery of growth'[62] and jeopardize their chances of re-election. At the same time, the low political salience that financial regulatory issues have during financial booms makes it more likely that arguments regarding the risks generated by inadequate regulatory policies will not resonate with elected politicians.[63] As a result of this political climate, during boom times regulatory agencies are likely to face pressures to be accommodating in the implementation of financial rules, thus hindering their capacity to "remove the punchbowl from the party" − particularly in areas such as prudential supervision and macro-prudential regulation which are more susceptible to economic and electoral considerations.[64]

At the same time, the pressures upon regulators coming from the political sphere may be reversed in the aftermath of crises or scandals. These events are likely to increase the political salience of financial regulatory policies among the broader electorate and can create incentives among elected politicians to be tough on the industry in order to extract electoral rewards.[65] According to different commentators, the financial reforms introduced after the crisis have not been immune from this sort of dynamic.[66] However, a crisis causing

---

[61] Sheng (this volume). See also Green (this volume).

[62] Cross (this volume).

[63] Warwick Commission on International Financial Reform (2009), *op. cit. in footnote* 41.

[64] See also Viñals and Fiechter (2010). 'The Making of Good Supervision: Learning to Say "No" '. IMF Staff Position Note SPN/10/08.

[65] Walter (this volume).

[66] According to different commentators, crisis-time regulatory politics may still introduce distortions in the regulation and supervision of financial markets by frequently leading to the possibility of an excessive tightening of regulation in the moment when it is least desirable ("regulatory overkill"). For a discussion of the distortions in the content of regulations that characterize the policymaking in a crisis, see Green, Ridley (this volume).

a severe deterioration of economic conditions is likely to increase rather than weaken the influence of the financial sector over the timing and nature of the rules implemented. Periods of slow economic growth may reinforce concerns that regulation may .be preventing small businesses from accessing credit and damaging the recovery of the economy.[67] In particular, in those circumstances where an apparent trade-off exists between the mandate of regulatory agencies to bolster financial stability and the goal of promoting economic growth (such as in defining appropriate capital requirements for banking institutions), then political incumbents as well as a number of societal stakeholders are more likely to support financial industry groups in demanding a watering down of the regulatory measures introduced in the middle of the crisis.[68]

In sum, as a result of the influence that the broader electoral and economic cycles have over the regulatory process, the possibility that financial regulation will be captured by special interests must be regarded as cyclical rather than static phenomenon, alternating between periods of crisis and boom.[69]

1.3 Towards a policy agenda against regulatory capture

This diagnosis of the different determinants of capture in financial regulation reveals how this represents a more multifaceted and complex phenomenon than is portrayed in many journalistic and scholarly accounts. The potential that a piece of regulation will unduly favour certain special interests is influenced by a multitude of factors, such as the kind of mobilization this will raise among different stakeholders, the institutional context, the dominant ideas, as well as the broader political and economic context surrounding the policymaking context.

---

[67] Green (this volume).

[68] Walter (this volume).

[69] Warwick Commission on International Financial Reform (2009), *op. cit. in footnote* 41; Baker (2010), *op. cit. in footnote* 28; Johnson and Kwak (2010), *op. cit. in footnote* 1; Helleiner and Pagliari (2011). 'The End of an Era in International Financial Regulation? Towards a Post-Crisis Research Agenda". *International Organization* 65(3).

These different channels and mechanisms make the potential for regulatory capture a partly inevitable aspect of the financial regulatory process, given the information-intensive nature of financial regulatory policies and the proximity with market participants required for regulators to stay abreast of market developments. At the same time, while it is implausible that this risk may be eliminated from the regulatory process, the attempts of financial industry groups and other stakeholders to influence the content of regulation towards their interests and the other mechanisms of capture described above can be channelled through mechanisms designed to mitigate their impact.[70]

The remainder of this chapter will present a wide range of different safeguards and mitigation strategies that could reduce the potential that regulation will diverge from the public interest and unduly favour specific interests. These strategies will build upon the academic literature that has examined the making of good regulation, but also from the direct experience of different contributors to this volume in regulatory policymaking, both in finance and other sectors. For the sake of clarity, these measures will be divided across three broad policy approaches to mitigate the risk of capture: 1) measures promoting greater balance and diversity in the competition among different stakeholders; 2) reforms of the institutional context within which regulators operate; 3) opening up the regulatory process to different external checks and balances.

1.3.1 Rebalancing the participation of stakeholders in the regulatory process

Different proposals to mitigate capture have focused on redressing one of its main determinants, that is, the imbalance between the capacity of financial groups to have their voice heard in the policymaking process and those of other stakeholders, such as depositors, investors, and consumers, whom the proposed rules are

---

[70] Baxter (2011), p.188, *op. cit. in footnote* 14.

designed to protect. While for authors such as Johnson and Kwak this goal requires the breaking up of institutions too big to fail, to constrain their political influence,[71] others have focused on balancing the influence of these financial industry groups by strengthening the plurality of voices in the regulatory process.

The experience of other sectors reveals how the involvement of a plurality of stakeholders besides the producers targeted by the regulation in the regulatory process, such as other business groups, non-governmental organizations and consumer movement organizations, can play a crucial role in keeping the influence of the regulated industry in check and limiting the potential for capture for different reasons. First, in a complex policy environment such as finance, strengthening the plurality of voices and perspectives in the regulatory process is important to reduce the risks that regulators find themselves exposed to one-sided evidence from the regulated financial sector.[72] Second, as Kroszner and Strahan argue, 'competition among rival interest groups can increase the likelihood of beneficial reform. Rival groups have an incentive to battle each other in addition to battling the consumer. If they dissipate their efforts against each other, they are less likely to be able to support narrow special interest regulation.'[73] Third, measures seeking to strengthen the plurality of groups in the regulatory process may also be an important counter to the risk of groupthink and intellectual capture, to the extent that these groups are capable of bringing different ideas and perspectives into the regulatory process.[74]

Three broad views remain among the authors regarding what measures could be introduced to achieve this goal: first, the creation of participatory mechanisms; second, tripartism and proxy advocates; and third, strengthening the diversity of views within the financial industry

---

[71] Johnson and Kwak 2010, *op. cit. in footnote* 1.

[72] See Carpenter, Moss, Wachtell Stinnett (this volume).

[73] Kroszner and Strahan (2000). 'Obstacles to optimal policy: the interplay of politics and economics in shaping bank supervision and regulation reforms.' Center for Research in Security Prices, Working Paper 512, February 2000), p. 38.

[74] See Carpenter, Moss, Wachtell Stinnett (this volume); Farnish (this volume)

1.3.1.1 Creating participatory mechanisms

Mattli and Woods have argued that regulatory policies are less likely to deviate from the public interest when they are developed through 'participatory mechanisms that are fair, transparent, accessible and open', thus favouring the participation of those stakeholders that are less well connected to the regulators.[75] The main mechanism through which this principle has been translated into the financial regulatory process is by subjecting regulatory policies to public consultations. This approach is increasingly being accepted by most regulatory agencies, although this varies significantly across bodies.

However, as different contributors have argued, public consultations by themselves are unlikely to be sufficient to ensure that a plurality of stakeholders will be capable of having their share of the input into the regulatory process. On this note, various adjustments have been suggested to avoid the risk that consultations may be being conducted solely to discharge formal obligations, such as granting different stakeholders sufficient time to digest the implications of the rules proposed, publicly summarizing the position of the different stakeholders, and justifying how these positions have been treated with respect to the final decision.[76]

Moreover, in order to compensate for the informational advantage of industry insiders participating in these consultations, different authors have also suggested that regulators should grant full access to the information available to them, including, for example, their internal data and analyses.[77] Along the same lines, a regulatory agency may be given the power to generate and disseminate information to remedy the public's information disadvantage vis-à-vis the industry. According to Barkow, regulators must be given the power to 'make the public aware of pending issues so that industry is not the only one who knows about them', as well as 'the authority to study and publicize

---

[75] Mattli and Woods (2009), *op. cit. in footnote* 13.

[76] Mogg (this volume). For a discussion of the limits of existing consultations, see Ridley (this volume).

[77] Ayres and Braithwaite (1991). 'Tripartism: Regulatory Capture and Empowerment.' *Law & Social Inquiry*, 16(3): 435-96. Ridley (this volume); Currie (this volume).

data that will be of interest to the public and help energize the public to overcome collective action problems and rally behind the agency'.[78]

These and other measures used to generate and disseminate information and enhance transparency in the consultation process are described not only as prerequisites to allow an informed debate among different stakeholders, but also as tools allowing 'the smaller, less well-funded interests (notably consumer interests and SMEs) to engage in the issues, possibly against the deep pockets of the incumbents'[79].

1.3.1.2 Tripartism and proxy advocates

The introduction of participatory mechanisms is in itself however unlikely to be effective in levelling the playing field and achieving an adequate participation from a plurality of stakeholders. In a highly technical area such as financial regulation, the financial industry groups with the greatest technical expertise continue to be best positioned to take advantage of these mechanisms, while those stakeholders with diffuse membership are constrained in their capacity to take advantage of the channels of access to the policymaking process.

Other authors have therefore discussed the creation of alternative mechanisms to empower the mobilization of groups with a diffuse membership such as consumers, investors and other entities, such as granting these groups a privileged position within the regulatory process, termed "tripartism" by Ayres and Braithwaite.[80] Within the context of financial regulatory policymaking, Raeburn has called for a 'form of affirmative action' on the part of regulators to strengthen the voice of those real economy interests whose representation is more fragmented.[81] Farnish has stressed the need to create the conditions for a more proactive engagement of regulators with consumer groups,

---

[78] Barkow (2010). 'Insulating Agencies: Avoiding Capture Through Institutional Design.' *Texas Law Review*, 89(1): 15-79, p.59.
[79] Currie (this volume).
[80] Ayres and Braithwaite (1991), *op. cit. in footnote* 76.
[81] Raeburn (this volume).

for instance by investing in processes to gather real-time intelligence from groups, designing consultations in ways that make better use of consumer representatives' limited resources, and creating direct routes for designated consumer groups to present complaints to which regulators need to respond within a defined timeframe.[82]

However, the capacity of consumer groups and NGOs to effectively engage in the policymaking process continues to be constrained by the fact that most of these bodies active in financial regulatory policymaking are too small, disperse, and underfunded. For other commentators, however, the objective of redressing the imbalance of power between consumers' and firms' resources and strengthening the voice of the former in the policymaking process requires a more direct intervention by policymakers. One mechanism would be for policymakers to subsidize the creation of consumer groups. This is for instance the approach adopted in the case of Finance Watch, an organization comprising different consumer groups, retail investor associations, housing associations, trade unions, foundations, think tanks, and NGOs, whose creation was sponsored by the European Parliament during the crisis with the objective of establishing a more effective counterweight to industry lobbying in regulatory debates.

Another solution relies instead on the creation of "proxy advocates" within regulatory institutions. These are internal agencies tasked to provide regulators with expertise and information from a consumer perspective, to challenge regulatory policies, and to represent the public interest at large in the decision making process.[83] This mechanism is common outside of finance, where different utilities regulators have established standing panels of consumer representatives to provide expert consumer input.

Similar mechanisms have also been established within finance by various US insurance regulators, the European Commission (the

---

[82] Farnish (this volume).

[83] Schwarcz (forthcoming). Preventing Capture Through Consumer Empowerment Programs: Some Evidence from Insurance Regulation. In: *Preventing Regulatory Capture: Special Interest Influence, and How to Limit It*, by Carpenter and Moss (forthcoming). Cambridge, Cambridge University Press.

Financial Services User Group), and the British FSA (Consumer Panel). However, the capacity of these bodies to truly represent consumer perspectives in the regulatory process is constrained by different factors such a limit to the resources allocated to such bodies, as well as their location within the organization. For this reason, Farnish has called for supplementing internal proxy advocates with independent external consumer bodies that may benefit from greater independence, capacity to set their own agenda, and capacity to speak out publicly if they disagree with the decisions of regulators.[84]

1.3.1.3 Strengthening competition within the financial industry

While the strategies described above seek to mitigate capture by increasing the capacity of consumers of financial services and other non-financial parties to act as counterweights to the producers' interests, this strategy is less applicable to the case of those markets where the counterparties are not retail consumers but rather other financial groups, such as in the case of wholesale markets.[85] A variety of authors have therefore advocated the introduction of measures to encourage the emergence of countervailing forces against the risk of capture from within the industry and to promote a greater engagement of those financial groups with a material incentive for stronger regulation.[86]

Some industry practitioners have argued that it is in the long-term interest of the financial industry to promote a strong regulatory infrastructure capable of achieving stability and restoring confidence in the financial system. However, short-term competitive concerns, rather than long-term interests in a more stable regulatory environment, seem to have dominated in a range of circumstances the engagement of financial groups in the policy arena. For instance, in the case of banking regulation, the capacity of investors in bank debt to

---

[84] Farnish (this volume). See also Ridley (this volume).

[85] Ridley (this volume).

[86] Porter (this volume). Walter (this volume). Helleiner and Porter (2010). 'Making Transnational Networks More Accountable.' *Economics, Management and Financial Markets*, 52.

act as a countervailing force to the management of banks is constrained by the dispersed nature of the investor community, the short-termism of part of it, and factors constraining market discipline such as deposit insurance schemes or the moral hazard created by "too big to fail" institutions.[87] Similarly, in the case of the regulation of hedge funds, the incentives for banks that provide these investment vehicles with leverage to lobby in favour of safer standards may be affected by the fact that many of the same banks also sponsor hedge funds. Moreover, the mobilization of powerful industry groups is particularly difficult in the case of complex systemic risk regulation, though the industry as a whole would have a strong incentive to address this kind of risk.

Authors have therefore suggested that regulatory mechanisms should be devised to better align the participation of financial industry groups in the policymaking process with the promotion of stronger regulation. Strachan has proposed the establishment of a 'standing body of practitioners' reflecting the composition of the financial services industry as a whole and therefore less susceptible to the demands of particular interest groups.[88] Porter suggests that giving rewards to 'whistleblowers' who reveal regulatory violations could give rise to a set of firms with a strong interest in preventing regulatory forbearance and capture. Similarly, requiring banks to issue contingent capital – bonds that convert into equity in time of crisis – may strengthen the incentives for bondholders to promote strong prudential regulation.[89] Helleiner and Porter propose to maintain some separation between the ownership of clearinghouses and dealers, so that the former will retain 'an incentive to protest against regulatory initiatives that would create opportunities to undermine or bypass clearing arrangements'.[90] The internal attitude of financial firms towards the regulatory process may be altered through changes to liability rules. For instance, Baxter argues that extending the fiduciary duties of the board and of top executives to cover others as

---

[87] FSA (2009), *op. cit. in footnote* 17.
[88] Strachan (this volume).
[89] Porter, this volume.
[90] Helleiner and Porter (2010), op. cit. in footnote 85.

well as shareholders may also affect the incentives of the industry towards regulatory policies.[91]

In sum, the objective of promoting a greater plurality of voices and perspectives in the regulatory process can be achieved not only by opening up the rulemaking process to stakeholders outside of the financial industry that are currently under-represented, but also by actively promoting a greater engagement of those stakeholders within the financial industry with a material interest in preventing capture.

1.4 Reforming the institutional context

Measures which seek to mitigate capture by incorporating a wider range of stakeholders in the regulatory process are unlikely to be effective in cases in which the institutional context within which the stakeholder input is processed into regulatory policies is perceived as favouring certain interests over others. Similarly, these measures are unlikely to be able to address the problem of capture during the process of financial supervision, which is based on a continuous interaction between the supervisor and the firm that is supervised. A second approach to mitigate the risk of capture has therefore focused on addressing those institutional biases which create incentives for regulators to favour financial industry groups under their supervision.

Granting regulatory agencies statutory independence and insulating the regulatory process from political horse-trading and short-term pressures of politicians interested in appeasing politically influential special interests have frequently been presented as the primary institutional fix to protect the diffuse interest of the general public against the risk of capture.[92] Independence is a particularly valuable safeguard against capture in those areas that are more susceptible to economic and electoral considerations, such as prudential supervision and macroprudential regulation, where regulators are more likely to be subject to strong pressures not to lean against the wind during

---

[91] Baxter (this volume).

[92] For a review of this literature, see Barkow (2010), *op. cit. in footnote* 77. The importance of statutory independence has been discussed in this volume by Mogg (this volume), Green (this volume), and Diplock (this volume).

boom times. Regulatory independence remains an important safeguard to allow regulatory authorities to resist capture and to conduct themselves with a "through the cycle" mentality and resist the forces toward leniency during periods of economic booms.[93]

However, the statutory autonomy of regulatory agencies is not in itself a sufficient safeguard against the risk of capture, especially when some institutional features of the agencies may have the impact of biasing the conduct of regulators towards certain groups. As Barkow has argued, 'under modern conditions of political oversight, other design elements and mechanisms are often just as important to an agency's ability to achieve its long-term mission relatively free from capture'.[94] The institutional design elements discussed in this chapter regard 1) the mandate of regulatory agencies, 2) their internal decision making procedures, 3) the staffing and recruitment practices of regulatory agencies, and 4) the way regulatory agencies are funded.

1.4.1 Mandate

Different authors have acknowledged how the mandate which regulators receive from parliament in legislation may affect the possibility that the conduct of the regulatory agency will be captured by special interests. Barkow argues that giving regulatory agencies a broad jurisdiction makes it more likely that they will be able to resist pressure from narrow groups. At the same time, if a regulatory agency is given 'conflicting responsibilities that require the agency to further the goals of industry at the same time that it is responsible for a general public-interest mission', it is likely that 'industry pressure and a focus on short-term economic concerns that are easily monitored will trump the long-term effects on the public that are harder to assess'.[95]

From this perspective, the approach common to many financial regulatory bodies of postulating a broad range of duties and placing

---

[93] Valencia and Ueda (2012). Central Bank Independence and Macro-prudential Regulation. IMF Working Paper, WP/12/101.
[94] Barkow (2010), p.17, *op. cit. in footnote* 77.
[95] ibid. p. 50.

upon the regulator the responsibility of balancing these duties is described by different authors as particularly problematic.[96] Ambiguities in the mandate of regulatory and supervisory agencies, or the presence of more distinct objectives, may lead regulatory agencies to unduly prefer one at the expense of others and to create opportunities for firms seeking to exploit those situations where supervisors can exercise discretion.[97] Clearly identifying a primary duty of the regulators could support them in asserting their independence of politicians and special interests.[98]

1.4.2 Internal decision making procedures

Besides the formal mandate of regulatory agencies, other proposals have focused on the internal processes through which regulatory decisions are taken that may make regulators more likely to unduly favour narrow interests. For instance, various authors have discussed how periodically rotating regulatory staff, similar to the rotation policy that exists for auditing purposes, may play a role in preventing supervisors from developing an excessive affinity to the market participants they regulate or an excessively narrow understanding of their responsibilities.[99] According to Strachan, the same objective could also be pursued by subjecting the approach of individual supervisors to the scrutiny of an internal peer review process, as well as by ensuring that the most important decisions, such as those 'around capital, liquidity, the overall supervisory evaluation and enforcement action' are taken by a committee rather than by individual supervisors.[100]

Reforms in the internal decision making procedures may also be adopted in order to ensure that the development of regulatory policies takes into account a broader set of concerns and voices. For instance, authors have suggested that all policy proposals should be

---

[96] Walter (this volume); Currie (this volume).
[97] Walter (this volume); Strachan (this volume).
[98] Currie (this volume); Green (this volume).
[99] Strachan (this volume); Sheng (this volume); Baxter (this volume).
[100] Strachan (this volume).

subject to an impact assessment to identify the implications for the real economy,[101] or should be assessed against a consumer checklist.[102] Currie has also discussed the empowering of internal panels to perform an internal audit function, checking whether the 'regulatory decision making had placed the consumer and citizen interest at the heart of its processes from the outset'.[103]

Moreover, internal adjustments in the organizational elements and decision-making processes of regulatory agencies are also instrumental in addressing the issue of intellectual capture. For instance, exposing key decisions to a wider group of people with different backgrounds and mind sets may play an important role in mitigating the risk of intellectual capture which derives from the proximity that develops between firms and their supervisors.[104] The Independent Evaluation Office (IEO) of the IMF has recommended to 'actively seek alternative or dissenting views by involving eminent outside analysts on a regular basis in Board and/or Management discussions', and to better reflect areas of significant disagreement and minority views in internal documents. Another set of proposals from the IEO has focused on 'strengthen[ing] the incentives to "speak truth to power"', such as by encouraging staff to challenge the views of the management and of the country authorities supervised by the Fund, as well as by giving staff 'the possibility of issuing reports without the need for Board endorsement'.[105] Along these lines, different authors have suggested that regulatory agencies should institutionalize within their structure a 'devil's advocate' figure to raise contrarian viewpoints,[106] or create internal advisory boards 'to challenge and think the unthinkable'.[107]

---

[101] Raeburn (this volume).

[102] Farnish (this volume).

[103] Currie (this volume).

[104] Currie (this volume); Strachan (this volume).

[105] IEO (2011). 'IMF Performance in the Run-Up to the Financial and Economic Crisis: IMF Surveillance in 2004–07', Independent Evaluation Office of the International Monetary Fund.

[106] Kwak (forthcoming), supra footnote 26. See also Carpenter, Moss, Wachtell Stinnett (this volume).

[107] Currie (this volume).

Finally, internal adjustments in the processes through which regulatory policies are designed and implemented could also be introduced to mitigate the cyclicality of regulatory capture. In particular, different authors have discussed how formal mechanisms could be introduced to review the legislation and regulatory approach periodically, 'irrespective of whether a crisis or scandal has taken place and irrespective of the general health of the economy', in order to mitigate the impact of the electoral and economic cycle over the content of regulation.[108]

1.4.3 Staffing and recruitment

Another set of proposals has sought to mitigate the incentives for regulatory agencies to unduly favour the regulated industry by looking at such agencies' staffing and recruitment practices, and in particular to protect them from the "revolving doors" phenomenon.

Two competing approaches have emerged on this issue. Some commentators have called for steps to constrain, as much as possible, the appointment into regulatory positions of people with industry backgrounds that may create frequent impartiality conflicts or to bar regulators from finding employment within industries that might have benefited from their work in the past.[109] The Governor of the Bank of England, Mervyn King, has argued that the best way to improve supervision and regulation should be to 'create people who believe that it is a public-service calling to work in the Bank of England and spend a good chunk, if not all, of their career as banking supervisors'.[110]

On the other hand, other authors have stressed that regulation and supervision of complex financial activities requires the kind of technical expertise and understanding of the economics and business

---

[108] Green (this volume); Ridley (this volume). The danger associated with this proposal is that the periodic review may occur during the wrong point in the cycle, creating new opportunities for certain actors to seek to water down the regime.

[109] See proposal by US Senator Ted Kaufman cited in Lin (2010). SEC's 'revolving door' under scrutiny. MarketWatch. 16 June 2010.

[110] Cited by Masters (2012).

models of the industry and therefore that this is likely to be found uniquely among those people with a direct experience working in the financial services industry.[111] As a result, seeking to dissuade the exchange of people across regulatory agencies and the firms they regulate may be detrimental, insofar as this limits the capacity of regulatory agencies to recruit people with the relevant expertise. Contrary to what is argued by Mervyn King, some have argued that public policies should encourage, rather than restrict, the exchange of people between the industry and regulatory agencies – through secondments, structured training programmes for supervisory staff,[112] internships for their staff to financial institutions outside of the jurisdiction being supervised,[113] or by developing a multistage career pattern in both sectors.[114]

Different approaches have therefore been suggested to allow regulatory agencies to acquire the expertise needed from the market, while seeking to mitigate the conflicts of interest which that may give rise to.

One set of proposals has focused on injecting greater transparency into the movement of people between regulatory agencies and the financial industry, for instance by requiring public disclosure in a registry of the history of those ex-regulators who represented clients before their former agency, or, more broadly, requiring regulatory agencies to disclose publicly the ties of individual regulators with the private sector.[115] Other proposals have focused on the establishment of "cooling off periods", stipulating a minimum number of years required before regulators are able to seek employment with interests that may have significantly benefited from

---

[111] Che (1995). 'Revolving Doors and the Optimal Tolerance for Agency Collusion.' *RAND Journal of Economics*, 26(3): 378-97. GAO (2011b). Maskell (2010). 'Post-Employment, "Revolving Door", Laws for Federal Personnel', Congressional Research Service. See also Ridley, Strachan, and Walter (this volume).

[112] Strachan (this volume).

[113] IIF (2011). *Achieving Effective Supervision: An Industry Perspective*, Institute of International Finance.

[114] Ridley (this volume).

[115] POGO (2011), *op. cit. in footnote 47.*

the policies they formulated, or prohibiting new employees from the industry to be involved in matters related to their former private-sector employer.[116]

An alternative approach has focused instead on calibrating the scope of employment restrictions according to the level of seniority. Currie has suggested that tougher standards for pre- and post-employment restrictions should apply to senior executive teams and to the board of regulatory institutions, allowing in the latter case 'no conflicts and no immediate past involvement with any of the major players'.[117] This approach would rectify the anomalous presence of people with direct involvement in the banking industry that characterizes the most senior positions and the board of different financial regulatory bodies, while still allowing these institutions to recruit the required expertise in the market.

Another set of mitigating strategies relies on complementing the presence of regulatory staff with direct experience from the financial industry with a group of career supervisors who identify their long term future with its public service aims and objectives and who have a more questioning attitude towards the latest market trends and innovations.[118] In a similar vein, Green argues that while some of the skills required to provide effective supervision can be 'brought in from the market', the broader understanding of the wider market environment as a whole – a prerequisite for effective supervision – 'only comes with a certain minimum supervisory experience in terms of both length and breadth of service'.[119]

Finally, an alternative approach would be to balance the recruitment of regulators with current knowledge of the industry with people who possess a diversity of professional experiences and training.[120] For instance, Raeburn has argued that financial regulatory agencies need

---

[116] Helleiner and Porter (2010), *op. cit. in footnote* 85. and POGO (2011), *op. cit. in footnote* 47.

[117] Currie (this volume).

[118] Strachan (this volume)

[119] Green (this volume)

[120] Currie (this volume), Raeburn (this volume), and Farnish (this volume).

to recruit individuals whose backgrounds qualify them to recognize the impact of regulatory policies beyond the 'usual suspects' of the participants in financial markets.[121] This approach is particularly important in injecting greater intellectual diversity into the activities of regulatory agencies and to reduce the risk of groupthink. As Chwieroth argues, recruitment procedures represent a 'pathway through which new beliefs can be transmitted' to the organization, and organizations that recruit uniquely among individuals with a specific type of training remain particularly vulnerable to developments within that sector or profession.[122] For instance, the IMF has in the past broadened its recruitment patterns in order to 'bring to the Fund a small number of career staff who might approach policy questions from a new and somewhat different perspective',[123] seeking in this way to counter the criticisms presented against the organization for displaying "less intellectual diversity than the Pentagon".[124]

1.4.4 Funding of regulatory agencies

A final set of institutional reforms has identified the source and the level of funding of regulatory agencies as the key to mitigating the internal incentive problems that may make regulators prone to be captured. The difference in salary between the private and public sectors remains one of the primary determinants of the revolving doors phenomenon, as inadequate funding limits the capacity of regulatory agencies to retain experienced staff. Furthermore, limited resources constrain the capacity of regulatory agencies to conduct research, generate knowledge, and to be a source of new ideas, thus increasing the risk that regulators will defer to the financial industry and rely excessively on its information.[125]

---

[121] Raeburn (this volume).

[122] Chwieroth (2009). *Capital Ideas: The IMF and the Rise of Financial Liberalization.* Princeton, NJ, Princeton University Press, pp. 249-50.

[123] IMF Administration Department, cited by Momani (2005). 'Recruiting and Diversifying IMF Technocrats.' *Global Society,* 19(2): 167-87.

[124] Finnemore, in: IMF (2002). 'Governing the IMF.' Transcript of an Economic Forum, International Monetary Fund.

[125] Walter (this volume); Fullenkamp and Sharma (2012), *op. cit. in footnote* 59.

Unfortunately, the resources available to regulatory agencies have often failed to keep up with their expanding responsibilities. For instance, while from 1939–2009 the number of SEC employees has little more than doubled, the number of shares trading hands each day in the US has increased more than twenty times.[126] Also, the recent investigation in the UK into the failure of the Royal Bank of Scotland has raised concerns regarding the inadequacy of the funding of regulatory agencies, as the task of supervising a bank with a presence in over 50 countries and employing 226,400 people was fulfilled at the beginning of the crisis by a team comprising only four-and-a-half members.[127] This discrepancy in the resources available has been aggravated by the response to the crisis, as the significant expansion in the remit and responsibilities of different regulatory agencies has in some cases been followed by denials of adequate funding to perform these additional tasks.[128] From this perspective, increasing the resources available to regulatory agencies may be regarded as one way to mitigate the risk of capture. This would allow regulatory bodies to increase their capacity to recruit and retain experienced staff and decrease their reliance on the financial industry.

Nevertheless, different views remain regarding what kind of funding model would achieve this goal while reducing the possibility of regulatory capture. The government represents the most natural source of additional funding, though this may increase the risk of capture by giving politicians undue influence over the regulatory process, and in particular by giving the government the power to "starve" the regulator of resources in order to constrain its operations.[129] Indeed, Walter has argued that systematic under-resourcing of regulatory agencies in the

---

[126] Grocer (2010). Want to Fix SEC's Revolving Door? Give the Agency More Money. *Wall Street Journal*, 16 June 2010.

[127] FSA (2011). 'The failure of the Royal Bank of Scotland.' Financial Services Authority Board Report, London, Financial Services Authority, section 3.3. The investigation has concluded that 'the approach to resourcing the supervision of the largest banks was fundamentally flawed and, critically, the resources applied were far too low adequately to meet the challenges of supervising RBS', pp.279-80.

[128] Baxter (this volume); Ridley (this volume).

[129] Strachan (this volume); see also Diplock (this volume)

United States in the period before the crisis represented 'a common legislative tactic that contributed to the undermining of effective regulation'.[130]

However, the alternative of funding the activities of regulators through a levy upon specific financial institutions, or more broadly on the financial system,[131] has the potential to exacerbate the problem of capture by increasing regulators' sense of obligation towards the firms that fund their activities.[132] An alternative to these two funding models proposed by Currie is that of a mixed model differentiating between the source of the funding and control over it, where funding comes mainly from the industry but the government oversees the level of funding.[133] However, given the difficulty for any of these mechanisms to raise sufficient funding for public sector salaries to be able to compete with those in the financial industry, Baxter has discussed the importance of developing non-monetary forms of compensation in the public sector, as well as the importance of boosting the 'reputation and prestige' of regulatory agencies.[134]

Moreover, attempts to mitigate the risk of capture by raising the resources of regulatory agencies may be reinforced by the introduction of measures to better align the compensation structure of regulators with the public interest. Various authors have called for regulating the compensation of regulators in a way which is similar to the regulation of bankers' bonuses. Such proposals include the suggestion of deferring the majority of regulators' pay, so that a regulator would lose a portion of it should shortcomings in his actions

---

[130] Walter (this volume). The former chairman of the SEC Arthur Levitt argued that during his tenure Congress constantly threatened the SEC with budget cuts if it pursued more assertive regulatory efforts. See Barkow (2010), *op. cit. in footnote* 77. Fullenkamp and Sharma (2012), *op. cit. in footnote* 59.

[131] E.g. see Hardy (2006); ibid. According to proposed legislation presented by the US Treasury in December 2011, the cost of the newly created Federal Stability Oversight Council will be raised by collecting semiannual fees from US bank and foreign banks, as well as nonbank institutions that fall under the supervision of the Federal Reserve.

[132] Strachan (this volume).

[133] Currie (this volume).

[134] Baxter (2011), *op. cit. in footnote* 14.

come to light, or to require a portion of regulators' deferred compensation to be invested into a fund which provides capital insurance to financial companies.[135]

In sum, there appears to be a range of important prerequisites for regulators to be able to carry out their duties without unduly favouring certain special interests: a clear and unbiased mandate, adequate internal procedures which expose regulatory decisions to a variety of views, an adequate framework to manage conflicts of interest from the revolving door issue, and appropriate funding.

1.5 External checks and balances

The policy measures discussed above have sought to mitigate the risks of capture from the inside by correcting not only stakeholders' access to the regulatory process, but also the institutional elements that may bias regulators towards the regulated financial industry. However, other policy approaches have focused on subjecting the regulatory process to a set of external checks and balances and ensuring that regulatory authorities are constantly supervised, held accountable, and challenged.

In theory, the conduct of regulatory agencies and the possibility that these will unduly favour special interests are already subject to multiple checks. A first set of checks is provided from their board and other internal review mechanisms. A second line of defence comes from the scrutiny of parliamentary committees or branches of government to which regulatory agencies are periodically required to respond and which ultimately remain the 'guardians of the balance of interests' in a democratic context.[136] Third, the media, as well as a plurality of NGOs, research institutes, consumer groups, and business groups both outside and within the financial sector all play a key role

---

[135] Bebchuk and Spamann (2010). 'Regulating Bankers' Pay.' *Georgetown Law Journal*, 98(2): 247-87. Kane (2010). 'The Importance of Monitoring and Mitigating the Safety-Net Consequences of Regulation Induced Innovation.' *Review of Social Economy*, 58. Fullenkamp and Sharma (2012), *op. cit. in footnote* 59. For a discussion see Barth, Caprio and Levine (2012), p. 227, *op. cit. in footnote* 1.
[136] Strachan (this volume).

in making elected policymakers more attentive to the broader impact of regulatory policies on their constituency.[137]

In practice, however, the effectiveness of checks to ensure that special interests have not acquired a disproportionate influence is severely constrained. The oversight of parliaments may be affected by short-term electoral incentives. The composition of the boards of regulatory agencies may skew their actions. The informational asymmetry and limited transparency which often characterize financial regulatory policymaking, combined with the often limited resources public interest groups have at their disposal, may limit such groups' capacity to scrutinize the operation of regulatory institutions. As Baxter argues, 'these traditional checks seem inadequate to ensure a balance of interests because so many regulatory decisions, from emergency lending by the Fed to daily regulatory sanctions or approvals go unnoticed'.[138]

Different proposals to mitigate the risk that regulatory agencies will be captured by special interests have therefore focused on strengthening the external checks surrounding the regulatory system or on creating new ones. Four sets of proposals are discussed in this chapter: 1) measures to enhance the transparency of the policymaking process; 2) measures to strengthen scrutiny by the judicial system; 3) the creation of independent expert bodies; and 4) checks from other regulators at the national and international level.

1.5.1 Transparency

One of the easiest ways to promote greater accountability and to favour the monitoring of instances of undue influence of special interests is to increase the transparency of the financial regulatory process.[139] For instance, different commentators have suggested that

---

[137] For the role of the media in preventing capture, see Dyck, Moss and Zingales (2008). 'Media versus Special Interests.' NBER Working Paper Series No. 14360. For the role of NGOs and other groups see Scholte and Schnabel, eds. (2002). *Civil society and global finance*. London, Routledge, and Porter (2005). *Globalization and Finance*. Cambridge, MA, Polity.

[138] Baxter (this volume).

[139] Currie (this volume); Baxter (this volume).

regulatory agencies should be required to publish on their websites details regarding their meetings with industry representatives, to make publicly available which groups comment on a regulatory proposal and whether they would be affected by the proposal together with the content of their response, as well as how the views of these groups have been taken into account in reaching the final conclusions.[140] Measures to enhance the transparency of the relationship between regulators and the regulated industry would be particularly valuable in the implementation phase of regulatory policy, where the confidentiality of supervisory relationships may make it more difficult to detect cases of capture.[141]

Some of the measures which seek to enhance the disclosure of information between regulators and different firms have been criticized on the basis that they could force firms to disclose commercially sensitive information that may be used by their competitors. From this perspective, too much transparency would have the negative effect of deterring firms from sharing their information with regulators. Moreover, during the crisis the Federal Reserve has during the crisis resisted the demands to disclose information regarding its emerging lending activities. However, according to Baxter, existing restrictions on the disclosure of information with regard to the interaction between regulators and the regulated firms 'have ended up protecting the central bank and financial institutions from political and shareholder accountability more than preserving financial stability'.[142]

There are however objective limits to what greater transparency can achieve in detecting instances of capture. Unlike in the area of central banking, there are objective limits to the possibility of quantifying and communicating the extent to which the objectives of regulation are met. Moreover, even if all the relevant information were released to the public, this does not guarantee that there will be stakeholders with the resources and incentives to process it and monitor regulators' actions.[143]

---

[140] See The Regulatory Information Reporting Act introduced by Senator Sheldon Whitehouse in July 2011; Strachan (this volume); Mogg (this volume).

[141] Walter (this volume)

[142] Baxter (this volume).

[143] Barth, Caprio and Levine (2012), p.12.

1.5.2 The legal system

Another potential source of external checks against the risk of capture could come from the legal system. As the experience of other sectors reveals, granting the right for different stakeholders to appeal some regulatory decisions in the courts, either owing to process failures or to substance, may provide an external check over those situations where regulatory decisions are not based on solid evidence and where special interests play an excessive influence.[144] According to Magill, the greater independence of judges from the political system and their longer tenure may make them less prone to being captured than regulators.[145] Moreover, the presence of a legal review process may also have indirect benefits by favouring the accountability of regulators. As Currie argues, the presence of an external legal review may make the regulator 'much more mindful of the need to ensure that its decisions comply with its statutory duties and are well reasoned and grounded in fact'.[146]

However, similar to the measures to increase the level of transparency discussed above, the application of this approach in the financial regulatory sphere incurs some severe limitations. The scope of financial regulatory decisions that can be subjected to judicial checks as a mechanism to detect instances of capture is limited by the nature of financial regulatory policies. In particular, the slow nature of judicial review frequently clashes with the technical complexity of financial regulatory issues, the difficulty of clearly identifying instances when regulators have deviated from the public interest, and the fast pace of the issues regulators have to deal with on a daily basis. While some authors present judicial review as a factor which levels the playing field, allowing the weaker stakeholders to challenge episodes of capture by those in a stronger position, this solution may also have the opposite effect of empowering those parties with more resources

---

[144] Magill (forthcoming). 'Courts and Regulatory Capture.' In: *Preventing Regulatory Capture: Special Interest Influence, and How to Limit It*, by Carpenter and Moss (forthcoming). Cambridge, Cambridge University Press; Mogg (this volume); Currie (this volume).

[145] Magill (forthcoming), *op. cit. in footnote* 143

[146] Currie (this volume).

since these are in a better position to take advantage of this mechanism.[147]

1.5.3 Expert review bodies

Given the limitations to the existing checks on the regulatory process, different authors have proposed the creation of external independent watchdogs with the responsibility of checking the operations of regulatory authorities in order to detect deviation from the public interest.

For instance, Barth, Caprio, and Levine have called for the creation of an independent institution called the "Sentinel" whose unique power would be to acquire information required to assess financial regulation and to provide an expert and independent assessment of financial policies, thus allowing an informed debate.[148] Along the same lines, Omarova has advocated the creation of a "Public Interest Council" in charge of advising Congress and regulators with respect to issues of public concern.[149] Baxter has proposed a more limited solution in the form of a self-funding consulting organization that could be consulted on key financial regulatory issues, to be established on the model of the MITRE organization, a not-for-profit organization created in the US to conduct research on national defense issues.[150] Howard Davies has discussed the possibility that a 'Sentinel-like body' could be set up by the financial industry itself.[151]

While these bodies would be staffed by experts and focus uniquely on financial regulatory issues, other proposals have instead suggested that this public interest check over financial regulatory policies should

---

[147] Barkow (2010), *op. cit. in footnote* 77.

[148] Barth, Caprio, and Levin (2012), op. cit. in footnote 1; Levine (2010). 'The Governance of Financial Regulation: Reform Lessons from the Recent Crisis.' BIS Working Paper 329.

[149] Omarova (2012). 'Bankers, Bureaucrats, and Guardians: Toward Tripartism in Financial Services Regulation.' *Journal of Corporation Law*, 37(3).

[150] Baxter (this volume).

[151] Davies (2010). 'Comments on Ross Levine's paper "The governance of financial regulation: reform lessons from the recent crisis".' BIS Working Paper 329. See also Levine (2010), *op. cit.* in footnote 147.

be performed by a body whose remit goes beyond finance. Examples in this regard are the "Office of Regulatory Integrity", as proposed by US Senator Sheldon Whitehouse in the Regulatory Capture Prevention Act of 2011, or the Australia's Productivity Commission discussed by Walter.[152] As Walter argues, 'requiring all legislation/rule setting to pass through a general public interest review process would help because the controversial concept of the "public interest" should be defined transparently and in general terms rather than on a sectoral basis'.[153]

Finally, the case for the establishment of Sentinel-like bodies has been presented not only at the national, but also at the international level. In particular, Diplock has proposed the creation of a public interest oversight body composed of international experts with no active regulatory roles, tasked to make recommendations to the members of the international regulatory community regarding to what extent international standards meet the test of public interest.[154]

However, important concerns have been voiced regarding the effectiveness and viability of subjecting the work of regulatory agencies to the scrutiny of expert public interest bodies, in particular as to how it would be possible to finance these bodies without further depriving existing regulatory institutions of resources,[155] and to what extent the highly political task of actually defining "public interest" on a given regulatory issue can be 'entrusted to a group of disinterested "wise men"'.[156]

1.5.4 Checks from other national and international regulators

Given the political difficulties in creating and funding new Sentinel-type bodies, an alternative source of checks and balances against capture may be provided by other regulatory agencies. Not only does the division of regulatory responsibilities across different agencies

---

[152] Walter (this volume).
[153] Walter (this volume).
[154] Diplock (this volume).
[155] Baxter (this volume).
[156] Davies (2010), *op. cit. in footnote* 155.

make it more difficult for any single group to dominate the regulatory process, but it also creates the potential for each regulator to represent a source of reciprocal oversight against undue interference of special interests in the work of other bodies. This kind of reciprocal oversight is particularly likely when different agencies have competing mandates, as well as when they are subject to consultation requirements or shared oversight over certain markets.[157]

From this perspective, recent innovations introduced in different countries in response to the financial crisis have improved the conditions for such reciprocal checks and balances to emerge. For instance, the crisis has led in different countries to bodies with macroprudential mandates, which may provide a system-wide perspective and challenge the undue influence of special interests in specific sectors.[158] Newly created institutions such as the Consumer Financial Protection Bureau in the US or the Financial Conduct Authority in the UK have been given an explicit mandate to protect consumer interests in the regulation of financial products.[159] The crisis has also led to the creation of institutions such as the US Office of Financial Research, which according to Barth, Caprio, and Levine 'might in theory act like a Sentinel'.[160] The creation of bodies such as the US Financial Stability Oversight Council, which includes the major regulatory institutions, has opened up a new platform to foster communication between regulatory bodies.

Reciprocal oversight on the work of regulatory authorities might also be provided at the international level. Over the years, different mechanisms have been created to subject national regulatory agencies to the scrutiny of international institutions. The East Asian financial crisis of 1997-8 has led the International Monetary Fund and the World Bank to expand their remit to include periodic reviews of the financial system of their member countries through the Financial Sector Assessment Program (FSAP) and the Reports on the Observance of Standards and Codes (ROSC). However, the

---

[157] Barkow (2010), *op. cit. in footnote* 77.

[158] Briault (this volume).

[159] Barkow (2010), op. cit. in footnote 77.

[160] Barth, Caprio and Levine (2012), p. 225, *op. cit. in footnote* 1.

effectiveness of this review process has, frequently been questioned, particularly given the capacity in the past of individual countries to block the publication of these reports and the limited power of international institutions to challenge their most important countries.[161]

Alternatively, national regulatory authorities could themselves provide international checks as they monitor their peers' activities in foreign countries. The international competitive dynamics which characterizes many financial markets mean that foreign regulatory authorities will have a strong incentive to denounce their counterparts, should they engage in regulatory forbearance and weak compliance in the implementation of internationally agreed standards which may give their domestic firms a competitive advantage vis-à-vis their foreign competitors.[162]

Innovations introduced since the crisis have created opportunities for national regulatory authorities to monitor the conduct of their counterparties and to identify national departures from international rules that lack reasonable public interest justifications.[163] G20 countries have agreed to be subject to periodic peer reviews conducted under the aegis of the Financial Stability Board (FSB), both on a thematic and on a country basis. The FSB has also been given the authority to propose exceptional measures for countries lagging behind in the implementation of internationally agreed standards, including blacklisting non-cooperative jurisdictions.[164] The FSB, in the conduct of its peer reviews, has established procedures to manage bilateral complaints regarding other countries' non-adherence to internationally agreed standards, potentially tilting the playing field in favour of their national firms.[165] Similar peer reviews will also be conducted at the European level by the newly established European supervisory authorities to monitor the implementation of the single

---

[161] Walter (this volume).

[162] Strachan (this volume).

[163] Walter (this volume).

[164] Helleiner (2010). 'What Role for the New Financial Stability Board? The Politics of International Standards After the Crisis.' *Global Policy*, October 2010.

[165] Strachan (this volume).

rulebook among different European countries. Furthermore, the potential for host-country authorities to monitor instances of regulatory capture in the policies implemented by their foreign counterparties has been increased through the creation of "colleges of supervisors" to supervise internationally active firms, from banks to insurance firms. Pressures from foreign authorities through peer reviews and colleges of supervisors may play a valuable role in preventing the design and implementation of regulatory policies which may unduly favour home-country financial institutions at the expense of other jurisdictions.

In sum, it is important to acknowledge how some of the institutional innovations that have been set in motion during the response to the crisis have the potential to increase the level of external scrutiny against the risk of capture.

1.6 Conclusions and summary of the contributions to this volume

This chapter has sought to shed light on the challenges brought about by the continuous and intense interaction between financial regulators and market participants, which characterizes the regulatory policymaking process in finance, and elucidates the numerous mechanisms that may cause the content of regulatory policies to diverge from the public interest and unduly favour special interests. While the multifaceted nature of regulatory capture and the complexity of financial markets make this risk an inevitable aspect of the regulatory process, this chapter has illustrated a variety of policy approaches through which such risk can partly be mitigated, by enhancing the plurality of voices in the policymaking process, correcting those institutional elements which may bias regulators' actions in favour of special interests, and reinforcing external scrutiny over the regulatory process.

The breadth of the approaches reviewed above and the choice not to focus on a single set of measures reflects the difference of opinion among the contributors to this volume and the literature on the appropriate approach. It is also an acknowledgement that none of these remedies alone is likely to address the multifaceted nature of the problem of capture. Moreover, as the relationship between regulators and the regulated industry assumes different forms in different contexts and countries, so too must the policy approach adapt to these different environments.[166]

However, a central theme that emerges from the discussion of these various approaches is the acknowledgment that measures to ameliorate the integrity of the regulatory process are more accessible than is often acknowledged. While some of the policy recommendations discussed in this chapter require rather broad legislative reforms, important adjustments to mitigate the risk of capture can be found in more easily attainable changes in the governance of regulatory agencies, or inside the financial industry. The regulatory agenda that has emerged since the aftermath of the crisis has neglected such "low hanging fruits" and largely focused on fixing gaps in the regulation of specific sectors or industries. The analysis developed here highlights the fact that paying attention to the process through which financial regulation is designed and implemented is equally important in order to build a more resilient financial regulatory system.

The rest of this chapter briefly summarizes the content of the contributions to follow.

The first section of the publication invites contributions from the academic community. **Lawrence Baxter** (Chapter 2) discusses the 'elusive nature' of the concept of capture in financial regulation and identifies different mechanisms to mitigate its extent. **Daniel Carpenter**, **David Moss** and **Melanie Wachtell Stinnett** (Chapter 3) discuss the lessons for financial regulatory policymaking from a recent collaborative project (Preventing Regulatory Capture: Special Interest Influence, and How to Limit It), arguing that capture is both less absolute and more preventable than is typically recognized. **Stefano Pagliari** and **Kevin Young** (Chapter 4) empirically analyse the different business groups and other stakeholders that make up the rulemaking phase in financial regulation and examine potential mitigating strategies emerging from the unique ecology of interest groups that characterize financial regulatory policymaking. The analysis by

---

[166] Currie (this volume).

Andrew Walter (Chapter 5) focuses instead on the implementation phase, highlighting how the more opaque, extended, and complex nature of this phase may offer new opportunities for the industry to capture policy.

The second section offers the perspectives of the regulatory community by including the contributions of former senior regulators. **Clive Briault** (Chapter 6) discusses the UK experience since the late 1990s, arguing that the broader political, social, and cultural context within which regulators operated played a key role in informing the attitude of regulators towards the financial industry. **Jane Diplock** (Chapter 7) discusses the role of capture in the international sphere and proposes the creation of a public interest oversight body to strengthen the integrity and credibility of international standard-setting bodies. **David Green** (Chapter 8) looks at how financial regulation is characterized by a cycle of fluctuation between a period of regulation or supervisory behaviour that in retrospect appears to have been excessively slack, and regulation which appears to have been excessively demanding. **Andrew Sheng** (Chapter 9) examines different types of regulatory capture in financial regulation and what incentives drive its existence, discussing in his conclusion different ways to deal with this problem. **David Strachan** (Chapter 10) argues that it is inevitable that legitimate claims from different stakeholders may open the policymaking process to the risk or to the perception of capture, and discusses a series of safeguards which may be employed to bolster the integrity of, and confidence in, the rulemaking and supervisory process.

The third section of this report includes contributions from representatives of financial industry associations and other stakeholders such as consumer groups and non-financial end users. **Gerry Cross** (Chapter 11) looks at how the regulation of financial services is particularly prone to the risk of "cyclical capture" and discusses what measures the financial industry can take to avoid the situation where boom periods in the economy may erode the quality of supervision. Writing from her perspective as a consumer advocate, **Christine Farnish** (Chapter 12) discusses different measures to strengthen consumers' input in an environment in which financial services firms have a built-in advantage in terms of knowledge, data, and resources. **Richard Raeburn** (Chapter 13) examines the difficulties faced by corporate end users of financial services in dealing with the round of financial regulation since 2008 and looks at the different measures to ensure that the financial regulatory process takes account of its impact on the real economy. **Adam Ridley** (Chapter 14) reflects upon his involvement in financial regulation of the investment banking community and other financial sectors, arguing that capture from the financial industry remains only one of the pathologies that affects the regulatory policymaking process.

The fourth and final section brings together the contributions of policymakers and academics that have reflected upon the experience of other sectors outside of finance. **David Currie** (Chapter 15) looks at his experience as a telecommunications regulator, discussing the lessons from his experience with regard to the importance of the marching orders that regulators receive from the legislatures, the selection processes for key regulatory positions, the revolving doors, funding, and the need to build internal checks. **John Mogg** (Chapter 16) subsequently reflects upon his experience as chairman of the gas and electricity regulator in Great Britain. He suggests that the risks of capture come from a broader set of participants than is commonly acknowledged and emphasizes the importance of preserving the independence of regulatory authorities. Finally, **Tony Porter** (Chapter 17) offers an insight into the problem of capture in the financial regulatory arena from the experience of regulation of the automobile industry, another highly globalized industry with a small number of powerful producers whose regulation has significant repercussions for society at large.

Section 1

An Academic Perspective

2.0 Understanding Regulatory Capture: an Academic Perspective from the United States

Lawrence G. Baxter[1]

2.1 Introduction

In the wake of the Financial Crisis of 2008, the huge Deepwater Horizon oil spill in 2010, and other industrial catastrophes, the media and academic journals are now replete with charges of that industries have captured their regulators. There are well-documented reports of constantly revolving doors in which the regulators and the regulated frequently change places, of huge amounts spent by industries in lobbying both legislators and regulators, and of close social relationships that exist between senior regulators and executives. A recent Bloomberg BusinessWeek profile describes the "chummy relationship" between the chairman of Citigroup, Dick Parsons, and the Secretary of the United States Treasury, Timothy Geithner, whom Parsons apparently calls "Timmy" – a term that one leading Wall Street analyst observes 'does not exactly acknowledge

---

[1] Lawrence Baxter is professor of practice of law in the Duke Law School. He has published extensively in the areas of United States and global banking and regulation; and administrative law. He began his academic career at the University of Natal in South Africa, where he held tenure from 1978 to 1984. In 1995, Baxter joined Wachovia Bank in Charlotte, NC, serving first as special counsel for Strategic Development and later as corporate executive vice president, founding Wachovia's Emerging Businesses and Insurance Group and its first eBusiness Group. He served as chief eCommerce officer for Wachovia Corporation from 2001 to 2006 before returning to Duke in 2009.

the authority of the Secretary, a post once occupied by Alexander Hamilton'.[2]

Sometimes it seems almost as if the United States Treasury (not to mention the staff of the White House itself) is run by a cadre of officials who were either recently members of Goldman Sachs or who had spent most of their waking hours interacting with the CEOs of Goldman, JP Morgan, Citi and other New York banking giants. One might be excused for assuming that the atmosphere between Big Finance and its regulators more accurately resembles the congeniality of an exclusive club than the formal relationship between regulators and a powerful industry. One might then also reasonably wonder whether such "chums" might treat each other rather more favourably than strangers[3].

"Capture" has therefore become a prominent element in public policy debates on financial regulation. As a theory of private distortion of public purpose, the concept seems important for diagnosing regulatory failures culminating in the 2008 Financial Crisis (Crisis) and for lessons on how to prevent future crises. The capture of financial regulators by elements of the financial industry is now often offered to explain why regulators did not take apparently obvious action to curb excessive industry practices that might have contributed to the Crisis, and as a reason for delayed implementation and substantial dilution of rules designed to reform the financial system.

2.2 Capture: an elusive concept

"Regulatory capture" has long played an important role in efforts to explain alleged regulatory failure. Suggesting that one interest group among many in a field contesting for recognition of their disparate

---

[2] Mayo, M. (2012). Exile on Wall Street: One Analysts Fight to Save the Big Banks From Themselves. Hoboken, N.J. Wiley. It is perhaps worth noting that the same profile observes that Parsons 'also got along well with [Comptroller of the Currency, John] Dugan, whom Parsons calls a "good guy". Leonard, D. (2011). 'Dick Parsons, Captain Emergency', Bloomberg Businessweek, 24.03.2011, available online at http://www.businessweek.com/magazine/content/11_14/b4222084044889.htm.
[3] See Johnson, S. (2009). 'The Quiet Coup.' The Atlantic, May, and Johnson, S. and J. Kwak (2010). 13 Bankers: The Wall Street Takeover and the Next Financial Meltdown. New York, Pantheon Books.

interests has seized control of the umpires, such that the game is no longer taking place on a level playing field, or that regulatory systems are even created by a strong interest group in order to stifle competition, capture is used by proponents of both regulation and deregulation to make their case. In a world of giant financial institutions, powerful chief executives, and huge bonuses despite poor financial performance, it seems that capture is to blame, one way or the other. For those in favour of more regulation, the industry's ability to influence regulators must be curbed. For those in favour of less regulation, one of the reasons for reducing regulatory influence is to prevent favoritism by captured regulators.

Capture is a perplexing concept when invoked in any area of economic regulation. It is frequently misdiagnosed because critics 'leap from an event (however embarrassing) to make large-scale inferences about an agency's entire culture', and it is often mistreated because 'there is far too much fatalism – some of it strategic, no doubt – about the possibility of ameliorating capture or even preventing it'[4]. The concept is generally problematic because it is at once a theory of legislative and regulatory motivation and a vituperative accusation levelled at results unfavorable to one of the contesting groups, even if those results might indeed strike the right balance among competing interests – "we wuz robbed", as many a losing boxer and his trainer have grumbled at the end of a fight. The accusation is likely to be made even if the actual result was the right one, or one that was inevitable given the legislative mandate under which the regulator is operating.

Capture might also manifest itself in various forms, ranging from the blatant (for example, where an official is bribed to make a decision) to the more nuanced types of 'deep' or 'cultural' capture that involve a consanguinity among elite classes of regulators and executives[5]. In the

---

[4] Carpenter, D. & D. Moss (2012). 'Introduction.' Draft chapter (as of 28.10.11) in: Carpenter and Moss, eds (forthcoming). Preventing Regulatory Capture: Special Interest Influence, and How to Limit It.

[5] Hanson J & Yosifon D, (2003), *The Situation: An Introduction to the Situational Character, Critical Realism, Power Economics, and Deep Capture*, 152 University of Pennsylvania Law Review. 129, 202–84; Kwak (forthcoming). 'Cultural Capture and the Financial Crisis', Draft chapter (as of 24.10.11) in: Carpenter, D. and D. Moss, eds (forthcoming). Preventing Regulatory Capture: Special Interest Influence, and How to Limit It.

latter situation, regulators and executives might share similar backgrounds, traditions, understandings of the markets and fundamental philosophies, talk to each other frequently and almost exclusively, share implicit understandings; the quintessential "old boys' club". Thus an appearance of impartiality on the part of a regulator might belie an inherent bias that, in various subtle ways, systematically favours that part of the industry with which the regulator most closely identifies.

2.3 Capture in financial regulation

When one starts to apply the notion of capture to financial regulation, the concept becomes more problematic than ever. In the United States (US), for example, additional elements bedevil the analysis.

There are various kinds of financial regulators. Some, for example the Office of the Comptroller of the Currency (OCC), are specifically directed to favour the industry they charter. The OCC is a prestigious agency within the Treasury Department founded back in 1863 primarily to create and propagate a national (or federal) banking system, which was intended to smother the chaotic state-chartered system that had enjoyed a monopoly in US banking after the demise of the Second Bank of the United States (1836). National banks, in the words of the US Supreme Court in 1873, are 'national favourites'. Though seldom expressed in such blunt terms, the growth and prosperity of the national banking system continues to be vigorously promoted by the OCC as a part of its implicit mandate under the National Bank Act. State-chartered banks, the tenacious counterparts to national banks, also continue to survive under the aegis of their own state chartering agencies. Bank holding companies have likewise enjoyed considerable protection by the agency directly responsible for approving their formation and promoting their prosperity, the Board of Governors of the Federal Reserve System (Fed). As we saw during the Crisis, both the Fed and the Treasury make no bones about the fact that when financial stability is threatened they consider it their first duty to protect the banks from failure in order to preserve the entire financial system. It is often declared that the passage of the Dodd-Frank Act in 2010 has put an end to the notion that any financial institution will be considered too big to fail, but few believe that this is really how the Act will be applied in another crisis.

Quite apart from these "chartering" agencies, there are other important kinds of financial regulators, such as the Federal Deposit Insurance Corporation (FDIC), the Consumer Financial Protection Bureau (CFPB), the Securities and Exchange Commission (SEC), the Commodity Futures Trading Commission (CFTC), and state insurance commissioners. Each has a different specific mission. The FDIC acts as manager and protector of the federal deposit insurance funds, and as receiver for banks and systemically important holding companies and non-bank financial institutions when they fail. The CFPB acts as a market umpire to protect consumers from improper financial products and promote proper market disclosures. The SEC and CFTC protect the overall transparency and integrity of the securities, futures and derivatives markets. State insurance commissioners regulate the insurance activities of the financial companies, no matter how large. These various agencies have often taken differing positions, sometimes in direct opposition to each other or to the Fed or the OCC. Very public examples of such clashes range from disputes over the reporting of loan loss reserves, the eligibility of trust preferred securities as appropriate components of capital, and the ability of a holding company to shelter its derivatives business inside its insured bank subsidiary. In this respect the regulatory fragmentation of the US system, far from being the chaotic structure for which it is often criticized, provides some of the "factional" elements that James Madison in the Federalist No. 10 considered so important for generating a sound result through partisan competition. So, although the public focus tends to be on the Fed and the Treasury, it is not self-evident exactly whom has been captured or how the captured agency might be able to act in the face of powerful conflicting regulatory interests without being exposed for improper bias. With this regulatory array it would be difficult in practice for any particular sector of the industry to secure the comprehensive capture of financial regulators.

The problem with capture as an analytical concept in financial regulation goes even deeper. Capture presupposes the competition of clearly delineated, divergent interests in which one stakeholder seizes control or exerts improper influence over the regulatory arbiters who are meant to be upholding an objective public interest. This idea might make some sense in the case of market regulators, such as the SEC, CFTC and CFPB, where the regulatory structure assumes a division between public (regulatory) action and private (industry and consumer) interests, in which the former strikes a balance over the contesting claims of the latter. But is this really an accurate depiction of the structure of financial markets and their relationship to financial regulators?

It is true that the activities of private market participants require financing and that this financing has generally come from non-governmental lenders and investors. In this respect banks have perhaps always been "private". However, in performing a critical role in government finance the largest banks have also long possessed a "quasi-public" character even as "private" entities. The system of national banks created by the US National Bank Act of 1863 was deliberately created to establish a national currency and provide financing to a severely cash-strapped federal government during the Civil War. For this reason, the courts recognized national banks to be not only 'national favourites' but also 'instrumentalities of the state'[6]. Such status had also earlier been extended to the First and Second Banks of the United States, which operated under direct congressional charters as quasi-central banks and this recognition took place long before the creation of a US central banking system in 1913.

These entities enjoyed quasi-public status because of the public functions they perform. Most important is their role as transmission belts of monetary policy, through which the central bank manages the money supply. They also play a central role as primary dealers and investors in huge volumes of public debt. Dealing and investing in government debt has long received privileged regulatory treatment,

---

[6] Baxter, L.G. (2012). 'Betting Big: Value, Caution and Accountability in an Era of Large Banks and Complex Finance', Review of Banking and Finance Law, 31 (Fall 2012, forthcoming)

exemption from the prohibitions otherwise placed on US banks against dealing and investing in private equity (the Glass-Steagall wall) and, when it comes to US government obligations, even from the prohibition against proprietary trading under the Volcker Rule. In addition, banks in the US are also critically important repositories for other failing financial institutions in situations where government simply lacks the resources to liquidate those institutions. Vivid examples of this "receivership" role are the acquisitions of Bear Sterns and Washington Mutual by JP Morgan Chase and of Merrill Lynch by Bank of America during the Crisis in 2008[7].

These public roles are important: they imply that large banks, despite the "private market" rhetoric, are semi-public institutions. In this context capture can become a confusing concept. After all, if banks perform public functions, why would there not be capture – perhaps even in both directions? Intense bank-regulatory influence would seem to be essential for the proper discharge of the quasi-public functions described. Capture, from this perspective, is simply inevitable and may be to a certain extent actually desirable. We do want exchanges of expertise in complicated areas of financial regulation. We do want experts as regulators, and regulatory experts as financial executives. We depend on constant interaction between the industry and regulators; indeed, bank supervision would be hard to imagine without it. And we would want some degree of coordination between government and banks for the implementation of monetary policy and the maintenance of financial stability.

2.5 Addressing capture with institutions and processes

If this view is correct, then the "problem of capture" in financial regulation might be better reframed in less tendentious terms. Some degree of capture is surely inevitable. If capture is understood as becoming undesirable when the degree of influence by one legitimate stakeholder in the regulatory process over another has become unbalanced, then avoiding or reducing the distortions created by capture – that is, disproportionate industry influence – becomes

---

[7] Ibid

essentially a question of promoting principles for maintaining transparency and accountability. Because they focus on a systemic process, no single solution is likely to prevent distortions on its own.

These principles can be grouped into five general categories: adequate regulatory capacity; meaningful transparency; meaningful access by stakeholders; external checks; and internal checks.

2.5.1 Adequate regulatory capacity

Americans treat regulators rather badly. Financial regulators are underpaid relative to the market for their skills; they are also the first to be blamed when congressional and presidential policies fail. Sometimes regulators deserve castigation but very often they are placed in the impossible position of having to carry out grossly ambitious, whipsawing and often incoherent legislative and executive mandates with inadequate resources. The recent huge extension by the Dodd-Frank Act to their regulatory mandate, followed by subsequent denials of congressional funding, provides a clear example of the regulator's predicament. Basically this is because, despite a general American acceptance of the importance of regulation,[8] the most effective short-term political strategy is to treat regulation as if it is a fundamentally illegitimate intrusion into a preordained free market. Of course this view is both historically and functionally absurd, but it is much easier to sell in the sound bites of Disneyworld economics and election year politics.

America also has a complicated regulatory framework that would have delighted cartoonists Heath Robinson and Rube Goldberg. This ramshackle regulatory structure is often criticized as a source of regulatory confusion, buck-passing and failure. My personal view is that this concern is overblown: there are many ways to structure sound regulatory institutions, and the US economy is massive enough to justify a multiplicity of specialized agencies. Perhaps it is just as well they are sometimes at odds with each other.

---

[8] Kwak, J. (2012b). 'Americans Like Regulation.' The Baseline Scenario, 13.03.2012, available online at http://baselinescenario.com/2012/03/13/americans-like-regulation/

Instead, the more important factors for ensuring adequate regulatory capacity are that:

I.   the missions of the agencies be clearly defined and coordinated;
II. the regulatory agencies be adequately funded;
III. regulators be properly incentivized through public funds, not promises of ultimate private reward from those they regulate;
IV. regulators possess or can obtain expertise that understands the businesses they regulate; and
V.   regulators be rotated, just like executives in good companies, so that they do not develop too narrow a focus of their responsibilities or too close an affinity with those they regulate.

All of these factors for regulatory adequacy are, of course, easier said than done. In financial services, pay disparities between regulators and the industry are particularly acute, notwithstanding the somewhat higher salaries paid by the financial agencies[9]. Other forms of incentives, such as enhanced status and special appeals to public minded recruits, might be important[10].

Unfortunately an obstacle is that public hostility toward regulators seems to be getting worse, not better, as election year rhetoric surrounding budget cuts intensifies. Yet the trade-off is as obvious as it is inevitable: the less resource capacity the regulators possess, the more dependent they will have to be on the industry they supervise[11].

2.5.2 Meaningful transparency

Adequate input by all significant stakeholders is required by the principle of participatory democracy and is surely vital for developing informed policy and its accurate implementation under the circumstances of the market and the industry. Given the extremely

---

[9] Philippon, T. and A. Reshef (2008). 'Wages and Human Capital in the U.S. Financial Industry: 1909-2006.' NBER Working Paper, No. 13405.
[10] Baxter, L. G. (2011). ' "Capture" in Financial Regulation: Can We Channel it Toward the Common Good?' Cornell Journal of Law and Public Policy, 21(1): 175-200.
[11] McCarty, N. (2012). 'Complexity, Capacity and Capture', Draft chapter (as of 07.13.11) in: Carpenter, D. and D. Moss, eds (forthcoming). *Preventing Regulatory Capture: Special Interest Influence in Regulation and How to Limit It.*

technical nature of finance and the close relationship between banking and government, it is natural that industry and regulators will develop very close associations. This closeness surely distorts perceptions over time and inevitably precludes consideration of other interests that ought also be placed in balance.

Various tools and techniques exist or have been proposed for promoting a proper balance. Sunlight through transparency – that Brandeisian 'best of disinfectants'[12] – remains as sound as ever. Bankers resist transparency for various reasons. They are practised in strictly protecting client confidentiality and they do not want to share information that might be useful to competitors. Together with central bankers they also fear that disclosure would reveal financial institution dependence on liquidity supports, and that this knowledge would be misunderstood by the markets and lead to runs on institutions and perhaps even to general financial instability.

These arguments against transparency are dubious. The first – protecting client confidentiality – is usually not endangered when detailed but anonymized bank information is disclosed, and if a client position is so large that it would be recognized this information is usually known to the market anyway. The second – protecting information from competitors – is no more important than in any other industry, so it is unclear why banks should enjoy a special privilege in this regard. And the third – protecting the market from misunderstanding the liquidity needs of banks – seems really to have ended up protecting the central bank and financial institutions from political and shareholder accountability more than preserving financial stability. For example, the Fed fought tooth and nail to resist Freedom of Information Act demands by two news media for disclosures relating to its emergency lending during and soon after the Crisis. When disclosure was finally forced, the information proved very embarrassing for both domestic and foreign financial institutions and the Fed itself. Had the Fed's actions been known during the passage of the Dodd-Frank Act, different policy choices might well have been

---

[12] Brandeis, L. (1913). 'What Publicity Can Do', *Harper's Weekly*, Dec. 20, 1913, available at: http://www.law.louisville.edu/library/collections/brandeis/node/196.

made, both regarding the support powers of the Fed and the permissible scale and operations of financial institutions.

The greater transparency imposed on the Fed by Dodd-Frank has helped produce more informed views on financial regulatory policy. Basel II and III also strive to promote greater disclosure to the markets. Additionally, more rigorous disclosure requirements could help prevent biased decision making that might arise from the revolving door between regulators and their industry. Greater disclosure all round would at least enable other stakeholders and the media to focus a spotlight on improper collusion.

2.5.3 Realistic stakeholder access

Participatory democracy also implies meaningful access to the process of regulation by all legitimate stakeholders. In the financial world this problem is particularly acute because financial institutions possess immense influence by reason of their size, resources and lobbying power. There is a strong argument for correcting this imbalance through devices and institutions that strengthen the ability of other stakeholders – customers, smaller financial institutions, specific niche industries, and so on – to represent their interests and be properly heard and responded to by the agencies that are charged with recognizing and protecting their interests.

Such correctives can take various forms. General public comment during the rulemaking process is one important vehicle but, as scholars have demonstrated, business comment appears to have much more influence than private inputs[13]. When it comes to the highly technical dimensions of financial regulation, such as working out the details of the Volcker Rule, the collective action problems for the general public seem particularly profound. Their mass action comments are often composed of little more than worthless form

---

[13] Yackee J & Yackee S (2006). *A Bias Toward Business? Group Influence on the U.S. Bureaucracy*, 68 J. POL. 128 and Yackee S (2012). "Reconsidering Agency Capture During Regulatory Policymaking." in Daniel Carpenter and David Moss (Eds.), *Preventing Regulatory Capture: Special Interest Influence, and How to Limit It* (forthcoming)

letters[14]. Industry input is much better organized and informed, and because of this it is also much more influential.

There are other possibilities. Ayres and Braithwaite propose a model of 'tripartism', in which non-industry groups would have full access to all the information before regulators, a seat at the negotiating table during the deal making process, and standing to sue or prosecute that is equal to that of the regulator itself[15]. Another approach might be to use a model from public utility regulation, where utility regulators in many jurisdictions are expressly charged by their authorizing legislation to consider and uphold the public interest. In some situations this role is institutionalized by the specific creation of a representative of the public interest who is engaged in the decision making process. A potential model for applying tripartism in financial services regulation can perhaps also be found in insurance regulation, where some states have developed proxy advocates for supporting the public interest in regulatory proceedings[16].

2.5.4 External checks

Various external checks surround the modern regulatory process, some more effective than others. The media can cast light on the process and generate public review. Congressional committees and inspectors general often engage in far-reaching investigations of the actions of the financial regulators, sometimes with very critical effect. Some judges, too, have strongly criticized the leniency of agencies in settlements with the industry, as was most recently demonstrated by Judge Rakoff's rejection of two settlements by the SEC against Bank of

---

[14] Krawiec, K. (2011). 'Don't "Screw Joe The Plummer": The Sausage-Making of Financial Reform. Working Paper, 09/2011, available at http://scholarship.law.duke.edu/faculty_scholarship/2445/.

[15] See Ayres, I. and J. Braithwaite (1991). 'Tripartism: Regulatory Capture and Empowerment', *Law & Social Inquiry*, 16(3): 435-96. and Ayres, I. and J. Braithwaite (1992). *Responsive Regulation: Transcending the Deregulation Debate*. New York. Oxford University Press

[16] Schwarcz, D. (2012). 'Preventing Capture Through Consumer Empowerment Programs: Some Evidence from Insurance Regulation.' Draft chapter (as of 28.10.11) in: Carpenter, D. and D. Moss, eds (forthcoming). *Preventing Regulatory Capture: Special Interest Influence in Regulation and How to Limit It*.

America and Citigroup. (Judge Rakoff's decision to reject the Citi settlement has been remanded by the Second Circuit Court of Appeal for having gone too far.) Perhaps there is greater scope for judicial checks on the excessive influence of particular stakeholders, though this check remains limited and highly dependent on the specific nature of disputes[17]. Finally, as already noted, the agencies themselves are sometimes at odds with each other in ways that enrich the public debate, necessary to promote sound policy outcomes.

These traditional checks seem inadequate to ensure a balance of interests because so many regulatory decisions, from emergency lending by the Fed to daily regulatory sanctions or approvals, go unnoticed. Furthermore, when it comes to complex and highly technical rulemaking, the relative expertise of interested parties can be extremely lopsided, with industry representatives having by far the greater knowledge and understanding of the issues and, as a result, effectiveness of comment in the rulemaking process. Groups of independent experts are not well organized into coherent committees capable of providing sufficient balance to the cacophony of pro- or anti-industry views[18].

This imbalance seems likely to distort how the agency perceives the issues and interprets its empowering legislation, even if there might in fact be alternative views just as important yet inarticulately held by stakeholders who lack the basic competence to represent them.

Such shortcomings in the representative process have led to various suggestions for new external checks on the regulatory process. The author has proposed a self-funding and independent consulting organization that would have to be consulted on key issues of regulatory policymaking. An example of such a model in the US is the MITRE organization which is primarily focused on military contracting

---

[17] Magill, E. M. (2012). 'Courts and Regulatory Capture', Draft chapter (as of 11.29.11, cited with permission) in: Carpenter, D. and D. Moss, eds (forthcoming). *Preventing Regulatory Capture: Special Interest Influence in Regulation and How to Limit It.*

[18] Balleisen, E. (2011). 'The Global Financial Crisis and Responsive Regulation: Some Avenues for Historical Inquiry', *University of British Columbia Law Review*, 44(3): 557-87.

but which has indeed sometimes provided advice to financial agencies[19].

A much broader proposal is that of an agency or "Sentinel" that would have power to demand information, have expertise to evaluate this information and the financial policies being adopted by the agencies, and have the responsibility to report its views to Congress and the executive branch. With purview over the whole financial system, the Sentinel would bring a broader perspective to bear than might otherwise be held by the specific agency whose action is under review. Being independently funded and situated, the Sentinel would also be in a position to offer impartial views as between the various financial agencies[20].

Another broad proposal is a 'Public Interest Council' that would consist of an expert independent government agency appointed by Congress and located outside the executive branch, charged with participating in the regulatory process 'as the designated representative of the public interest in preserving long-term financial stability and minimizing systemic risk'. Like the Sentinel, the Council would possess neither legislative nor executive powers; it would, however, have wide authority to collect information from both government agencies and private market participants, conduct investigations, publicize its findings and advise Congress and regulators to take action 'with respect to issues of public concern'[21].

The difficulty with each of these ideas is that they are predicated on a substantive public interest that can be identified in some detached way by experts. Yet it is unlikely that any of the agents in the process would acknowledge or even perceive that their positions were not in fact the best ones for the public interest, and it is has become naive to

---

[19] Baxter, L. G. (2011). ' "Capture" in Financial Regulation: Can We Channel it Toward the Common Good?' *Cornell Journal of Law and Public Policy*, 21(1): 175-200.

[20] See Barth, J. R., G. Caprio Jr. and R. Levine (2012). *Guardians of Finance: Making Regulators Work for Us*, Cambridge & London, MIT Press and Levine, R. (2010). 'The governance of financial regulation: reform lessons from the recent crisis.' BIS Working Paper 329.

[21] Omarova, S.T. (2012). 'Bankers, Bureaucrats, and Guardians: Toward Tripartism in Financial Services Regulation.' *Journal of Corporation Law*, 37, forthcoming

expect otherwise. As one critic of the Sentinel idea has put it, 'it is misleading to suggest that these [regulatory] judgements do not have a strong political dimension to them. They cannot be put on autopilot, or entrusted to a group of disinterested "wise men"'[22]. Proposing the addition of new layers to the regulatory process is also a questionable strategy, politically and financially. The regulators tend to under-resourced as it is, and regulatory burden in financial services has become a rallying cry for the industry, sometimes with good reason. In the United States at least, proposing to allocate yet more funds to yet more external public agencies would have little prospect of success in today's Congress.

Another promising and potentially meaningful check, however, is also emerging in the United States, following similar developments in the United Kingdom. This is a cadre of privately funded and diverse expert organizations akin to the "shadow banking committee" that played a prominent role in critique of financial regulatory policy in the United States in the 1980s and 1990s. The original shadow banking committee is now known as the Shadow Financial Regulatory Committee, an independent committee sponsored by the American Enterprise Institute. Additional examples are the Centre for Economic Policy Research, PublicCitizen, new deal 2.0, Project on Government Oversight (POGO) and Americans for Financial Reform.

In another chapter in this book, Christine Farnish, chair of Consumer Focus, describes the experience in the United Kingdom of such initiatives and their potential for promoting more effective consumer input on financial regulation. Bodies like these are independent of the industry itself and presumably reflect independent perspectives and accumulating financial expertise. One might anticipate that such organizations will develop the capability of providing extensive expert input into the regulatory process, with the muscle to assure public coverage and regulatory and congressional attention.

---

[22] Davies, H. (2010). 'Comments on Ross Levine's Paper "The governance of financial regulation: reform lessons from the recent crisis." ' BIS Working Paper 329.

2.5.5 Internal checks

One of the most effective means of restoring equilibrium in interests in financial services is not external checks and balances, but internal change within the industry itself. This might be through cultural change, perhaps a return to a more restrained approach to market competition, away from the trading culture and back to advisory professionalism. A frequently heard lament is for the days before Goldman Sachs became a public company, when the investment banking culture was dominant and personal liability more real. Viewed in this light the emphasis on increased capital levels – more skin in the game on the part of the owners of financial firms themselves and less reliance on other people's money – represents an attempt to restore a greater sense of personal responsibility for risk-taking.

There might also be other ways to adjust the internal attitudes of financial executives, such as changes to liability rules. For example, fiduciary duties can be extended to cover more genuine "clients", a matter on which the SEC presented recommendations for broker-dealers and investment advisers under the mandate of Section 913 of the Dodd-Frank Act (SEC 2011) and which is fiercely resisted by industry groups. Elsewhere, I have argued that the fiduciary duty of the board and top executives, traditionally focused exclusively on shareholders, should to be adapted to reflect the fact that a critical third party, though not always recognized, is inevitably present in the boardroom, namely the public that subsidizes the industry so heavily.[23]

These kinds of proposals tend to arouse great hostility from the industry, as we saw with the enactment of Section 404 of the Sarbanes-Oxley Act in 2002. Yet a vivid personal experience for me was the change in how fellow executives and I focused on financial reporting once we became aware that we were personally on the hook for their reliability. There is nothing like personal liability in the

---

[23] Baxter, L.G. (2012). 'Betting Big: Value, Caution and Accountability in an Era of Large Banks and Complex Finance', *Review of Banking and Finance Law*, 31 (Fall 2012, forthcoming).

midst of great corporate brumes to focus the mind on what is important.

2.6 Conclusion

Capture in the somewhat quasi-public industry of financial services is quite chameleonic. It is the seemingly perverse result of an unavoidably close and intense interaction between regulators and the industry, yet it is hard to imagine a financial services industry free of the phenomenon. The complex interaction between regulators and industry makes it hard to solve the problems of distortive influence through any one technique; instead, a more effective approach – to deploy a cluster of rather traditional solutions – continues to be necessary. This hardly comes as a surprise, given the exceptionally complex nature of financial markets, their volatile and rapid evolution, and the complicated and often conflicting policies that we support.

3.0 Lessons for the Financial Sector from 'Preventing Regulatory Capture: Special Interest Influence, and How to Limit it'

Daniel Carpenter[1], David Moss[2] and Melanie Wachtell Stinnett[3]

3.1 Introduction[4]

In the wake of the global financial crisis of 2007–09, regulatory capture has become at once a diagnosis and a source of discomfort. The word

[1] Daniel Carpenter is the Allie S. Freed Professor of Government and Director of the Center for American Political Studies in the Faculty of Arts and Sciences at Harvard University. Professor Carpenter focuses upon public bureaucracies and government regulation, particularly regulation of health and financial products. His latest book is 'Reputation and Power: Organizational Image and Pharmaceutical Regulation at the FDA' (Princeton University Press 2010).

[2] David Moss is the John G. McLean Professor at Harvard Business School and the founder of the Tobin Project. His academic research focuses on economic policy and especially the government's role as a risk manager. He has published numerous books and articles on these subjects, including 'When All Else Fails: Government as the Ultimate Risk Manager' (Harvard University Press, 2002). Professor Moss's most recent book is 'Government & Markets: Toward a New Theory of Regulation' (edited with E. Balleisen, Cambridge University Press, 2010). Professors Carpenter and Moss are the editors of 'Preventing Regulatory Capture: Special Interest Influence and How to Limit It' (Cambridge University Press, forthcoming).

[3] Melanie Wachtell Stinnett is the Director of Policy and Communications at The Tobin Project. She has published on trends in the United States Supreme Court's docket and served as Project Manager for the TARP Congressional Oversight Panel's "Special Report on Regulatory Reform," published to Congress in January 2009. Previously, she worked as a voter protection attorney during the 2008 presidential campaign and as an attorney in private practice focused on federal appellate litigation.

[4] The authors would like to thank John Cisternino and Yousef Gharbieh whose thoughtful contributions and unwavering commitment to the Preventing Regulatory Capture edited volume have significantly influenced and strengthened this essay.

"capture" has been used by dozens upon dozens of authors – ranging from pundits and bloggers to journalists and leading scholars – as the tell-tale characterization of the regulatory failures that permitted the crisis.[5] In addition, critics who doubt whether regulatory reforms will be sufficient draw upon capture as a source of widespread scepticism (if not despair) that nothing real can be changed. Seen this way, capture of financial regulation appears not only as a significant cause of the crisis, but also as a constraint upon any realistic solutions. Most of those solutions will, in this view, be watered down or dashed by captured regulators in the future.

Is capture truly as powerful and unpreventable as the informed consensus seems to suggest? When it prevails, does capture pose insurmountable obstacles to financial regulation, so much so that we ought to give up on regulation altogether? We write as part of a large-scale project that questions this logic and suggests that, indeed, capture may be preventable and manageable, including in the realm of financial oversight.

In this essay, we first detail how questions arising from the drive for financial regulatory reform in the wake of the crisis encouraged a focus on "preventing capture" and the development of an edited volume on the subject: Preventing Regulatory Capture: Special Interest Influence and How to Limit It.[6] We then turn to a discussion of the central thesis of Preventing Regulatory Capture, arguing that capture is both less absolute and more preventable than is typically recognized. Focusing on several case studies in Preventing Regulatory Capture, we next examine prevention strategies that are already in place across regulatory agencies. In the conclusion, we consider recommendations from Preventing Regulatory Capture that may be particularly relevant to managing special interest influence in the financial sector.

---

[5] See, e.g., Daron Acemoglu & Simon Johnson, 'Who captured the Fed?' Economix Blog, The New York Times, March 29, 2012, available at http://economix.blogs. nytimes.com/2012/03/29/who-captured-the-fed/ (accessed April 30, 2012); Daniel Kauffman, 'Corruption and the Global Financial Crisis', Forbes, January 27, 2009; Gary Becker, ' "Capture" of Regulators by Fannie Mae and Freddie Mac', available at http://www.becker-posner-blog.com/2011/06/capture-of-regulators-by-fannie-mae-and-freddie-mac-becker.html (accessed July 21, 2011); and Gerald P. O'Driscoll, Jr., 'The Gulf Spill, the Financial Crisis and Government Failure', Wall Street Journal, June 12, 2010.
[6] Preventing Regulatory Capture: Special Interest Influence and How to Limit It (D. Carpenter & D. Moss, eds, Cambridge University Press, forthcoming).

3.3 How financial regulatory reform illuminated the need for research on "preventing capture"

In early 2008, a group of social scientists convened to consider the state of scholarship on regulation as part of a research initiative organized by the Tobin Project, an independent and non-profit research organization based in Cambridge, MA. While research on government failure had come a long way since the mid-twentieth century, scholarship on what distinguishes government success from failure had been less robust. It was as if medical researchers had spent decades identifying cases of medical error, without offering a complementary understanding of how (and when) doctors operated successfully to improve patients' lives. A new focus was needed to better understand not only cases in which government failed, but also cases in which government succeeded and the conditions under which each occurred. In 2010, this research effort produced a first edited volume – Government & Markets: Toward a New Theory of Regulation[7] – which explored both the promises and the pitfalls of regulation, and ultimately aimed to identify strategies for improving regulatory governance.

The financial crisis of 2007–2009 gave palpable urgency to this on-going research initiative. As financial regulatory reform took centre stage in Washington, DC, policymakers were faced with a great range of complex issues, tasked with addressing the risks and benefits inherent in everything from derivatives markets to systemically significant financial institutions. To get up to speed on such highly specialized subjects, legislators and their staffs often turned to outside experts for input. At various points during the regulatory reform process, scholars involved in the Tobin Project's research efforts were asked to share their perspectives on the problems of financial regulation, and to give advice on potential solutions.

As these conversations progressed, preventing capture emerged as an important issue for policymakers. Throughout 2009 and 2010, both the House of Representatives and the Senate were considering bills that would establish a new agency with independent authority to

---

[7] Government & Markets: Toward a New Theory of Regulation (E. Balleisen & D. Moss, eds, Cambridge University Press)

protect retail consumers of financial products, an idea initially developed by Professor Elizabeth Warren. At the same time, both houses of Congress were exploring options for how to manage systemic risk throughout the financial system, proposals which ultimately gave rise to the Financial Stability Oversight Council. With respect to both efforts, the question arose repeatedly: was it possible to design agencies in ways that would protect or insulate them from capture?

This question was on policymakers' agendas, and it became increasingly clear that it should be on the research agenda of academics as well. At the time, scholars affiliated with the Tobin Project were able to offer recommendations on how legislators might prevent capture based on their own experience and expertise. Yet, the relevant literature was disturbingly thin, with a notable lack of attention to the question of capture prevention. There is, of course, a long history of work in the tradition of Bernstein, Huntington, Stigler, and their contemporaries on the perceived state of regulatory capture in government. However, while there have been some notable contributions over the past several decades,[8] research on strategies for preventing capture remains at an early stage. To make progress in this area, we would first need to agree on a precise

---

[8] See, *e.g.*, Mathew D. McCubbins, Roger G. Noll, Barry R. Weingast, 'Administrative Procedures as Instruments of Political Control', *Journal of Law, Economics, & Organization*, 3(2), Autumn, 1987, p. 247; Jean-Jacques Laffont and David Martimort, 'Separation of Regulators Against Collusive Behavior', *RAND Journal of Economics*, 30(2), Summer 1999, pp. 233, 257; Terry M. Moe, 'The Politics of Structural Choice: Toward a Theory of Public Bureaucracy', in Oliver E. Williamson, ed., *Organization Theory: From Chester Barnard to the Present and Beyond*, expanded edition, New York: Oxford University Press, 1995, p. 147; Daniel Carpenter, 'Protection without Capture: Product Approval by a Politically Responsive, Learning Regulator', *American Political Science Review*, 98(4), November 2004, pp. 613-31; Steven P. Croley, *Regulation and Public Interests: The Possibility of Good Regulatory Government*, Princeton: Princeton University Press, 2008, pp. 143-44; David Moss and Mary Oey, 'The Paranoid Style in the Study of American Politics', *Government and Markets: Toward a New Theory of Regulation*, edited by Edward Balleisen and David Moss, Cambridge: Cambridge University Press, 2010; Alexander Dyck, David A. Moss, and Luigi Zingales. 'Media versus Special Interests', NBER Working Paper Series, No. 14360, September 2008, p. 31; and Gunnar Trumbull, *Strength in Numbers: The Political Power of Weak Interests*, Cambridge: Harvard University Press, forthcoming.

definition of capture, introduce clear standards of evidence for determining the extent to which capture succeeds in turning regulatory decision making against the public interest, and explore the reach of special-interest influence in practice (paying particular attention to why such influence may be more limited in some contexts than others). The forthcoming edited volume from the Tobin Project, Preventing Regulatory Capture, aims to address this suite of questions.

3.4 A new scholarly understanding of regulatory capture

The central thesis of the volume is that regulatory capture[9] is partly – and perhaps largely – preventable. This proposition marks a departure from earlier scholarship and commentary that tended to consider capture to be largely inevitable and ubiquitous, often on the basis of limited evidentiary support. From our perspective, the primary problem with the traditional capture argument boils down to the tenuous link between theory and observation. In certain instances in the literature, capture has been misdiagnosed, inferred on the basis of undesired regulatory outcomes in the absence of careful empirical or observational analysis. In part as a consequence, the literature has not focused on methods to prevent or treat undue special interest influence since capture has often been seen as unavoidable. In many cases, these studies generated calls for deregulation, on the grounds that no regulation would be better than regulation captured by industry.

---

[9] In *Preventing Regulatory Capture*, we begin with the following definition: 'regulatory capture is a result or process by which regulation (in law or application) is, at least partially, by intent and action of the industry regulated, consistently or repeatedly directed away from the public interest and towards the interests of the regulated industry'. Hewing closely to this definition, we posit that to properly diagnose capture a researcher would need to (a) identify a defeasible public interest, (b) show action and intent by industry, and (c) show policy shift away from the public interest as a result of the intentional action of industry. Only by meeting these criteria can scholars distinguish capture from a host of other factors that shape regulation. Even more importantly, scholars can then determine the degree to which capture is diminishing a regulation's contribution to the public good and the extent to which mitigation and prevention techniques are, and can be, effective.

In contrast to this earlier literature, however, the case studies in Preventing Regulatory Capture suggest that capture is rarely, if ever, absolute. Contributors to the volume carefully examined a range of agencies and found that capture was far from complete in many cases, as there were clear limits and checks on industry influence. As a result, it seems reasonable to think that there was not "strong" capture in these cases of the type Stigler and his contemporaries might have predicted – that is, capture so damaging that society would be better off if the regulation did not exist at all. Rather, a more nuanced story emerged across several regulatory arenas to suggest that some cases of "capture" prove not to be that at all, and that even when industry does exert significant influence, regulations can still be at least partly – or even largely – successful in serving the public good.

For example, focusing on the question of how best to use history to diagnose capture, David Moss and Jonathan Lackow conduct a thorough historical analysis of a key decision made by the Federal Radio Commission in 1927.[10] That year, the FRC opted not to expand the broadcast band, a decision widely assumed in the subsequent economics literature to have been a clear-cut case of capture by incumbent broadcasters (who presumably wanted to avoid additional competition on an expanded radio band). However, in re-evaluating the historical record, including additional source material that had not previously been considered, Moss and Lackow find that the FRC's decision was supported by all of the relevant interest groups at the time, from radio manufacturers to radio listeners, and that incumbent broadcasters were among the most divided on the issue. Given that the preferences of a broad range of stakeholders were reflected in the decision, there is little basis for characterizing it as having been captured by a narrow industry interest. Moss and Lackow suggest that previous observers may have let their faith in theory get the better of them in diagnosing this as a case of regulatory capture, particularly when hard historical evidence strongly pointed the other way.

---

[10] Throughout this essay, we refer to chapters in the forthcoming volume, *Preventing Regulatory Capture*, by author name only, with no corresponding page citations for direct quotations. At the time of writing, the volume is in manuscript form and pagination has yet to be finalized.

Similarly, in a detailed case study of the Food and Drug Administration's decision making over a period of several decades, Daniel Carpenter finds no evidence of "strong" capture of the kind that Stiglerian theory would have predicted. In a historical analysis of the expansion of the FDA's statutory mandate in the 1930s and subsequent decisions through the 1960s, Carpenter finds that a capture hypothesis is not supported by the historical record or empirical analysis of Congressional voting patterns. Indeed, working with a coalition of allies, including women's groups and consumer unions, the FDA was able to secure passage of a new enabling statute expanding its authority to include gatekeeping power over drugs, among other things. Carpenter notes that 'the predominant influence upon the agency during this period came from a set of multiple constituencies and audiences at the nexus of academic pharmacology, government and university scientists, and industry'. Industry was certainly involved and at one point did 'blunt the FDA's initiative' through allies in Congress, but its influence was not controlling and did not rise to the level of capture. According to Carpenter, the passage of the FDA's enabling legislation in 1938 and 1962 'offers a stark rejection of capture-based hypotheses'.

In a separate study of three public health agencies, Mariano-Florentino Cuéllar also finds evidence 'contravening some of the more aggressive versions of the now-commonplace "agency capture" theory'. Cuéllar examines major decisions made by the USDA, the FDA, and the CDC in recent decades: an effort to regulate food-borne pathogens in the 1990s, an initiative to assert jurisdiction over tobacco in the 1990s, and an evolution toward a greater role in health surveillance, respectively. Drawing on a rich historical record, Cuéllar finds evidence of competing interests in all three cases, often with the regulated industry opposing the outcome. As put by Cuéllar, 'these examples complicate, at least in the public health context, the idea that agencies are largely unable to overcome resistance in order to pursue important policy innovations bearing more than a plausible relationship to advancing social welfare'. Indeed, in all three cases the agencies 'broke new ground in protecting the public health', despite significant opposition from industry.

What these case studies and others[11] in Preventing Regulatory Capture suggest is that capture is not absolute. Across a range of agencies, the studies in Preventing Regulatory Capture uncover evidence of multiple stakeholders successfully influencing regulatory outcomes. These findings call into question any narrative of "strong" capture, where industry controls the regulator to an extent that the public would be better served if the regulation under consideration did not exist at all. Instead, special interest influence seems to manifest in degrees. In some cases, industry might be participating in a manner not contrary to the public interest, or may have no discernible effect. In other cases, industry influence can be so significant as to rise to the level of capture, but it is generally of the type that we would call "weak" capture. In contrast to "strong" capture, which would render a regulation detrimental to the public interest, "weak" capture describes a situation where industry influence may limit or undermine a regulator's efforts to serve the public interest, but not so much that society would be better off without the regulation.[12] In such cases, the question at hand is how to treat the problem of capture, without throwing the proverbial baby out with the bathwater.

3.5 Strategies to prevent regulatory capture

If we understand special interest influence to exist along this spectrum, as opposed to being uniform and inevitable, we must reject the conclusion that deregulation is the appropriate response in all cases. Deregulation may be appropriate in selected cases, but it

---

[11] In an illuminating study of the Minerals Management Service (MMS), implicated and widely criticized after the Deepwater Horizon explosion and Gulf oil spill of spring 2010, Christopher Carrigan provides evidence in his contribution to Preventing Regulatory Capture that even claims about the capture of this agency are relatively weak. And in a study in the volume on mining inspections by the Mine Safety and Health Administration, Catherine Hafer and Sanford Gordon provide enlightening new quantitative evidence that countermands simplistic capture explanations of regulatory behaviour in this realm.

[12] In the Preventing Regulatory Capture volume, we also discuss the difference between "entry-barrier" capture of the sort that erects new regulations as a means of facilitating the power of incumbent firms, and deregulatory capture which vitiates public interest regulation in favour of a wide variety of alternative interests.

cannot serve as the "go-to" or default solution when capture is diagnosed within a regulatory agency or a policy regime. A new framework that accounts for the diverse types of special interest influence opens the door to a fresh examination of potential solutions, ranging from deregulation in certain cases to treatment or prevention in many others. Indeed, the case studies in Preventing Regulatory Capture suggest that capture is likely a treatable condition in many contexts and point to numerous strategies already in place in the regulatory system to constrain undue special interest influence where it might emerge.

If we turn back to the case studies by Carpenter and Cuéllar discussed above, each is suggestive of existing mechanisms to prevent undue special-interest influence in regulation. With respect to the FDA, Carpenter notes that the active participation of an alliance of actors in the decision making process likely helped to prevent industry from exerting overwhelming influence. In the case of the public health agencies, Cuéllar emphasizes that the agencies' scientific expertise, broad statutory mandates, and alliances with civil society and political appointees enabled them to push forward with regulation in the public interest, even where industry was applying sizeable pressure in a different direction. Taken together, these case studies suggest, among other things, that strategies to enhance the participation of non-industry actors during agency decision making could potentially help to keep industry influence in check.

Indeed, several contributors in Preventing Regulatory Capture emphasize a similar point: involving a diversity of interests in the decision making process can help to prevent industry capture and mitigate lesser degrees of special interest influence. For example, in a chapter on the Department of Transportation, Susan Webb Yackee conducts an empirical analysis of comments during rulemaking and finds that while business influence is prevalent, 'it is not dominant and does not rise to the level of capture'. In an environment where industry is lobbying the regulator proactively and consistently during the rulemaking process, Yackee concludes that industry influence nevertheless does not dominate policy outcomes. Why is industry influence not controlling here? Among other things, Yackee identifies the participation of sub-national officials in the comment process as a valuable counterweight. Noting that state-level transportation officials are often implementing DOT policy and thus have access to technical information and data, Yackee argues that 'sub-national officials may provide a previously underappreciated deterrent to agency capture during regulatory policymaking'.[13] Put simply, they may 'provide a foil to business interests'.

While Yackee highlights a somewhat organic means of diversifying the input reaching a regulator, another option is to establish consumer empowerment programs with this discrete purpose. In his contribution to Preventing Regulatory Capture, Daniel Schwarcz examines programs intentionally designed to give voice to the public interest in the arena of state insurance regulation, where industry has 'substantial influence over regulatory outcomes'. He examines two types of consumer empowerment programs – proxy advocacy and what scholars Ian Ayres and John Braithwaite have called 'tripartism'[14] – through three detailed case studies of their implementation in California, Texas, and the National Association of Insurance Commissioners. For cases in which there is one clear consumer perspective, Schwarcz finds that having a proxy advocate appointed within the government can be most effective because the advocate 'appears to influence regulatory results primarily by providing regulators with expertise and information from a consumer perspective, rather than by applying political pressure'. However, where there are multiple consumer interests at stake, Schwarcz argues that tripartism is more effective at counteracting the industry perspective, in part because in such cases the regulator needs to hear from numerous advocacy groups, all of which can be empowered and reimbursed for their involvement in the regulatory process. Broadly, Schwarcz concludes that the consumer empowerment programs he studies are effective means through which to channel the consumer perspective into the regulatory process, arguing that a dual approach

[13] Nugent, John D. (2009). *Safeguarding Federalism: How States Protect their Interests in National Policymaking*. Norman, OK: University of Oklahoma Press.

[14] Ayres, I. and Braithwaite, J. (1991). 'Tripartism: Regulatory Capture and Empowerment', *Law & Social Inquiry*, 16: 435–96.

of proxy advocacy and tripartism be implemented to capitalize on the strengths of each.

Together, these four case studies suggest that strategies for capture prevention are already in place in several arenas and that these methods can potentially be exported to regulatory environments where undue special interest influence is manifest. The challenge going forward is to deepen our understanding of why certain strategies work effectively, build on those successes where possible, and use our enhanced understanding to develop and test new strategies that have not yet been tried. The need for such tools is perhaps particularly strong in the financial sector, where the tumult of the past few years has underscored the importance of regulation in the public interest, protected from industry capture.

3.6 Preventing capture in the financial sector

Before we turn to how the strategies discussed in Preventing Regulatory Capture might be applied in finance – a question that in many ways sparked this research inquiry – it might be helpful to ask whether "capture" in fact exists in the financial sector and, if so, in what form. Indeed, as the financial crisis of 2007–2009 unfolded, and regulatory responses were proposed and debated, we began to notice some common features of the dozens (if not hundreds) of claims being made about captured regulatory agencies. The claims had the benefit of seeming to fit neatly with the unfolding story, yet a disturbing commonality among them was a lack of solid evidence. It could appear, and often did appear, that regulatory agencies were being steered (consciously or not) by the very entities they were supposed to regulate. Yet in most cases there was little or no direct evidence linking the process (or events) of capture to the regulatory failures that everyone decried.

A targeted empirical assessment of whether and to what extent regulatory capture exists in the financial sector is beyond the scope of this short essay. However, what the case studies in Preventing Regulatory Capture tell us is that to the extent that capture does manifest in the financial sector, it likely does so in a variety of degrees and deserves an equally multifaceted response. One factor that may be relevant in identifying helpful strategies is the sheer complexity of modern finance. Indeed, the exceptional intricacy of financial products and relationships may well make regulators in the field prone to particular kinds of special interest influence. This argument is advanced by two contributors in Preventing Regulatory Capture: Nolan McCarty in a discussion of expertise in complex policy arenas, and James Kwak in a chapter on "cultural capture".

In brief, what both McCarty and Kwak argue (in part) is that the complexity inherent in the financial sector makes regulators particularly dependent on industry for expertise, and thus more likely than regulators in less complex arenas to be influenced by it. For his part, McCarty models regulation in complex policy domains, noting that in finance in particular experts who work in industry are paid a substantial wage premium, and many are trained in schools that tend toward an industry perspective at the outset. Consequently, 'bureaucrats find it very difficult to establish autonomous sources of information and expertise about the consequences of different policies'. McCarty concludes that 'as policy becomes more complex, regulatory outcomes are increasingly biased towards those preferred by the firm'.

Kwak's analysis of the prevalence of 'cultural capture' in finance complements, and perhaps reinforces, McCarty's conclusion. Defining cultural capture as the situation in which industry 'can shape policy outcomes through influences other than material incentives and rational debate', Kwak focuses on how group identification, status, and relationship networks can lead regulators to privilege the interests of industry advocates. Kwak's analysis suggests that the 'increasing complexity of finance made it more difficult for agency employees to evaluate proposals on their merits, increasing the importance of proxies'. As Kwak argues, 'the more complex and information-intensive an issue is and the less capacity the agency has to devote to the issue, the greater the potential importance of cultural capture. Faced with uncertainty deciding between competing theories of the world and the public interest, people are more likely to fall back on the signals communicated by identity, status, or relationships'.

McCarty and Kwak's analyses suggest that capture-prevention strategies aimed at complex policy environments might be particularly helpful in the financial sector. One promising intervention along these lines is discussed earlier in this essay: that is, ensuring that regulators are provided with diverse sources of information. While such strategies could well be productive across a range of policy environments, there is reason to believe that interventions focused on increasing the diversity of information might be more productive than other approaches in complex policy environments. If financial regulators are prone to capture because industry exploits their need for expertise, then strategies aimed at increasing the diversity of high-quality information available to regulators could help to mitigate capture in this sector.

This reasoning would suggest that finding ways to establish effective consumer advocacy programs in the financial sector, along the lines of those examined by Daniel Schwarcz, may be helpful. Indeed, Kwak argues in favour of tripartism and he specifically recommends an official public advocate as a promising stratagem to prevent capture in finance. Similarly, developing opportunities for state-level actors to communicate directly with agency officials during rulemaking, and perhaps at other stages in the regulatory process, might also mitigate undue special interest influence, per Susan Yackee's study.

Kwak and McCarty offer some additional concrete suggestions regarding capture prevention in finance that bear mention here. Along the lines of Schwarcz and Yackee's guidance, Kwak recommends other ways that agencies might increase diversity of expertise, such as internal advisory committees staffed with academics, a "devil's advocate" housed within financial agencies, and negotiated rulemaking that would institutionalize the participation of many interests in the rulemaking process. With respect to institutional design, Kwak echoes the recommendations made by Preventing

Regulatory Capture authors Richard Revesz and Michael Livermore, who advocate enhancing OIRA's function as an external check on agency action (or inaction) that might be unduly influenced by industry.

There is some reason to believe, however, that when it comes to extremely complex financial activities, the field of options may narrow. McCarty's model leads him to conclude that the level of complexity involved in some areas of the financial sector would leave regulators so dependent on industry for expertise that the options available to protect against capture are rather constrained. McCarty argues that in some cases it might be better to prohibit extremely complex instruments completely than to try to design equally complex regulation. McCarty argues that under such circumstances, to prevent captured regulation, Congress should either ban the financial activity outright, or should consider either drawing a bright-line rule that requires little regulatory discretion or deregulating to avoid the damaging effects of a captured regulator.

3.7 A direction for future scholarship on preventing capture

With all this said, the research in this space has only begun to move toward better diagnosing, measuring, and preventing capture. Above all, a renewed focus among regulatory scholars on the prevention of capture is absolutely critical, and our hope is that Preventing Regulatory Capture takes a first significant step in this direction. The increasingly empirical approach to capture that we hope is exemplified in the volume promises not only a more realistic picture of the problem, but also the possibility of more finely tuned remedies. We hope as well that this shift toward the empirical in the study of capture presages a new orientation on government failure more generally, focused not just on whether failures exist, but also on how they play out in practice and how (and under what conditions) they can be prevented or minimized. Surely, there would be little satisfaction with cardiologists if they could tell us only that heart failure exists, without having much to say about how to prevent it or limit its effects. Political economists should face the same challenge with respect to government failure. Deregulation may be a valuable remedy in some cases, but it can hardly be the right remedy in all cases. Deeper and more detailed understanding is required, and it is our hope that Preventing Regulatory Capture constitutes at least a helpful step in the right direction, and a foundation upon which future scholars can build.

4.0 Who Mobilizes? An Analysis of Stakeholder Responses to Financial Regulatory Consultations

Stefano Pagliari[1] and Kevin L. Young[2]

4.1 Introduction

The making of financial regulatory policy is often a contested terrain in which a variety of stakeholders, ranging from trade associations to consumer groups, mobilize over and contribute to the process of contemporary financial rulemaking. As a number of contributions in this publication make clear, the characteristics of the engagement of different stakeholders constitute not only an important determinant of what rules will be implemented, but also of whether the regulation will unduly favour certain stakeholders over others. Despite this widespread recognition, existing scholarship in this area has failed to pay adequate attention to which stakeholders mobilize in the financial regulatory rulemaking process, and what this means for our understanding of how regulatory capture might be mitigated.

[1] Stefano Pagliari is a PhD Candidate at the University of Waterloo and a Research Associate at the International Centre for Financial Regulation. His work focuses on the political economy of the regulatory response to the global financial crisis. His published work appears in International Organization, Journal of European Integration, Journal of European Law and he is the Co-Editor (with Eric Helleiner and Hubert Zimmerman) of 'Global Finance in Crisis: The Politics of International Regulatory Change' (Routledge, 2009).
[2] Kevin Young is Assistant Professor in the Department of Political Science at the University of Massachusetts Amherst. Previously he was Post-Doctoral Fellow at the Neihaus Center for Globalization and Governance at Princeton University, and Fellow in Global Politics at the London School of Economics, where he completed his PhD in 2010. His core research interests include international political economy, interest groups and business lobbying, and the political economy of financial regulation. His recent published work appears in Review of International Political Economy and Public Administration.

This chapter will present the findings of a recent survey of written letter responses from stakeholders to financial regulatory consultations. Our analysis reveals a number of significant empirical trends in terms of which groups mobilize over financial regulation more than others, how and where stakeholder mobilization is different in finance as opposed to other areas of regulation, and whether or not the recent financial crisis has affected these trends. We show evidence that while the mobilization of stakeholders outside the business community is very low, financial regulatory policies also attract the mobilization of a greater diversity of business participants than is commonly acknowledged by theories of regulatory capture.

Our analysis is divided into three parts. In the first part we review some of the existing literature which has explored why the rule setting phase of financial regulation is understood to be associated with a very particular kind of stakeholder mobilization. In the second part we explicate results from a new dataset on response letters to financial regulatory policy consultations by different kinds of stakeholder groups. The third part then lays out some of the implications of our findings.

4.2 Sectoral diversity in the financial rulemaking process – a review of the literature

The interaction with different business groups, consumer groups and other stakeholders through formal consultations and bilateral meetings represents a central mechanism through which regulatory authorities gauge information regarding the impact that different regulatory decisions may have on different groups, as well as their general sentiment. In a complex environment such as in financial markets where the outcome of regulatory policies is characterized by a significant degree of uncertainty, the capacity to continuously receive information and feedback from stakeholders is deemed crucial to produce informed regulatory policies and limit their unintended consequences.

At the same time, the characteristics of mobilizing different groups which seek to influence the rulemaking process are also considered to be one of the factors influencing the potential that regulation will be captured by special interests. In this regard, regulatory capture is understood as more likely to occur in those instances where the mobilization of a narrow range of groups directly targeted by a given regulation will dominate the policymaking process, while other, more diffuse groups such as consumer groups will be hindered from making their mark. In contrast, when stakeholder mobilization is more diverse the opposite effect is anticipated. A more diverse set of stakeholders mobilizing would ensure that regulators are exposed to a greater variety of information and perspectives, as well as reduce their dependency on the information received by any single group of stakeholders, reducing the risk of capture.

From this perspective, the literature on financial regulatory policymaking in particular has often presented finance as an area particularly prone to capture. A number of reasons have been posited as likely to constrain the plurality of stakeholders mobilizing in financial regulatory policymaking. First, the technical complexity that characterizes financial regulatory debates increases the information asymmetries between the financial groups directly targeted by the specific piece of regulation and other stakeholders, thus limiting the capacity of the latter group to actually engage.[3] Second, the temporary horizon within which the costs and benefits of regulatory measures will manifest themselves varies across different stakeholders. While the costs imposed by more stringent regulatory policies are more readily apparent to the financial industry group being directly targeted, the impact of financial regulatory policies on other stakeholders may be more indirect and difficult to decipher in the short-term, thus limiting the incentives of these groups to mobilize.[4] Third, even when the costs of different regulatory solutions are also easier to detect in the short-term for those stakeholders that are only indirectly affected, the capacity of stakeholders, such as investors and consumers of financial

---

[3] Baker (2010). 'Restraining regulatory capture? Anglo- America, crisis politics and trajectories of change in global financial governance', *International Affairs*, 86(3): 647-63.

[4] Mattli and Woods (2009). *In Whose Benefit? Explaining Regulatory Change in Global Politics*, The Politics of Global Regulation. Mattli and Woods. Princeton, NJ, Princeton University Press.

services, to mobilize to protect their interests is constrained by the diffuse nature of these stakeholders and the limited organizational resources available to overcome collective action problems.[5] Fourth, the informal institutional context within which financial regulatory policies are developed is frequently described as constraining the mobilization of a plurality of stakeholders. The participation of financial industry groups is facilitated by the existing network they share with regulators, fostered by the common professional experiences, training, and revolving doors that link these actors together in a common "policy network".[6] The existence of this tight-knit community between regulators and the financial industry groups under their surveillance is often seen as an obstacle hindering the mobilization of those outsiders seeking to "break in" to the relatively closed financial regulatory policy network.[7]

Thus for a range of different reasons existing scholarship suggests that the plurality of stakeholders involved in financial regulatory policymaking should be quite low. While there is widespread agreement on this point, some scholarship emphasizes the cyclical nature of such a condition. Specifically, events such as financial crises or corporate scandals are understood to bring the distributional consequences of financial regulation into sharper focus, thus better enabling different stakeholders to assess the distributional consequences of financial regulation. In turn, such dynamics create a window of opportunity for policy entrepreneurs that would not normally mobilize to engage in the policymaking process, and add greater plurality to the regulatory debate.[8] For this reason, we might expect the diversity of actors involved to increase in the aftermath of crises and scandals.[9]

[5] Olson (1965). *The Logic of Collective Action: Public Goods and the Theory of Groups*, Harvard University Press.

[6] Young (2012). 'Transnational regulatory capture? An empirical examination of the transnational lobbying of the Basel Committee on Banking Supervision.' *Review of International Political Economy*.

[7] Lall (2011). 'From failure to failure: The politics of international banking regulation.' *Review of International Political Economy*.

[8] Mattli and Woods (2009), *op. cit. in footnote* 2.

[9] Culpepper (2011). *Quiet Politics and Business Power: Corporate Control in Europe and Japan*, Cambridge, Cambridge University Press.

4.3 An empirical investigation of stakeholder mobilization in finance

While there are strong theoretical reasons why the diversity of stakeholders active in the financial regulatory arena may be constrained, this characteristic of the financial regulatory process is an empirical question. Furthermore, it is one frequently assumed but not assessed empirically in a systematic fashion. Who mobilizes in the financial regulatory policymaking process?

One key empirical resource for answering this question is provided by the common tendency in recent years for financial regulatory agencies to open regulatory proposals to formal consultative processes. Since the early 2000s in particular, regulatory agencies have undertaken policy consultations which ask for formal written comments by interested groups. Although policy consultations do not represent the only mechanism available for advocacy, the publicly available written responses to these consultations do provide a relatively systematic "trace" of which actors tend to mobilize in response to different regulatory policies.

As part of a larger study,[10] we generated a new dataset composed of the written responses of different stakeholders to a variety of policy consultations. These policy consultations took place in a wide variety of institutional contexts, in a number of different countries, and across a time period between 1997 (when data first started to become available) and 2012. While most of our data includes responses from the United States, our dataset also includes responses from Canada, Germany, and the United Kingdom. Given the greater relevance of financial regulatory policymaking occurring at a supranational level, we have also included different policy consultations held by the European Commission, as well as from international regulatory institutions such as the Basel Committee on Banking Supervision and the International Organization of Securities Commissions. In total we coded 13,466 comment letters in response to 292 different policy consultations across finance and other sectors, covering a total of 58

---

[10] This section draws upon data and analysis in 'Leveraged Interests: The Role of Corporate-Financial Coalitions in the Regulation of Finance' by Pagliari and Young (2012). Currently Under Review. Available at www.stefanopagliari.net

different governance bodies, ranging from the US Food and Drug Administration to the Canadian Council for Insurance Regulation to the Directorate-General for Internal Market within the European Commission.[11]

Table 1: Percentage of Respondents to Financial Sector Consultations

Respondent	Percentage of Total Comment Letters
Trade Unions	1.47
Consumer Groups	1.15
Research Institutions	3.65
NGOs	6.67
Business Groups	87.06

Table 1 summarizes the different kinds of stakeholders who respond to consultations around financial regulatory policies. These findings show how the diversity of interest group mobilization around financial regulatory policymaking appears relatively constrained. In this sense, NGO mobilization is a relatively rare occurrence. So too is the mobilization of interest groups representing more "diffuse" constituencies, such as consumer protection groups and trade unions.

Private business organizations – composed of firms, associations, and coalitions of business groups – clearly dominate financial regulatory policymaking. Yet the business community is a heterogeneous group. Which kind of businesses respond to financial sector consultations? To answer this question, we broke down this category according to the sector and industry of the different business respondents. For each policy consultation we have differentiated between three different groups of respondents: 1) those business groups that were directly targeted for regulation ("Target Group"); 2) other financial business groups who are not the direct target of the regulatory measure

---

[11] Of this total, 146 consultations concerned financial regulation of some kind, with 6379 response letters coded. 158 consultations concerned areas of regulation other than finance, with a total of 8196 response letters coded. For a more detailed description of the dataset see the Appendix in Pagliari and Young (2012).

("Sectoral Cohabitants"); and 3) business respondents from outside finance ("Outsiders"). For instance, in the case of banking regulation, banks and banking associations would be the "target group", credit rating agencies or insurance companies would be "sectoral cohabitants", while manufacturing companies or agricultural associations would be "outsiders". The results of this analysis, summarized in Table 2, show how financial sector consultations are characterized by a plurality of different kinds of business respondents, with almost a quarter of the respondents being non-financial business groups.

Table 2: Percentage of Business Reponses to Financial Sector Consultations

Category of Business Respondent	Explanation of Category	Percentage of Total Comment Letters
Target Group	The respondent is the direct target of regulation.	45.12
Sectoral Cohabitant	The respondent is in the financial sector, but is not being targeted directly.	29.94
Outsider	The respondent is outside the financial sector.	24.95

The importance of non-financial business groups in financial regulatory debates has further been increased in the regulatory response to the global financial crisis. Using September 2008 as a dividing line among all written response letters, Table 3 illustrates the composition of respondents to financial sector consultations before and after the global financial crisis, with the column on the right calculating the percentage change over the two periods.

Table 3: Percentage of Respondents to Financial Sector Consultations, Before and After the Global Financial Crisis

Respondent	Pre-Crisis	Post-Crisis	% Difference
Trade Unions	0.31	2.02	+548
Consumer Protection	1.48	1.00	−32.41
Research Institutions	4.40	3.29	−25.07
NGOs	2.26	8.77	+288.73
Business Groups	91.56	84.92	−7.25
of Business Groups:			
Target Group	46.88	44.22	−5.66
Sectoral Cohabitants	35.19	27.24	−22.58
Outsiders	17.93	28.53	+59.08

These results suggest that the plurality of groups mobilizing over financial regulatory policymaking has changed in some important ways since the crisis. In particular, the number of trade union organizations, NGOs, and non-financial end users of financial services has increased significantly since the crisis, thus significantly diversifying the sectoral origin of groups which mobilize and limiting the predominance of financial industry groups targeted by regulation.

But how unique is the mobilization of stakeholders around financial regulatory policies compared to the regulation of other sectors? In order to assess this question, we also compared these financial consultations to a wide variety of consultations around regulatory policies concerning other sectors of the economy. In this regard, we selected consultations within sectors which each had (varying) similarities with the financial sector and which also emerge in discussions of regulatory capture. Specifically, we included consultations on the regulation of the energy sector, the health care industry, the agricultural sector, and the media and telecommunications industry. Table 4 illustrates our comparative results, showing the percentage of respondents across different sectors.

Table 4: Percentage of Respondents to Consultations in Different Regulated Areas

Respondent	Agriculture	Energy	Telecoms	Health	Finance
Trade Unions	1.07	1.12	1.06	0.32	**1.47**
Consumer Protection	0.74	0.94	0.92	1.83	**1.15**
Research Institutions	5.23	3.97	1.42	9.06	**3.65**
NGOs	14.22	9.14	3.48	10.84	**6.67**
Business Groups	78.74	84.83	93.12	77.94	**87.06**
of Business Groups:					
Target Group	83.18	69.68	84.07	64.71	**45.12**
Sectoral Cohabitants	5.71	11.07	11.28	19.10	**29.94**
Outsiders	11.12	19.25	4.65	16.19	**24.94**

Taken together, these results illustrate a number of empirical regularities that may be significant for understanding the dynamics of private sector influence in the policymaking process and the potential for capture. The first pattern which emerges in this data is the low level of civil society organizations such as NGOs as respondents to financial sector consultations. Financial regulation features a very low level of engagement of consumer protection groups, although this is not strikingly different from other regulated sectors. Research institutions are less engaged in financial regulatory consultations than in most other sectors – a surprising finding given the highly technical nature of financial regulation.

A second pattern is the significantly greater diversity of business groups that tend to mobilize in response to financial sector consultations. When it comes to financial regulation, there appears to be greater mobilization of business groups that are not directly targeted by regulation than in any other sector, both from within the same sector ("Sectoral Cohabitants") than from the rest of the economy ("Outsiders"). Interestingly, only the regulation of the energy sector features a comparable number of outsiders mobilizing.

These results stand in contrast to the expectations of those theories of regulatory capture which have postulated that the diversity of actors mobilizing around financial regulatory policies would be hindered by collective action problems and information asymmetries. Instead, the analysis in this section reveals how the mobilization of groups surrounding the development of financial rules is different from what we find in the regulation of other areas, and most importantly, more sectorally diverse than theories of regulatory capture assume. This anomaly can be explained in part by considering the special position that the financial sector occupies in the rest of the economy and the numerous ties that link financial firms with the real economy, either directly or indirectly. Since numerous financial regulatory policies are likely to have an impact over the rest of the economy, this may create strong incentives for a broader range of business groups to mobilize.

4.4 Policy implications

What are the policy implications of this analysis for the potential that a piece of financial regulation will unduly narrowly favour the stakeholders being regulated? Our analysis above suggests two broad implications.

On the one hand, the relative under-representation of stakeholders outside of the business community, in particular consumer advocates, NGOs, and trade unions within financial sector policymaking compared to other areas of economic policymaking, suggests that the likely diversity of perspectives and concerns that reach the regulatory process is limited in important ways. Non-business groups have the potential to represent diffuse interests in society that might be under-represented by the business community. The greater diversity of actors who mobilize within the business community might be interpreted as limiting the risk that any onset of special interests will disproportionately influence the policymaking process, by creating greater potential for these groups to "balance" each other out.

However, there are other reasons to suggest that the opposite outcome might result. Manufacturing firms that mobilize over financial regulation do not necessarily advocate opposing positions as do banks when it comes to bank regulation; nor is it necessarily the case that agricultural stakeholders oppose the views and the advocacy of institutional investors. Owing to the unique structural location of finance in the economy – as private progenitors and managers of credit – the short-term preferences of non-financial business groups might actually be more often aligned with financial sector groups than opposed to their positions.

Indeed, since the financial crisis in particular efforts to regulate numerous areas of finance, such as hedge funds, banking, and derivatives regulation have featured cross-sectoral business coalitions comprising both financial and non-financial business groups.[12] In this context, financial industry groups have actively altered their lobbying strategies in order to tie their interests to those of other non-financial stakeholders, highlighting the diffuse costs of new regulatory rules. One example of such a strategy is the fact that the publication of the Basel III agreement was preceded by a publication of the Institute of International Finance (IIF), the main association representing internationally active banks, which denounced the costs the implementation of the Basel III agreement would pose on the real economy. The IIF asserted these costs would be as far as eight

---

[12] See Pagliari and Young (2012) for an explication of this phenomenon.

times higher than those estimated by the Basel Committee.[13] Hedge Fund associations such as the Alternative Investment Management Association (AIMA) have directed their opposition to the Alternative Investment Fund Manager Directive (AIFMD) by highlighting the costs that the regulation would pose for pension funds across Europe, declaring that '[i]f they suffer lower returns as a result of the Directive, it's not only Europe's pension funds but Europe's pensioners of both today and tomorrow who will suffer'.[14] Banks that act as derivative dealers have claimed that the measures introduced by US Congress to regulate OTC derivatives markets would cost US companies as much as $1 trillion in terms of capital requirements, thus decreasing their capacity to generate employment opportunities.[15] In many of these and other instances financial industry groups have been joined by non-financial businesses and trade associations who share similar concerns and partially overlapping policy agendas.

This strategy has often been effective as elected politicians are generally wary of introducing regulatory measures that may negatively affect employment and growth, in particular during a period of weak economic growth. Under these conditions, regulators are likely to face strong pressures from a plurality of business groups as well as their political masters to be more lenient in the implementation of regulatory policies that may harm the economy, or if a trade-off exists between the goal of bolstering the safety of financial institutions and preserving the flow of credit to the rest of the economy.

In these cases, the mobilization of a broader variety of business groups inside and outside finance does not necessarily mitigate the capacity of financial groups to capture the policymaking process, but may actually reinforce their influence in the policymaking process. The acknowledgement of this possibility has led important commentators

---

[13] IIF (2010). 'Interim Report on the Cumulative Impact on the Global Economy of Proposed Changes in the Banking Regulatory Framework', Institute of International Finance.

[14] AIMA (2009). 'European Directive Could Cost European Pension Industry 25 Billion Euros Annually', London, Alternative Investment Management Association.

[15] ISDA (2010). 'US Companies May Face US $1 Trillion in Additional Capital and Liquidity Requirements As a Result of Financial Regulatory Reform, According to ISDA Research', International Swaps and Derivatives Associations.

and policymakers to flag 'deceptive lobbying',[16] wherein Representative Barney Frank warned against the risk of financial institutions 'taking the end users in effect as hostages to get out from under some of these requirements'.[17] The extent of such practices and others like it is unknown, but it does appear that financial industry groups tend to be increasingly savvy at connecting their own advocacy endeavours to the fate of other groups in the business community.

How is it possible to ensure that the mobilization of business groups in financial regulatory policymaking mitigates rather than reinforces the influence of those special interests? First, the relative under-representation within financial regulatory policymaking of stakeholders from outside the business community compared to other sectors suggests that public policy intervention should be deployed towards enhancing the capacity of voices outside the business community to participate in the regulatory process. The objective of redressing some groups' underrepresentation may also require the pooling of resources to subsidize the mobilization of existing consumer groups, or the creation of independent agencies tasked to represent these concerns in the regulatory process.[18]

Second, beyond granting channels of access to the policymaking process, public policy intervention should be directed towards facilitating the capacity of those groups for whom the impact of the regulation in question is less immediate, such non-financial end users, in order to allow these groups to assess the impact that specific financial regulatory issues will have on them. For instance, granting full access to the information available to regulators, including their data, analyses, and draft texts, could compensate, at least in part, for the information asymmetry between the financial industry groups target of regulation and other stakeholders.[19] These mechanisms may reduce

---

[16] Johnson (2011). 'Deceptive Lobbying on Derivatives', *New York Times*, Economix Blog, 17 February 2011.

[17] Paletta (2010), 'Late Change Sparks Outcry Over Finance-Overhaul Bill', *Wall Street Journal*, 1 July 2010.

[18] Schwarcz (forthcoming). 'Preventing Capture Through Consumer Empowerment Programs: Some Evidence from Insurance Regulation', in *Preventing Regulatory Capture: Special Interest Influence, and How to Limit It*, by Carpenter and Moss (forthcoming). Cambridge, Cambridge University Press.

the risk that the mobilization of non-financial stakeholders will not occur uniquely around the information provided by financial industry groups targeted for regulation.

Third, regulators should play a more careful game when setting out new regulatory reforms. Interest group advocacy can be conceived as an 'informational subsidy'[20] to policymakers' efforts to understand the impact of regulatory policies. This may be helpful in particular circumstances, but it is only logical that most outside stakeholders have incentives to over-represent this impact. The distortions that this may bring to the policymaking process may be mitigated by developing a more standardized and transparent process of cost-benefit analysis within the regulatory policymaking process itself, by endowing regulatory agencies with more capacity to conduct robust impact analysis before policies are released, as well as by delegating the task of estimating the costs of regulatory policies to independent task forces capable of providing an independent and expert assessment.

Fourth, the anticipation of a widespread mobilization of financial and non-financial groups around the implementation of regulatory policies which may potentially impact the real economy signifies that regulators need to be given a clearer mandate regarding how to navigate the trade-off that often exists between bolstering financial stability and protecting the flow of credit to the real economy. This represents a grey area in the mandate of regulatory agencies and such ambiguity creates room for undue influence in the regulatory process of short-term political pressures. At the same time, greater independence from the political process is required to allow regulators to withstand widespread pressure which could emerge during a downturn to water down the implementation of reforms in order to limit any negative impact on the real economy.[21]

---

[19] Ayres and Braithwaite (2006). 'Tripartism: Regulatory Capture and Empowerment', *Law & Social Inquiry*, 16(3): 435-96.

[20] Hall and Deardorff (2006). 'Lobbying as Legislative Subsidy', *American Political Science Review*, 100(1): 69-84.

[21] See Green (this volume), and Valencia and Ueda (2012), 'Central Bank Independence and Macro-prudential Regulation', IMF Working Paper, WP/12/101, International Monetary Fund.

4.5 Conclusion

In this research note we have explored the unique kind of stakeholder mobilization that surrounds the rule-setting phase of financial regulation. Explicating some results from a new dataset on response letters to a variety of different regulatory policy consultations, we illustrated two important features of financial regulatory policymaking. First, financial regulation appears to be associated with a less plural degree of stakeholder mobilization when it comes to non-business groups such as NGOs, trade unions and consumer groups. Second, we demonstrated that when it comes to the mobilization of different stakeholders within the business community itself, financial regulation is associated with a great plurality of groups which mobilize.

While this latter result might be interpreted as limiting the ability of financial industry groups to exercise excessive influence' over the regulatory process, we have argued that there are reasons to think otherwise, since many non-financial business groups share similar concerns about the diffuse costs of financial regulation. Different policy adjustments are required to ensure that this business plurality may function as a mitigating factor against the risk of capture, rather than amplifying the influence of special interests.

5.0 Regulatory Implementation and Capture

Andrew Walter[1]

5.1 Introduction

As noted in the introduction to this publication, most of the debate over the so-called capture of the policymaking process by private financial sector interests[2] has focused on the rulemaking process. However, there is no compelling a priori reason to believe that private influence over rulemaking constitutes the most important form of policy capture. Capture might also be important during the implementation process, not least because this can be even more opaque, extended and complex than rulemaking. Generally, capture in the implementation phase will be problematic if it produces outcomes that entail additional deviations from the public interest (to the extent this can be defined). Two general kinds of such deviation are of interest: formal non-compliance, when actors openly resist

---

[1] Andrew Walter is Reader in International Political Economy at the London School of Economics and Political Science (LSE) and Academic Director of the TRIUM Global Executive MBA programme. He specializes in the political economy of international money and finance. He is also a Research Associate in the Department of Management at the LSE, and is on both the governing Council and Executive Committees of Chatham House (London), on the Academic Advisory Board of the International Centre for Financial Regulation (London), and the editorial board of the *Review of International Studies*. His forthcoming book, edited with Professor Xiaoke Zhang, is *East Asian Capitalism: Diversity, Change, and Continuity* (Oxford University Press, 2012). Other recent books include *China and the United States in the Global Order* (Cambridge University Press, 2011, with Rosemary Foot), *Governing Finance: East Asia's Adoption of Global Standards* (Cornell University Press, 2008), and *Analyzing the Global Political Economy* (Princeton University Press, 2009, with Gautam Sen). He is currently researching the political consequences of financial crises.

[2] For definitions of capture, see the Introduction. Here, I use capture as a shorthand term for excessive private sector influence over public policy outcomes.

implementation of agreed rules that approximate the public interest, and "mock" compliance, when actors engage in formal compliance with such rules but behave in ways that negate their intent.[3]

The implementation phase can be more subject to the influence of organized interests than the rulemaking process, for three main reasons. First, regulators may attain some distance from national politics and organized lobbies when they negotiate in international peer networks, whereas implementation remains largely a national affair (with the important exception of the EU). Second, interest groups often mobilize in the implementation phase as specific details of regulatory proposals take shape. Third, as has occurred since 2008, crises can delegitimize conventional ideas and empower entrepreneurial policymakers arguing for greater regulatory stringency, but firms and organized economic interests generally are much less prone to Damascene conversions.[4] Extended implementation phases can provide such interests with new opportunities to regroup. They may challenge new regulation in contexts in which their political leverage and access to institutional veto points are greater, or persuade policymakers and supervisory agencies to engage in regulatory forbearance.

This contribution therefore focuses mainly on capture in the post-rulemaking phase and the possibilities for its mitigation. However, I first point to potential interdependencies between excessive private sector influence over rulemaking and over post-rulemaking policy outcomes. It draws on my previous research on financial regulatory outcomes in the East Asian context, which is a useful corrective to the empirical focus of the contemporary capture debate on advanced Western countries.[5]

---

[3] In 'Governing Finance' I define "compliance" in a more encompassing sense than "implementation", a term I reserve for the actions of public sector actors. Here I use the two terms interchangeably. See Walter A. (2008), *Governing Finance: East Asia's Adoption of International Standards*, Ithaca, NY, Cornell University Press.

[4] Extensive business sector opposition to Roosevelt's New Deal is one example. Over 2009-11, the growing assertiveness of financial firms in the US and Europe in opposing a variety of post-crisis regulatory proposals is another.

[5] Walter A. (2006). 'From Developmental to Regulatory State? Japan's New Financial Regulatory System.' *The Pacific Review*, 19(4), pp. 405-28; Walter A. (2008). *Governing Finance: East Asia's Adoption of International Standards*, Ithaca, Cornell University Press.

5.2 Interdependencies between rulemaking and implementation

For various reasons there is likely to be a trade-off between the intensity of industry influence attempts at the rulemaking and post-rulemaking phases. This is because influence attempts in the rulemaking process can be both costly and risky (e.g. attempts to exercise voice in the political process via lobbying or campaign contributions, or deployments of exit threats), whereas firms may judge that they will have more success in diluting the impact of rules in the implementation phase.

Political and legal institutions are likely to affect the nature of this trade-off. For example, US firms may devote so many resources to influencing the rulemaking phase because the legislative process is relatively open to such influence compared to their ability to influence supervisory agencies in the implementation phase. In political systems with relatively stringent electoral finance rules and in which political power is less fragmented than the US (for example the UK), industry may have fewer points of influence in the rulemaking phase; firms may choose to concentrate their resources on influencing implementation outcomes. In political systems with weak enforcement capacity this strategy might be especially attractive.

We should also consider how perceived differences in the degree of capture across different jurisdictions can reverberate across borders and influence the nature of industry mobilization. For example, the perception in the US and UK that German and French politicians and regulators were overly influenced by relatively highly leveraged and undercapitalized national banks may have helped to mobilize American and British bankers and regulators to push for greater attention to the monitoring of implementation of Basel III and to details such as risk-weighting practices.[6] Such counter-mobilizations might sometimes be useful, and it is a reminder that it is usually wrong to assume that industry preferences are homogeneous.

Macroeconomic and electoral cycles can also have a powerful influence on both phases and the nature of any capture in them.

---

[6] Barker, A. and B. Masters (2012). 'Paris and Berlin seek to dilute bank rules', Financial Times, 22 January.

Rulemaking in the immediate aftermath of crises or scandals, when the financial sector is distressed and politically unpopular, may be less amenable to industry capture than in tranquil times (Sarbanes-Oxley, Dodd-Frank and Basel III in different respects reflect this post-crisis tendency). Elections that follow closely on a crisis or scandal can produce political competition to be tough on the industry both in rulemaking and supervision, whereas elections at a greater distance may permit more industry influence as media and public attention wanes. It is often said that reformist zeal fades with economic recovery, but it may be that the absence of durable recovery permits financial firms to achieve greater influence over the timing or nature of implementation, or to have post-crisis rules rewritten or diluted. The current debate between the Basel Committee, some national regulators and the financial industry over the growth implications of Basel III and related rules is characterized by considerable uncertainty about the true nature of the trade-off between financial stability and growth, let alone about where the social optimum lies. Political incumbents are likely to be more inclined to accept industry's more pessimistic assessments and arguments for regulatory leniency in a low growth environment.

5.3 Capture in the implementation phase

Implementation can offer new opportunities for industry to influence policy in a way that is often less transparent than lobbying over rulemaking. The confidentiality of the supervisory relationship can produce deviations of supervision from legislative intent ("agency slack"). Sometimes supervisors can be subject to direct capture due to bribery (not unknown in countries such as Indonesia, Korea, and Japan) or to more indirect forms of influence due to the socialization effects that can result from close proximity to firms (this may be more likely in jurisdictions where supervisors confront the largest and most sophisticated global banks). Japan's system of amakudari involved underpaying supervisors on the implicit understanding that they would later be employed in their retirement as directors in the firms they supervised. The ending of this system after the scandals of the 1990s — and new related rules prohibiting private firms from entertaining supervisors – may have had the unintended effect of reducing supervisory knowledge of the financial sector.

Related to this, capture in the implementation phase can also result from the (sometimes deliberate) under-resourcing of supervisory agencies. The systematic under-resourcing of regulatory agencies in the United States including the Office of Thrift Supervision and the SEC over the past decade or more was a common legislative tactic that contributed to the undermining of effective regulation. Such under-resourcing can increase the knowledge asymmetries between supervisory agencies and the industry and facilitate excessive supervisory deference. Even today, independent government inspectors point to the inadequate resources of crucial supervisory agencies, including the Federal Housing Finance Agency, responsible for the regulation of Fannie Mae and Freddie Mac[7]. An extreme case can be found in Korea's Ministry of Finance and the Economy, which before the 1997 crisis provided for only one individual to be responsible for the supervision of the whole non-bank financial institution sector, an area in which supervision was notoriously lax.

Agency discretion can also facilitate capture. Innovative and risk-tolerant firms inevitably seek to exploit areas of regulation in which ambiguity and supervisory discretion are greater. Relevant examples since the early days of the Basel capital adequacy regime include industry lobbying to influence supervisory treatment of hybrid capital and of the risk-weighting treatment of trading book assets. Key supervisory agencies such as the Federal Reserve during the Greenspan years exercised considerable discretion in yielding to industry pressure (from the major commercial banks) to interpret Depression-era legislation such as the Glass-Steagall Act in ways that hollowed it out from within well before it was repealed in 1999. Firms may also seek to exploit opportunities where supervisors can exercise discretion in the treatment of regulatory breaches. A costly example is

---

[7] FHFA [US Federal Housing Finance Agency] Office of the Inspector General (2012). 'FHFA-OIG's Current Assessment of FHFA's Conservatorships of Fannie Mae and Freddie Mac', *White Paper* WPR-2012-001, March 28.

the treatment by the UK FSA of the largest UK bank, RBS, in the years leading up to its failure in 2008. The FSA's (2011) report into this failure revealed a number of occasions on which the FSA raised concerns with RBS management about its risk management practices but failed to take firm action. On one occasion the FSA was apparently persuaded by RBS's chief executive to dilute the force of its concerns about its risk management practices in a letter to the bank's board[8]. Such failures of supervisory enforcement may be especially likely during tranquil periods and when, as in the US and UK before the crisis, regulatory philosophy and the political consensus are conducive to non-intervention.

Governments, regulators and firms can also collude in the practice of regulatory forbearance, which involves the discretionary non-enforcement of prudential rules. It is not always easy to decide whether this reflects private sector "capture" or if it is driven by reasonable government understandings of the public interest. In the decade from the mid-1990s in Japan, regulators and the government tolerated an extraordinary reliance of major Japanese banks on deferred tax assets (DTAs) to meet their Tier I capital requirements. From the perspective of many foreign critics, this reflected deep capture of policymakers by a collectively insolvent banking sector and the inability of the Japanese political system to deal effectively with zombie banks and firms. From the perspective of Japanese policymakers, this regulatory forbearance was a necessary policy response to the collapse of the bubble economy and to the severe political constraints on the public recapitalization of banks – something many Western governments and banks are now in a far better position to appreciate.

Another relevant example is provided by South Korea during the 2001-2 downturn, when extensive and hidden regulatory forbearance by the government concerning banks' loan accounting and capital requirements were probably instrumental in saving distressed industrial firms such as Hynix and the economy in general from further

---

[8] FSA [UK Financial Services Authority] (2011). *The Failure of the Royal Bank of Scotland: Financial Services Authority Board Report.* London: FSA pp. 279

dislocation at a time of weak demand and continuing deleveraging[9]. The Korean and Japanese authorities were only doing what has since become conventional wisdom – varying real capital requirements in a countercyclical fashion.

5.4 Mitigation possibilities

Since different kinds of policy capture are shaped by underlying political, legal and social institutions it is implausible to believe that it can be eliminated. Reducing capture in the rulemaking process in a country like the United States may require fundamental reforms to electoral campaign finance and to the legislative process, reforms that may be politically unrealistic. Nor is private influence always incompatible with the public interest. As noted above, industry preferences are often heterogeneous and the extent to which the public interest is undermined by private influence depends considerably upon which private interests (if any) prevail. Simon Johnson and others have argued that the growth of mega-banks has facilitated deep policy capture by excessively large, too big to fail institutions – and that the only viable solution is the radical Rooseveltian one of breaking them up. But there seems to be little political appetite for this solution either in the United States or at the level of the G20, where the main focus has instead been one of requiring modest additional capital charges and closer supervisory attention of SIFIs. This may mean that the prospects for reducing the level of influence over policymaking by the largest financial institutions are very limited.

Given this apparent political reality, how might the capture that can result from the close proximity of supervisors to large firms (something that is likely to increase after the recent crisis) and from agency discretion be limited? It is not easy to see ways around these potential avenues for capture, except to build in cross-checks through extensive information disclosure and robust independent auditing of policy decisions. However, we should recall that supervisory reliance

---

[9] See chapter 6 in Walter, Andrew (2008)

on other actors (e.g. auditors, ratings agencies, independent directors) as a cross-check and source of information was often ineffective in the past and that these other actors may themselves be even more subject to capture than supervisory agencies.

A better international regime would also be one in which national departures from international rules that lack reasonable public interest justifications are discouraged through open peer review. The proceedings and results should be published. Done well (via persuasion rather than by enforcement threats), this can empower national authorities to resist domestic interests pushing for undesirable defections. It may also help to prevent the unravelling of the international rulemaking and implementation processes. If, for example, in the implementation of Basel III, European governments are perceived as diluting the new standards in various ways for their own advantage, this incentivizes banks elsewhere to lobby for retaliatory non-implementation. There are obviously strong incentives for governments to engage in mutual non-aggression pacts. But it seems essential that for peer review to be effective (as in the WTO panel process and unlike in IMF financial sector assessments) the reviewed party should not be able to block reports or to excise politically sensitive material.

Greater transparency as regards regulatory forbearance would also be worthwhile, requiring supervisors to subject discretionary departures to independent and transparent review (perhaps to national auditors as well as to international bodies like the FSB and European Commission). It would assist this if key bodies such as the Basel Committee and the FSB also made clear that there can be a positive public policy justification for such forbearance, which after the Asian crises of the late 1990s became a taboo. In fact, Basel III reflects some recognition of this in that the countercyclical and capital conservation buffers will supposedly permit a reduction in regulatory capital during downturns. But questions remain about the reputational consequences of such envisaged relaxations – notably, for example, the European Banking Authority required a pro-cyclical tightening of the capital regime for European banks in the recent crisis. The fairly narrow range of the discretionary capital buffer may also be insufficient in a serious crisis (it is doubtful it would have been sufficient in the Japanese case), which could have the undesirable effect of pushing regulatory forbearance once again into the shadows (where, almost certainly, it lurks today).

An open system of peer review, with assessment of national policy justifications by qualified FSB/BIS/IMF staff, is likely to be more productive than attempts at enforcement. But effective implementation requires good rules and standards in the first place: national authorities have to be convinced that they make sense for international regimes to empower them to resist undesirable pressure from private sector interests. More private sector actors also need to be co-opted to support good regulation. Bank management and creditors currently have few additional incentives in the medium term to align their behaviour with the public policy objectives of the post-crisis era and have strong incentives to lobby governments to adopt negotiating positions and implementation plans that do not serve the broader public interest [10](Admati et al. 2010). If this persists, there will be little that peer review can do to achieve better financial regulation.

A final question is how much more prone financial sector rulemaking is to capture than other industries. Should we be providing solutions to capture problems in finance without addressing similar problems in other sectors? Requiring all legislation/rule-setting to pass through a general public interest review process would help, because the controversial concept of the "public interest" should be defined transparently and in general terms rather than on a sectoral basis. Review bodies like Australia's Productivity Commission process may offer a useful model as they can help to subject most policymaking to the same kind of independent, general interest test. Permitting and encouraging other organized interests (consumer groups, organized labour, small business, etc.) to submit public comments could also help to increase both the transparency and legitimacy of regulation, something in which the financial sector has a significant interest.

---

[10] Admati, Anat R., Peter M. DeMarzo, Martin F. Hellwig, and Paul Pfleiderer (2010). 'Fallacies, Irrelevant Facts, and Myths in the Discussion of Capital Regulation: Why Bank Equity is Not Expensive', *Rock Center for Corporate Governance at Stanford University Working Paper* No. 86, *Stanford Graduate School of Business Research Paper* No. 2065, August.

Section 2

A Regulator's Perspective

6.0 Regulatory Capture, Political Dominance or Collective Intellectual Failure? A View from a Former UK Regulator

Clive Briault[1]

6.1 Introduction

In this chapter I focus mostly on the UK experience since the late 1990s, from which I draw three main conclusions:

- first, that the UK experience suggests that any "capture" of the regulators took the form of capture by politicians rather than by industry; however
- second, that the main issue in the UK – and elsewhere – ahead of the current financial crisis was a collective intellectual failure; and therefore
- third, any solutions need to focus more on collective intellectual failure than on regulatory capture.

[1] Clive Briault is a Senior Adviser on regulation at KPMG in London, an adviser to a number of supervisory authorities in Europe, a programme leader at the Toronto Centre for Leadership in Financial Supervision, and has acted as a consultant to the IMF, World Bank and Asian Development Bank. He is also managing director of Risk and Regulation Consulting Limited and a non-executive director of a financial services company in the UK. Clive joined the Bank of England in 1980. His roles there included Head of Monetary Assessment and Strategy (1991-1996), and Head of Capital and Wholesale Markets Division (from 1996-1998). He joined the Financial Services Authority at its formation in 1998 as Director of Central Policy, and was Director, Prudential Standards from 2001 to 2004. Clive was Managing Director of Retail Markets at the FSA from April 2004 to April 2008. The points expressed in this paper are those of the author and do not represent those of any organization to which he is affiliated.

6.2 What is regulatory capture?

My preferred definition of regulatory capture would be where regulators are induced to act differently to how they would otherwise have acted in the absence of influence from outside parties. These parties might include the industry, consumers, politicians, the media and others. This might be evidenced by regulators favouring one or more interested parties at the expense of the broader public interest, and not regulating on the basis of a well-informed understanding of technical issues, market developments, and industry and consumer practices. But it cannot be evidenced simply by the amounts of funding, lobbying, communication channels, and "revolving door" movements of staff between the regulators and other parties.

6.3 Institutional design

A commonly made argument is that regulatory capture is facilitated by inadequacies in the institutional context in which regulators and supervisors operate. The UK Financial Services Authority (FSA) was supposed to be a model of independence, accountability, transparency and consultation.[2] This framework was praised in a number of official reports[3] ahead of the current financial crisis.

The FSA made active use of a practitioner panel and a consumer panel (both established on a statutory basis under the Financial Services and Markets Act 2000), and a non-statutory small firms panel. This was reasonably effective in encouraging and developing a consumer input to policymaking as a counterweight to practitioner input, even if the consumer panel inevitably faced difficulties in terms of resources and generating a consumer view on a wide and complicated range of issues. Indeed it is therefore unfortunate that this input is being weakened under the new institutional arrangements in the UK, where

---

[2] Clive Briault, 'The rationale for a single national financial services regulator', *Financial Services Authority Occasional Paper 2*, May 1999.
[3] As referred to in the letter from Callum McCarthy to Tony Blair, 29 May 2005. Published on the FSA website under the 'Freedom of Information Act'.

the Prudential Regulatory Authority does not intend to establish any standing panels, and where the practitioner and consumer panels of the Financial Conduct Authority may operate from a weaker statutory basis than was the case with the FSA – because the new legislation has removed the earlier statutory requirement[4] for the regulator to explain in writing why it is rejecting advice offered by a panel.

However, the institutional design of the FSA was not sufficient to prevent the UK from being close to the epicentre of the financial crisis. So we need to look more broadly at the UK experience.

6.4 The political context

Regulation and supervision operate in a political, social and cultural context. This includes the prevailing political ideology – which might be generally in favour of free markets, or alternatively in favour of state intervention and even state ownership – and the attitude of the government to regulation – which might be to regard regulation as red tape and needless bureaucracy, or it might be in favour of more and tougher regulation. Even if a supervisory agency is "independent" in the sense of enjoying strong statutory protection from interference, it is likely to be influenced by the political climate.

The shift to a free market ideology reached its pinnacle in political terms with Margaret Thatcher in the UK (Prime Minister from 1979 to 1990) and Ronald Reagan in the US (President from 1981 to 1989). This was manifested in various ways, including faith in markets, deregulation in the financial and other sectors, and the promotion of home ownership[5].

---

[4] Financial Services and Markets Act 2000, Section 11(3).

[5] The free market ideology gave strong support to the benefits of a property-owning democracy, a theme that has continued more or less unscathed through successive US and UK governments ever since. In part, this was based on empirical evidence (especially in the US) that home ownership encouraged more stable and more law-abiding neighbourhoods, better educational attainment by children, and higher rates of participation in local democracy. And, in part, a home-owning democracy was attractive because of the political benefits of the feel-good factor of rising house prices.

As explained by Bridget Hutter[6],

> 'in the 1980s/1990s a number of advanced industrial societies experienced a so-called "regulatory crisis". ... There was a strong deregulatory rhetoric, centred on alleged over-regulation, legalism, inflexibility and an alleged absence of attention being paid to the costs of regulation. Regulatory officials, policies, agencies and rules were all subject to criticism and political attack. They were accused of "burdening industry" and of inefficiency and ineffectiveness in their own operations. During the mid 1980s Britain witnessed waves of deregulatory initiatives concerned with the costs of compliance, the over-regulation of business and institutional reforms to control this.'

Successive UK governments established various tasks forces and units within the Cabinet Office and government departments to promote "better regulation". This culminated in the Hampton Report[7], which although carefully positioned as promoting more efficient approaches to regulatory inspection and enforcement without compromising regulatory standards or outcomes went beyond this mandate to equate good regulation with less regulation.

As part of the establishment of the FSA, the Financial Services and Markets Act 2000 included the desirability of facilitating innovation, the international character of financial services and the desirability of maintaining the competitive position of the UK within the seven "have regard to" principles which the FSA had to take into account when discharging its general functions.[8]

Politicians were joined by the industry, the media and other commentators in subjecting the FSA in its early days to a constant barrage of criticism of the costs of regulation, and to repeated claims

---

[6] Bridget Hutter, 'The Attractions of Risk-based Regulation: accounting for the emergence of risk ideas in regulation', *Centre for Analysis of Risk and Regulation Discussion Paper 33*, March 2005.

[7] Hampton Report, 'Reducing administrative burdens: effective inspection and enforcement', HM Treasury, March 2005.

[8] Financial Services and Markets Act 2000, Section 2(3).

that the FSA was 'over-mighty', 'judge, jury and executioner', and a 'bureaucratic leviathan'.[9]

The Financial Services Practitioner Panel stated in its Annual Report that 'rising compliance costs and the increasing burden of regulation in the UK generated by domestic regulation and governmental initiatives, as well as EU financial services legislation, are perceived by many practitioners to pose a serious threat to the international competitive standing of the UK financial services market'.[10] Similarly, successive Banking Banana Skins reports by the Centre for the Study of Financial Innovation (CSFI) highlighted 'too much regulation' as a key risk facing banks – indeed this factor was top of the list of risks in both 2003 and 2005.[11]

As Howard Davies, the first Chair of the FSA, commented, 'on every occasion that I appeared in Parliament as the Chairman of the FSA I was attacked for over-intrusive regulation. In the UK, the City of London was seen as a goose that lays golden eggs, which should on no account be frightened into flapping its wings and flying away.'[12]

In this sense politicians moved ahead of the financial services industry in promoting the benefits of a competitive, open and not unduly regulated financial industry, as a means of boosting growth, employment and tax revenue. Howard Davies observed that 'on the whole, banks [in the UK] did not have to lobby politicians, largely because politicians argued the case for them without obvious inducement'.[13]

Even the Prime Minister entered this territory, claiming that 'something is seriously awry when ... the Financial Services Authority

---

[9] Some of these criticisms are referenced and discussed in: Clive Briault, 'The rationale for a single national financial services regulator', *Financial Services Authority Occasional Paper 2*, May 1999.

[10] Financial Services Practitioner Panel, *Annual Report* 2003.

[11] 'Banking Banana Skins 2012', Centre for the Study of Financial Innovation, February 2012.

[12] Howard Davies, 'Comments on Ross Levine's paper "The governance of financial regulation: reform lessons from the recent crisis" ', Bank for International Settlements Working Papers 329, November 2010.

[13] ibid.

that was established to provide clear guidelines and rules for the financial services sector and to protect the consumer against the fraudulent, is seen as hugely inhibiting of efficient business by perfectly respectable companies that have never defrauded anyone'.[14]

Interestingly, in a letter rebutting these comments[15], the then Chair of the FSA Callum McCarthy stressed in the FSA's defence, among other things, the favourable views of internationally active firms when comparing their experiences of regulation in the UK with regulation in the US and the other main European financial centres.

Sir David Arculus, Chairman of the Better Regulation Task Force, gave a speech to staff of the Financial Services Authority on 29 June 2005 which emphasized this "better regulation is less regulation" approach, saying: 'I spoke to the Prime Minister and was delighted when he agreed to sponsor our report "Regulation: Less is More". ... We concluded that there were great economic benefits – an increase in GDP of more than one percent – from adopting the Dutch "One in, One out" approach.'[16]

Not surprisingly, the FSA's response to these pressures was to stress the proportionate nature of its regulatory interventions:

> 'the first thing that all regulators need to remember is that while regulation should bring benefit, it is also a source of cost to the financial sector. We are very mindful of this and determined to keep this cost to a minimum. In assessing the case for regulatory intervention, our starting point is to determine whether the market is able to deliver acceptable outcomes – or alternatively whether there is a significant market failure. Identifying whether or not there is a market failure is a first step – not a sufficient condition – in weighing up the case for regulation. ... For the FSA

---

[14] Prime Minister Tony Blair, 'Risk and the State', Speech at The Institute for Public Policy Research, 26 May 2005.

[15] Letter from Callum McCarthy to Tony Blair, 29 May 2005. Published on the FSA website under the Freedom of Information Act.

[16] Arculus D (2005), Chairman of the Better Regulation Task Force, Speech to staff of the Financial Services Authority, 29 June, available at: http://www.fsa.gov.uk/library/communication/speeches/2005/0705_sda.shtml

to consider regulatory intervention, there must be a market failure that relates to the objectives of financial regulation and the likelihood that such intervention will provide a net benefit.'[17]

6.5 Collective intellectual failure

However, did this political dominance actually change what regulators and supervisors would have done anyway? Would they have behaved differently in the absence of these pressures? I doubt it. Politicians, regulators, central banks and the industry all suffered from a collective intellectual failure ahead of the current financial crisis. As a result, all these parties failed to appreciate the nature and enormity of the risks building up in the financial system.

In the UK, the Turner Report[18] observed that the prevailing philosophy of supervision ahead of the current financial crisis was based on the assumptions that market forces and market discipline keep both the economy and individual regulated firms broadly on track, and that the senior management and boards of regulated firms have a strong and long-term interest in firms performing well. In contrast, the current financial crisis undermined both of these assumptions.

Indeed, as Alan Greenspan commented:

'all of the sophisticated mathematics and computer wizardry essentially rested on one central premise: that enlightened self-interest of owners and managers of financial institutions would lead them to maintain a sufficient buffer against insolvency by actively monitoring and managing their firms' capital and risk positions. When in the summer of 2007 that premise failed, I was deeply dismayed.'[19]

---

[17] Sants H (2005), Speech at the SHCOG / SIA Cross Borders Conference, 15 November, available at: http://www.fsa.gov.uk/library/communication/speeches/2005/1115_hs.shtml

[18] Financial Services Authority (2009), 'The Turner Review: a regulatory response to the global banking crisis', March.

[19] Greenspan A (2009), 'Speech to Economic Club of New York', New York, February, available at: http://online.wsj.com/public/resources/documents/EconClub.PDF

Frank Vibert refers to the most important source of regulatory and supervisory failure ahead of the financial crisis as 'cognitive failure': 'both market participants and regulators misread the signals from the market, ignored warning signs and were generally overconfident in their ability to ride out any turbulence'.[20]

Peter Nyberg, in his report on the build-up to the financial crisis in Ireland, refers to 'groupthink' – the tendency among homogeneous groups to consider issues within a single paradigm and not challenge basic premises – as a key contributory factor. Nyberg observed that the authorities 'noted macroeconomic risks and risky bank behaviour but appear to have judged them insufficiently alarming to take major restraining policy measures', that 'trust in a soft landing was consistent and, though not very well founded, continued until and during the crisis management period', and that 'the central bank seems not to have sufficiently appreciated the possibility that, while each bank was following a strategy that made sense, in the aggregate, when followed by all banks, this strategy could have serious consequences for overall financial stability'.[21]

To the limited extent that the warning signs were present it is not clear whether they were ignored because of cognitive bias or groupthink, or whether they were simply drowned out by the conventional wisdom of the day. For example, Warren Buffet may have described derivatives as 'financial weapons of mass destruction'[22], but others took a different view, such as Alan Greenspan: 'these increasingly complex financial instruments have especially contributed, particularly over the past couple of stressful years, to the development of a far more flexible, efficient, and resilient financial system than existed just a quarter-century ago'.[23]

---

[20] Vibert F (2010), 'When experts fail', *Central Banking*, 20(3), February.

[21] Nyberg P (2011), 'Misjudging Risks: the Causes of the Systemic Banking Crisis in Ireland', Department of Finance, Ireland, 19 April.

[22] Berkshire Hathaway Annual Report, 2002.

[23] Greenspan A. (2002), 'Remarks on International Financial Risk Management', Council on Foreign Relations, Washington, D.C., 19 November, available at: http://www.federalreserve.gov/boarddocs/speeches/2002/20021119/default.htm

In addition, Ben Bernanke noted that

'in addressing the challenges and the risks that financial innovation may create, we should also always keep in view the enormous economic benefits that flow from a healthy and innovative financial sector. The increasing sophistication and depth of financial markets promote economic growth by allocating capital where it can be most productive. And the dispersion of risk more broadly across the financial system has, thus far, increased the resilience of the system and the economy to shocks.'[24]

Reflecting this collective wisdom, regulators – not just the FSA, but the Basel Committee on Banking Supervision – also invested heavily in working with the industry to develop regulatory standards. The Basel Committee worked closely with the banking industry during the development of the Basel II Capital Accord[25] to produce an approach that allowed banks – subject to conditions – to use their own internal models to calculate the amount of capital they should hold against credit, market and operational risks. This was not regulatory capture, but reflected a generally held regulatory view that: major banks had improved their risk management to acceptable levels; the banking industry had valuable technical insights that could be built upon in developing regulatory capital requirements; and allowing banks to use internal models if they met the qualifying conditions would encourage banks with weaker risk management to improve their capabilities.

The Basel II Capital Accord was welcomed at the time by the FSA as a 'major achievement', representing 'many years of discussion,

---

[24] Bernanke B (2007), 'Regulation and Financial Innovation', Speech at the Federal Reserve Bank of Atlanta's 2007 Financial Markets Conference, Sea Island, Georgia, 15 May, available at: http://www.federalreserve.gov/newsevents/speech/bernanke 20070515a.htm

[25] Basel Committee on Banking Supervision (2004), 'Basel II: International Convergence of Capital Measurement and Capital Standards: a Revised Framework', Bank for International Settlements, June

consultation and sheer hard work by regulators, central banks, officials and the industry round the world'.[26]

In an intellectual climate in which new financial techniques such as securitization, secured borrowing and sale and repurchase agreements had made liquidity appear to be easier to generate by financial institutions – from retail banks to US investment banks – it was not surprising that liquidity risk generally dropped off international and national regulatory agendas.

As discussed by Ross Levine and Howard Davies[27], the FSA – and indeed the European Union – also took an accommodating view in 2004 by allowing US investment banks to operate in the EU under the Financial Conglomerates Directive on the basis that they were regulated to an 'equivalent' standard of prudential regulation by the US Securities and Exchanges Commission.

Nevertheless, some major regulatory and supervisory initiatives were launched during the pre-crisis period. The principles-based approach to Treating Customers Fairly, which turned one of the FSA's eleven Principles for Businesses into a campaign to improve customer-facing standards, was driven forward by the FSA in the face of industry opposition which claimed that the title of the campaign should be dropped because it implied that financial institutions were treating their customers unfairly.

Similarly, the Retail Distribution Review was also based on the premise of market failure, this time in a more structural sense, under which commission-led sales and advice and a focus on volume rather than quality generated poor outcomes for consumers. As Callum McCarthy observed, 'we have a system which serves neither the producer of the services nor the consumer of the services. ... The present remuneration model ... suffers from product bias, provider bias and churn.'[28]

---

[26] Sants, H. (2005), 'Overview of the FSA's implementation proposals for the Capital Requirements Directive and Basel II in the UK', Speech, 10 March.

[27] 'The governance of financial regulation: reform lessons from the recent crisis', Bank for International Settlements Working Papers 329, November 2010.

[28] McCarthy C (2006), 'Is the present business model bust?', Speech at the Gleneagles Saving and Pension Industry Leaders' Summit, Gleneagles, 16 September.

Both these initiatives were predicated on the assumption that financial institutions could exploit their market power and the asymmetries of information between consumers and product providers, contrary to the recent popular assertion that the FSA had always assumed that markets worked well.[29]

6.6 New paradigms

As a result of the current financial crisis, and in response to sharp shifts in the intellectual and political contexts, the mood music and regulatory and supervisory approach has shifted dramatically – especially with respect to capital and liquidity standards given the series of tougher regulatory requirements introduced by the Financial Stability Board and the Basel Committee[30], and a more assertive and intrusive approach to supervision[31]. Regulators and supervisors are now following a different intellectual paradigm. "This must never happen again" has become a political rallying cry, and banker and bonus bashing a populist sport as the realization dawned that financial sector profits had been privatized while the losses were socialized. As Ulrich Beck commented, 'what a priceless convert's comedy is being performed on the world stage'.[32]

Failures in risk management by many financial institutions also illustrate that an unjustified reliance on "science" may lead to an over-estimation of the ability to quantify, control and mitigate risks, as well as to the emergence of new and unanticipated risks[33]. Beck argues that modern society fails to recognize the danger that 'rationality, that is the experience of the past, encourages anticipation of the wrong kind of

---

[29] For example, Financial Services Authority (2009), *op. cit.* foonote 17; and Wheatley M (2012), 'My vision for the FCA', Speech at the British Bankers' Association, 25 January.

[30] Including 'A global regulatory framework for more resilient banks and banking systems', Basel Committee of Banking Supervisors, December 2010.

[31] See, for example, Vinals J and Fiechter J (2010), 'The Making of Good Supervision: Learning to Say "No" ', *IMF Staff Position Note*, May.

[32] Beck U, 'This free-market farce proves the state is crucial', *Guardian* blog 'Comment is free', April 2008

[33] Briault C (2010), 'Risk Society and Financial Risk', in: Bridget Hutter (ed.), *Anticipating Risks and Organising Risk Regulation*, Cambridge University Press, August.

risk, the one we believe we can calculate and control, whereas the disaster arises from what we do not know and cannot calculate'.[34] He identifies a 'fatal irony' arising from the 'futility with which the highly developed institutions of modern society – science, state, business and military – attempt to anticipate what cannot be anticipated'.

6.7 Ways forward

Since my main thesis is that the root of the problem ahead of the current financial crisis was collective intellectual failure, the main question here must be how such a failure could be prevented. This is not easy, but I do see three starting points.

First, we should at least be clear about the intellectual viewpoint that we want our regulators and supervisors to be following. Society needs to decide what it wants the financial sector to look like. The post-crisis mood is already driving regulators to take a risk-averse approach to delivering safety and soundness, financial stability and high standards of conduct, at the expense of the ability of the financial sector to contribute to economic growth and of consumers to make adequate provision for saving, investment and protection. But is this where we want to be? How safe, how boring, and how limited as a contributor to economic growth do we want the financial sector to be? The answers to this societal question need in turn to be reflected much more clearly and explicitly in the objectives and mandates of regulators and supervisors, in order that they deliver an agreed vision of the financial sector and strike the desired balance between safety and economic growth. Indeed, this clarity should be the bedrock on which the relationship between the regulator and the regulated is built.

This need for clarity is also of particular importance in limiting the negative externalities that emerge in the event of the failure of a major financial institution. Because of the difficulties in "internalizing" these negative externalities through incentive structures[35] we are

---

[34] Beck U (2006), 'Living in the world risk society', *Economy and Society*, 35(3), August.
[35] Briault C (2012), 'Incentive Structures', Paper presented at the ICFR/SUERF Conference on Future Risks and Fragilities for Financial Stability, London, 8 March.

moving towards an unattractive and inefficient reliance on regulatory and other interventions to limit the size, structure and business activities of financial institutions. An alternative would be to explore whether there is a third way here, which could build on a private/public partnership and recognize more explicitly that neither the addition of new incentives designed to take the market to the right solution nor ever more intrusive regulation are the best ways of identifying and building a role for financial institutions that reflects both private and social objectives.

Second, the shift in emphasis towards macro-prudential oversight – which many Asian countries introduced following the Asian crisis more than ten years ago, and which the rest of the world is now putting into place – should be of benefit if it results in a better informed debate on risks to financial stability, less groupthink, and a greater propensity to take action to address risks to financial stability. This should be an important shift from the earlier tendency of many central banks to produce long lists of risks in a Financial Stability Report, but then for the authorities to do nothing to address and mitigate these risks. However, if some risks are simply not spotted then no action to mitigate them will be taken. And mechanisms to encourage a diversity of views will not necessarily generate better outcomes if the majority view prevails but then proves to be incorrect.

Third, as I have argued elsewhere[36], financial market participants and policymakers therefore also need to recognize that not all risks can be anticipated and that resilience needs to be built to cope with risks once they do materialize. Hence, the importance arises of establishing credible and effective "resolution plans", under which major financial institutions could be resolved in an orderly manner with limited impact in terms of contagion to the rest of the financial sector, adverse effects on the wider economy, and costs to the taxpayer. However, both prevention and resilience are costly, so we need a proper debate on whether these are substitutes or complements and again an agreed vision on the way forward.

---

[36] Briault C (2010), 'Risk Society and Financial Risk', in: Bridget Hutter (ed.), *Anticipating Risks and Organising Risk Regulation*, Cambridge University Press, August.

7.0 Regulatory Capture and Global Standard Setters

Jane Diplock AO[1]

In this short thought piece I would like to reflect on the issue of regulatory capture by looking at the role of those who are charged with protecting the public interest in global standard setting. How can the users of global standards be confident that there is no regulatory capture of the standard setters and their outcomes, that the processes of standard setting are transparent and appropriate and the standards set are suitable for global adoption and enforcement in the public interest? In order to imbue confidence, there needs to be a mechanism to ensure there is no actual or perceived bias or outside influence in the standard setting process and that the processes of arriving at those standards are appropriate in the public interest.

There is no doubt that the global financial crisis has left us questioning the effectiveness of some global institutions and processes and asking ourselves about some accepted economic presumptions and views about how markets and capital structures really work in the globalized, technically enabled markets of the twenty-first century. Increasingly

[1] Jane Diplock was the Chairman of the Executive Committee of the International Organisation of Securities Commissions (IOSCO) until April 2011. She was first elected in 2004 and re-elected for a fourth term in June 2010. Jane was appointed Chairman of the New Zealand Securities Commission in September 2001, and reappointed in 2006 for a further five-year term, which ended in April 2011. Before this appointment, Jane was the National Director, Infrastructure and Strategic Planning, and New South Wales Regional Commissioner with the Australian Securities and Investments Commission. She has also held executive positions with Westpac Banking Corporation, and was Managing Director of the New South Wales Technical and Further Education Commission. She is a member of the Public Interest Oversight Board, a member of the board of Singapore Exchange Limited, a member of the board of The International Integrated Reporting Council and a number of international advisory boards.

the challenge of how to protect the public interest in standard setting for global interconnected markets has come to the fore.

Much of the analysis undertaken since 2008 has focused on our understanding of the factors which underpin financial stability and in particular the role markets play in financial stability. It has also become increasingly obvious that the globalized capital markets need global standards, uniformly implemented. Nowhere is this more important than in the area of disclosure by issuers and the audit of such firms to ensure investor confidence. It is equally important in capital markets standards.

The complex roles of the various players in global standard setting – policymakers, the regulators, and professional standard setters – suggest a conundrum we need to fully resolve before the challenges of governance of global institutions are settled. Much of the discussion in the literature on regulatory capture fails to distinguish between the role the policymakers, politicians and their ministries play in the establishment of domestic policy settings and regulatory remits, and the limits this can place on the roles undertaken by regulators and standard setters. To equate the roles of these two sets of players is to miss one important aspect of the complexity of the implementation of global standards.

My proposition is that, given the importance of global standards and the complexity of the relationships of stakeholders with those who set them, serious thought should be given to an institutional framework which can give the standard setting work the confidence of users and other stakeholders. This confidence is vital to ensuring global acceptance and implementation. It is also important to enhance the efficient allocation of global capital. The role of global standards has increased in importance over the past decade. Global standards have also become more complex, interleaving, and their scope and impact has increased enormously. I suggest that the governance of the standard setters has struggled to keep up with this increased importance and impact on the regulated community.

It has been recognized for standard setters in the accounting and auditing professions that there is a need for a mechanism to ensure that users can have confidence in the standard setting process. These mechanisms take varying forms, but in the area of securities market standard setters, the issue has not yet been addressed. Commentators have suggested that international standard setters are one step removed from the checks and balances obvious in the domestic arena and are therefore less transparent and may be more liable to capture. I do not agree that they are necessarily more likely to be captured, but perception is important for confidence. I do agree that some of the processes of international standard setters seem opaque, convoluted and less than transparent.

The focus of the G20 through the Financial Stability Board on the development of relevant global standards and their implementation has been a direct reflection of the importance of such standards and their implementation on global financial stability. The politicians who make up the G20 advocate this premise and at least in their public utterances seem to see that that their political futures depend on getting this right. In other words, the public choice is currently one which aligns their short-term political interests and the urgency to find stability for the global markets. This has not always been the case.

The tendencies of late – partial ("light-handed adoption") or non-adoption of global standards in financial regulation, in order to gain a perceived economic or comparative advantage – has, at least for the short-term, largely dissipated or is no longer fashionable. Does this mean that pressure to develop standards which are less rigorous, or directed towards the short-term interests of stakeholders rather than the public interest, necessarily abated? I am not convinced.

Standard setters generally agree that the credibility of global standards, agreed by consensus to be in the public interest and achieved through a rigorous and transparent process, is vital to ensure global adoption. Such standards often take a great deal of time to develop and need dedicated technical experts to ensure they are workable. The users of these standards need to be assured that they have been developed independently of interested parties and in a transparent manner.

The political or professional masters of those involved in standard setting understand the need for independence but also want accountability. They are often driven by short-term domestic political and economic concerns and influenced by their domestic constituents and their interests. From the contradiction between the long-term public interest and shorter-term concerns, a conundrum emerges. How can independence be assured for users and other stakeholders when the influence of those who fund or select the standard setters can lead to a perception of capture? Equally vital: how can the quality of process and output, and value for money, be assured by those who fund and select them?

The funding of standard setters and regulators is almost always linked in some way to a political or professional process. This is understandable, as practically it is difficult to have such a public service funded otherwise. Even if the process is "industry funded" then that funding model usually has political or professional oversight.

The perception of regulatory capture can arise in subtle ways. Funding is often a way of influencing regulatory bodies. Funding of regulators and standard setters by national governments means that the capability in resource terms of the standard setter or regulator and therefore their capacity to contribute to the standard setting process can be influenced by the political process. Similarly, a limited domestic legislative remit, ineffective laws which are impossible to implement, and legislative proposals which do not cover the field limit the capacity for regulators and standard setters to protect investors, to fully consider the needs of other stakeholders, and therefore to take the public interest effectively into account.

Can independence and accountability both be achieved? This is the challenge which faces all standard setters, including those setting global standards. At the global level both the IASB and IFAC have developed governance models which are designed to deal with this conundrum.

Regulators are generally seen as the proxy for the protection of the public interest. This proxy is useful but not perfect. They must act independently (the IOSCO Principles, for example, require it); yet, actual models of independence from the political process and therefore the lobbying process of stakeholders varies wildly. For instance, some securities markets regulators are political figures in the government of their jurisdiction. Others are selected from amongst political allies of those in power or from amongst those who have demonstrated alignment with the political or economic outlook of the government of the day. Some work closely with their finance ministries and others do not.

Much of this does not matter if when in the role the regulator acts in an independent way. Too close a relationship between the regulator and his political masters can lead to a perception of conflict of interest, or regulatory capture. In some cases the checks by the IMF and World Bank on regulatory performance of jurisdictions under the Financial Sector Appraisal Programme (FSAP) have been qualified if it appears the securities regulator is not acting in an entirely independent way. It is true that this rarely happens and that securities market regulators usually are found to act in an independent manner. Nevertheless, regulatory capture is sometimes alleged and the perception remains.

How can this perception be allayed? Just as the IMF and the World Bank check the status of the implementation of global standards through the FSAP programme and Reports on the Observance of Standards and Codes (ROSCs), there are suggestions that perhaps individual regulators should subject themselves to independent reviews of their operational efficiency and effectiveness; these could be published to ensure the transparency of their effectiveness and that they have been acting in the public interest. Despite the risk of there being some perception of potential conflicts or potential for regulatory capture, the regulator remains the best (if imperfect) proxy we currently have for an impartial public interest.

A similar perception issue arises in global standard setters whose expertise is drawn from the professional bodies. The perception that the setters of such standards may in some way consciously or unconsciously favour standards which will assist the profession rather than other users of standards, issuers and other stakeholders, can undermine confidence in those standards setters. In other words, the profession can appear to have captured the standard setting process.

The great efforts to ensure transparency of process and widest possible consultation assist in allaying this perception, but the fact remains that there is a growing realization that there needs to be institutional bolstering of confidence in the impartiality of standard setters. A particular example arose during the global financial crisis which illustrates the issue.

During the global financial crisis, standard setters, in particular the International Accounting Standards Board (IASB) and the Financial Accounting Standards Board (FASB), found themselves under considerable pressure to change the priority of the standard setting process and to change the standards they had set, in particular regarding ways to suit a clearly defined commercial agenda. This agenda was promoted by a number of banks and other financial institutions via a political lobbying process and was quite successful in gaining political traction in a number of jurisdictions. These financial institutions and their constituent stakeholders considered that the then applicable accounting standards had contributed to the crisis, and significantly, were making dealing with the crisis by some banks more difficult. They also had some more general complaints about the standard setting processes.

In 2009 the two accounting bodies set up the Financial Crisis Advisory Group, a group of international experts to assist them in considering the issues. The members had wide experience in the global markets and as Chairman of the Executive Committee of IOSCO, I was honoured to be among them. Chaired by Harvey Goldsmidt and Hans Hoogervost, the experts around the table were captains of industry, some current or retired banking and securities regulators, as well as standard setters from the profession.

The pressure the international standard setters were feeling was an interplay of attempted regulatory capture being played out on the global stage. It was a particularly interesting case study as it potentially brought together the issues of the perception of regulatory capture both of professional bodies and the regulators who were party to the discussions. It reflected a frustration with some in the political and business world that the independence of the global standard setters put them beyond their influence and direct reach.

Everyone who was involved in those meetings was aware of the high stakes the global financial community was playing for; this was a time of exquisite financial instability and stress. There were clearly vested interests in the business community that valued the disclosure revealed by fair value accounting. There were vested interests in the accounting standard setters at the table who had laboured very assiduously over the complex standards under discussion and were convinced of their usefulness. There were also securities markets regulators who were aware of their role as proxy for the public interest, in particular issuers and other stakeholders. There were banking regulators who were very concerned about the financial stability aspects of banking collapses and who had a view which did not align with some of those of the regulators, particularly a view on countercyclical approaches to provisioning and the accounting treatment that suggested. All members were critically aware of the importance of the issues: in almost every jurisdiction represented there were banks hovering on the brink of collapse and there was great public anxiety about the future of the global financial system. Swirling around all of these concerns was the issue of the independence of the global standard setters.

The Financial Crisis Advisory Group provided a buffer for the international standard setters from the attempt to influence their processes and outcomes. It reported that accounting standards had not caused the global financial crisis – a myth which had some appeal to some commentators and it asserted the importance of the independence of the global accounting standard setters. The FCAG report emphasized that standard setting independently undertaken with wide consultation and integrity would assist in resolving the crisis.

The issue of the conundrum of accountability and independence is not easily resolved. Structures such as the FCAG are useful to highlight the issue of attempted capture if the balance appears to be becoming dangerously and urgently uneven and where the usual processes of resistance to capture seem not to be working.

There need to be permanent institutional structural frameworks which will make such crisis interventions unnecessary. These structures need to be independently funded and empowered not only to oversee the process, but also outcomes for suitability.

It is for this reason that the standard setters for the International Accounting Standards (IFRS), the International Auditing Standards (IASs), as well as the standards for ethics and education of auditing professionals, have been refining their oversight processes. Both the IASB and IFAC realize that for confidence in the standards which they set, there needs to be an independent oversight mechanism to ensure that the standards they set have the confidence of users and other stakeholders. They see the necessity for a buffer to ensure that the perception of regulatory capture does not undermine confidence in the standard setting process.

In most aspects of accounting and auditing standard setting, the model has a board of truly independent experts to ensure the processes they follow are in the public interest. Trustees are the independent experts in relation to the IFRS Foundation and the Public Interest Oversight Board (PIOB) serves this role in relation to IFAC. The IFRS Foundation has recently completed its five-yearly constitutional review and has in its revised constitution reasserted the role of the Trustees in acting in the public interest.

In one very important accounting area, that of public sector accounting, there is currently no public oversight mechanism. The international adoption of accrual accounting by governments and their agencies lies woefully behind adoption of IFRS or US GAAP in the private sector. Recently IFAC requested the G20 to take up this issue as the current sovereign debt crisis has only served to illustrate the parlous state of disclosures by many governments and their agencies. Historically the setting of public sector standards has been undertaken by IFAC, yet oversight of accounting rather than auditing standards has traditionally been done within the IFRS Trustee framework. While there are valid arguments for either the IFRS Trustees or the PIOB to undertake the oversight, it is clear that the standard setting process should be undertaken by a body charged with the public interest to ensure confidence in the standard setting process and the standards.

What should the remit of any public interest oversight body be? Clearly it needs to ensure that the process of standard setting is transparent, that appropriate consultation takes place, and that the views of users and other stakeholders are properly addressed. However, I consider it needs to do more than to merely oversee due process. It needs to ensure that the standard setter is considering the right issues and that its agenda is appropriate in the public interest. It cannot be in the public interest that inappropriate, unworkable, or unenforceable standards are issued, or that the priority or progress of standard setters is influenced by processes other than those strictly in the public interest. The oversight body should ensure the correct priority is accorded standards and that the progress of the standards' development is appropriate in the public interest.

The work of the public interest body should be made publicly available and transparent. It should report back to the standard setter on the standards set and give advice publicly if it considers that any standard does not meet the public interest test. It should be able to recommend changes to the scope or detail of the standard if it considers it to be in the public interest to do so. It should also comment on the transparency of the process for arriving at the standard, the effectiveness of the consultation and the usefulness and capacity for global implementation of the standard.

The work of the public interest body should be prominent in the minds of users and other stakeholders to ensure that the confidence it is intended to imbue is actualized. This will require a sensible and balanced publicity approach to ensure the processes are understood and respected.

How should such a public interest body be funded? This is another difficult question. The funding of such a body needs to be at arm's length from the users and other stakeholders, yet it is precisely in their interests that it will work. Clearly, global public institutions such as the World Bank, the IMF, IOSCO, the IAIS, the Basel Committee, European Commission and others would have an interest in such a body. Also the IIF, stock exchanges, and global associations of asset managers, pension funds and so forth should also be interested in the work of such bodies. Through the mechanism of blind trusts funding should be managed completely at arm's length. Such funders will want to have some monitoring or accountability mechanism to ensure their funds are spent within the remit of the public interest body.

The role of the monitoring of public interest bodies is an equally important accountability mechanism. It needs to ensure the public interest body uses its budget wisely and is efficient in the use of resources supplied by those bodies. The relationship of monitoring should not be a remit to influence the standard setting process or outcomes in any way. Otherwise a perception of the possible conflicts outlined earlier would arise.

The three levels of accountability (standard setter, public interest oversight and monitoring body) are important to ensure that each level can adequately assuage the potential for conflicts which can emerge in the standard setting process. To suggest that regulators alone could assure the public interest without the buffer of an oversight board is to ignore the conflict and pressure that can emerge in that relationship between regulators and political forces. It may appeal to some in the regulatory community but will not give the level of confidence needed in my view to ensure the efficient allocation of global capital.

This leads me to a more controversial suggestion. If regulators are not a perfect proxy for the public interest, then perhaps the global standard setting process for securities regulation should now consider a public interest oversight mechanism to ensure that public interest considerations, greater transparency and due process are seen as evident in its standard setting.

IOSCO is the global standard setter and is currently reviewing its governance structure. A new governance structure has been agreed in Beijing in May 2012. I would like to suggest that consideration be given to a public interest oversight mechanism for IOSCO. A board of international experts who have no active regulatory roles could be established to give confidence to issuers and other stakeholders that due process, proper consultation and transparency is being undertaken in its important global standard setting work in the public interest. It would also advise IOSCO on whether the standard setting priorities were correct in the public interest and comment on the pace and progress of the standard setting process. Also, it would ensure that standards set were comprehensive, useful, enforceable, and able to be globally implemented.

Such a public interest body could draw on the newly agreed research function of IOSCO, by an independent reporting line, to ensure it was fully resourced with the latest research thinking around securities market regulatory issues. It could be funded by users and other stakeholders through an arms length funding mechanism and it would give increased confidence in the standard setting process. This suggestion is not entirely unlike the "Sentinel" suggested by Ross Levine in his book The Guardians of Finance, though it is more modest as it would not need to be resourced by a separate group of economic and financial research analysts. It is more ambitious as it would make recommendations and suggestions, not to domestic regulators but to the members of the international standard setting communities concerning the priorities and content of the standards as well as on process issues, and make these recommendations publicly available.

The past ten years have seen IOSCO develop from a network of regulators, meeting to set aspirational standards, to a vital part of the global financial infrastructure, with two seats on the Financial Stability Board, setting securities market standards implementable in all G20 countries and encouraged in all others. As standards become more operational, as jurisdictions see these standards more as compulsory for adoption rather than optional, and as the Financial Stability Board pushes for more auditing of jurisdictions' compliance, so political pressure and that of industry on standard setters is likely to increase. The impact of operational standards on individual jurisdictions' capital markets will mean greater scrutiny, both by the politicians in those jurisdictions as well as the investors and other user communities. The alignment of public choice between standard setters and politicians and their constituent interest groups is unlikely to continue for long, if indeed it ever truly existed. There will also be increased pressure by users and other stakeholders to ensure that the public interest remains preeminent in the standard setting process. Perhaps now is the time for IOSCO to also accept the public interest challenge that arises with its increased importance, relevance, and responsibility, and to form a public interest board.

The model of global standards setters – overseen by independent bodies charged with protecting the public interest – is one whose time has come. IOSCO remains outside this model, but it may find the concept a useful one as the standards it develops are increasingly being accepted and implemented globally and are of increasing importance to issuers, other users and stakeholders. Confidence that the public interest is protected and embodied in these standards is essential and a public interest oversight body may assist in this process.

8.0 Political Capture and the Regulatory Cycle: How Should it be Addressed

David Green[1]

8.1 Introduction

There has been much discussion about the risk of capture of regulators by the regulated, but rather less about the direct relationship between politicians and the regulator, what some have called "political capture". Nevertheless, this is central to the debate about the relationship between the regulator and the regulated because it is to politicians rather than the regulated community that regulators are ultimately accountable and it is politicians who write the legislation by which regulation and supervision is governed. The political climate or mood is at all times something that the regulator has to deal with, irrespective of whether legislation is in course of

[1] David Green has worked for over forty years as a central banker and financial regulator, principally in the Bank of England and the Financial Services Authority and is currently risk advisor at the Central Bank of Ireland. From 1968 to 1998, he worked in the Bank of England on a broad range of topics. From 1974 to 1977 he served as Private Secretary to the Managing Director of the IMF in Washington DC. From 1998 to 2004, he was Head of International Policy Co-ordination and EU Affairs for the FSA. In this role he was particularly engaged in the development of the Financial Stability Forum, the European single market in financial services and of the Lamfalussy committee structure. He was a member of the Banking Supervision Committee of the ECB where he represented successively the Bank of England and the FSA, and of the Banking Advisory Committee of the European Commission. He was Adviser on Public Affairs to the Managing Board of Euronext from 2004-5 and from 2005-2011 Adviser on International Affairs to the UK Financial Reporting Council as well as serving as Secretary of the International Forum of Independent Audit Regulators. He has published, jointly with Sir Howard Davies, "Global Financial Regulation - The Essential Guide", and "Banking on the Future: The Fall and Rise of Central Banking".

being changed. It is often, therefore, also through the influence of politicians that the regulated seek indirectly to bring pressure to bear on the regulators. This note attempts to explore this space further.

It is often recognized that there exists in financial regulation a cycle of fluctuation between a period of regulation or supervisory behaviour that in retrospect appears to have been excessively slack and regulation which, again in retrospect, appears to have been excessively demanding. This process inevitably impinges on the relationship between regulators and their political masters. The challenge is that it is difficult to observe at any point of time just where one might be in such a cycle, which is in its nature erratic and manifests differently in each phase, or consequently when and in which direction regulation should be adjusted.

This note suggests that the political process needs to recognize the existence of such a cycle through formal mechanisms to serve as a reminder of the need to be alert to such a cycle, of the risks of overshoot it carries with it, and of the need to adjust legislation accordingly. The political process also needs to recognize that supervisors need to be appointed who are equipped to handle the pressures which the existence of this cycle inevitably places on them.

8.2 The regulatory cycle

To give a stylized description, there are, of course, periods when there is not much political discussion, if any, about financial regulation. In this phase, politicians do not interfere significantly in financial regulatory policies, in part due to the inherent complexity of the issues, but mostly because of the absence of immediate electoral rewards associated with initiatives in this sector. Instead, politicians prefer to delegate regulatory and supervisory functions to independent regulatory agencies.

This state of affairs is usually interrupted by some incident – financial failures or lapses in conduct – which results in an outcome with politically unacceptable costs. It might be a BCCI, a Barings, subprime, Enron, RBS, Madoff, or any number of like incidents. Typically it will arise during boom conditions or, more likely, as they come to an end and the tide starts to go out, leaving uncovered the excesses of the recent past and the losses that they impose on users of financial services, and sometimes the taxpayer. Beyond providing important opportunities, sometimes the only ones, for market failures to be demonstrated, crises are likely to generate demands that never again should there be such shortcomings. Pressures for regulatory change may come from the general public, depositors, investors or policyholders who have suffered, usually encouraged by the press, and also perhaps from some parts of the financial sector who may feel that their competitors have been insufficiently stringently regulated with resulting disadvantage to themselves. As a result of these pressures, crises are likely to lead to a greater engagement on the part of politicians not implicated in the structure of the existing regulatory framework.

Crises will also create the political opportunity for reforms that are not necessarily directed to address genuine shortcomings uncovered by the crisis, but rather arise from pre-existing social and political objectives. The introduction of measures to regulate hedge funds in Europe after the crisis has been described through the analogy of a bar room brawl where you punch the person you had always wanted to hit rather than the person who started the fight. Similarly, the appointment of the Independent Commission on Banking in the UK has received criticism by some as appearing more directed to taking up pre-existing attitudes to the desired social role of banking and the proper response of regulation to this, rather than the particular defects in each of retail and investment banking uncovered in the crisis which provided the opportunity for reform initiatives.

Clearly there will be many cases where evidently-needed reform will only come about after a crisis or some other shock or scandal, as with the long-delayed imposition of consolidated supervision on US investment banks. However, there is also the risk that the political heat behind reform may lead to a situation of regulatory overshooting, as with some aspects of the Sarbanes-Oxley response to Enron and, quite possibly, with the massive increase in capital and liquidity requirements sought following the recent crisis.

It will take some time, at least a year, before mainstream political opinion reaches the consensus that change of regime is definitely needed and then much more time, say two years, to decide on what a new regime should look like, and then a further period, say another two years, for the new, stricter regime to come fully into force. By then, of course, conditions may well have changed; there may be little risk that the problem to be averted, possibly at considerable economic cost, will recur because markets are now alerted to it; or by then there may be reason to suppose that the remedy identified may not have been as well tailored to match the actual problem which had surfaced as had been generally supposed.

Typically after a while, usually in a period of slower growth, there will be increasing concern that excessively burdensome regulation is damaging the economy; regulation is thought to be being implemented over-strictly with too much attention to rigid rules; the international competitiveness of the local financial market place is thought to be being prejudiced; access to credit may be being denied to small businesses; innovation in general is said to be stifled, and so on.

After a period of time, those who form mainstream political opinion will reach a consensus that regulation needs to be relaxed. This follows pressure from regulated firms who feel their profitability and business opportunities are being unjustifiably impeded by bureaucratic obsession with improbable risks, or from potential borrowers, small businesses or aspiring homeowners who feel they are being starved of credit to which they should be entitled, or from civic leaders who are told that employment and tax revenue in their financial centre is depressed because of over regulation compared to other centres. It will be concluded that a lighter touch is needed, that innovation must be given a chance to prove its value, that credit standards should look to the longer term, and that regard should be had to international competition with more loosely regulated centres, and so on.

The process of determining the regulatory stance will then go into reverse. The mood will shift: the regulators will be expected to take account of it, and the legislative wheels will begin to turn. It will take a couple of years to reach agreement on a new regime and another couple of years to implement it. By this time the political and perhaps economic cycles will have turned again.

Although this cycle is an abstract concept, some examples may serve to illustrate how this phenomenon might manifest itself in practice. In the UK context one of the many motives behind the reforms resulting in the creation of the FSA was a sense that that the more judgemental approach to supervision pursued by the Bank of England, which was out of line with the much more legalistic approach of other major jurisdictions, lay behind the shortcomings which had allowed the BCCI and Barings affairs to happen. There was also a sense that the Bank was less likely to be rigorous in supervision because of its close involvement in markets and an excessive concern not to disturb them. The reforms enacted attempted to modify this approach and introduce much more evidence-based supervision which would have to withstand much stricter legal scrutiny and avoid the risk that judgement would be exercised inappropriately. Some of the regulated firms were supportive of this for the different reason that they thought that it would be easier for their lawyers to take advantage of a rule-based approach.

In fact, after a while as the economy picked up but regulation still contained a large content of "rules", pressure started to be generated for supervision to be "light touch". Although there was no provision for such a shift in the legislation, politicians, including the Prime Minister, started to make it clear, quite vocally, that this was what was expected (see Clive Briault in this publication). Risk in the financial system must have gone down, it was asserted, because of successful economic management, while excessive regulation was damaging both the interests of the UK as an international centre and the legitimate right of citizens to own a home, irrespective of likely ability to service debt, so that after a while the FSA itself was under pressure to use this same "light touch" language to take account of the prevailing mood.

Meanwhile, the Bank of England had taken seriously the political steer surrounding the 1998 reforms to stay out of supervision. Of course, once crisis struck once more, the previous direction of political guidance was sharply reversed, light touch fell out of favour, judgement was brought back into the supervisory rhetoric (though is not yet enshrined in legislation) and the Bank of England was given responsibilities in just those areas in which it had previously been judged as falling short. Of course, this very much simplifies and perhaps even caricatures what has taken place, but a description of this kind serves to highlight just how far the regulatory cycle can swing.

So far I have addressed regulation in a purely domestic context. However, account must increasingly be taken of the existence of such cycles in the international context, which may or may not be synchronized. In some periods, market participants will be looking at what other countries are doing, as will governments, to seek to shut down regulatory arbitrage opportunities; in other periods, they will seek to exploit them for themselves. An interesting contrast may be drawn between the demands for "light touch, principles-based" regulation in the middle of the last decade in the UK (in direct competitive reaction to the rule-based introduction of Sarbanes-Oxley in the US) with the demands in 2008-09 for a global regulatory response, as identical as possible, in response to the global financial crisis. This brief period of unanimity has, of course, dissipated as countries have found that the common regulatory solutions agreed internationally at unprecedented speed now look not so well suited after all to the circumstances of individual countries. The cycle is already turning in some jurisdictions, and as implementation of the previously agreed G20 reforms gets closer, there is demand in different countries to water down regulation, in part as a result of weakening political/electoral appetite for regulation and in part because slowdown in growth is reinforcing the argument that these reforms may hurt economic growth.

The fact that some countries are already in different phases of the cycle is also leading to a resurgence of competitive issues, with pressure to ease implementation, irrespective of the merits of the measures, if other countries fail to comply. This can be seen currently in relation to the Basel III implementation, or with requirements for the centralization of clearing of OTC derivatives markets. The widened circle of decision making on international standards, now including far more countries from the emerging markets, also contributes to the challenge of matching domestic political aspirations with the desire for an international level playing field.

So much is generally familiar. What is less commonly observed is that such cycles leave the supervisors themselves in a very exposed position. In its nature supervision will not eliminate failure or other shortcomings in outcome. Indeed, few regimes are constructed with the intention to achieve such an outcome because of the economic damage which would likely result. The consequence is that supervision is always hazardous. Furthermore, however, because of the intrinsic lags in the process just discussed, the regime the supervisors are legally obliged to operate will quite possibly be out of sync almost all the time, not just some of it, with what mainstream political opinion thinks should currently be the right approach. Thus any overshoot in either the direction of excessive strictness or slack in relation to current political expectations will be uncomfortable for the supervisors.

8.3 Policy recommendations

It is not straightforward to construct self-adjusting mechanisms which will minimize the potentially substantial economic costs arising from overshoot of regime or the direct costs involved simply in change of regime. There are, of course, various objective indicators in relation to the purely macroeconomic aspects impinging on the regulatory cycle which can be used for major cyclical economic variables, such as ratios of credit to GNP, but there may not be consensus on what macroprudential indicators of this kind may mean or how their indications may be used to take action.

Some of the Better Regulation tools are one starting point, particularly in the tightening phase, though they are also susceptible to misuse for particular political ends, particularly in the loosening phase, where an agency charged with policing better regulation can be politically tasked. The broad principles behind better regulation are that regulation and its enforcement should be proportionate, accountable, consistent, transparent and targeted, with proper regulatory impact assessments and post-implementation reviews undertaken. These tests, particularly in relation to proportionality and targeting, can help try to make it more likely than not that the changes undertaken are indeed related directly to the specific failing that has materialized and can help reduce the risk of cyclical overshot. As suggested above, sometimes the action taken is derived as much from more general current prejudice (see Ridley in this publication) as from a strict analysis of the market failure or regulatory gap involved leading to remedies directly tailored to address that failure or gap. Quite often the actions are directed to the wrong target or else are disproportionate to the risks involved and in turn this will quickly result in pressure to fudge implementation.

It may also be helpful to have set time periods for legislation to be reviewed root and branch irrespective of either the economic or political cycle, as with the decennial revision customary with Canadian banking legislation. These tools could include sunset clauses. Of course, a requirement for periodic review on a set timescale may run the risk that the review falls at an unhelpful point in the cycle and creates new opportunities for certain actors to seek to water down the regime. A review process also takes some time itself, during which circumstances can change. Nevertheless, it should help to ensure a more considered approach to getting the right overall balance because it may cut across those periods when there is strong desire for change in one direction or another.

So much for the legislative process; where are the supervisors left in the midst of such cyclical changes in climate? The first thing is for the board of a supervisory agency to ensure that the agency makes clear exactly how it interprets its legal mandate and what it intends to do to give effect to this. The framework surrounding supervision in terms of legislation, accountability or governance must make it clear that this is what a supervisor is required to do and recognize that the supervisor does not have leeway to diverge from the legal mandate governing it at the time it needs to decide to act (or not act as the case may be). If the legislature does not like what the arrangements are then it needs to change them, but it should not apply pressure for the supervisor to act at variance from the prevailing legal requirements. The regulator's governing body needs to be constructed in such a way as to be able to resist such pressure, which may be more difficult if it has been appointed by politicians or has substantial industry representation.

The other thing the board of a supervisory agency must do is to ensure that it acts as it says it will act, irrespective of pressures to change regime without legislative cover, and to give protection to staff that are under pressure to do otherwise. Failure to do what the agency has said it will do is perhaps the principal grounds on which disciplinary action against a supervisor is reasonable. Otherwise supervisors need protection from being held responsible simply because something has gone wrong. Such immunity is usually granted to some degree by legislation and needs to be reinforced politically. Some things will always go wrong at some point because of the intrinsic nature of supervision which should never be intended to achieve zero-failure and in practice never will, except by luck.

The discussion above has focused on shifts in political attitudes to regulatory policy and the need to be alert to harmful distortions that can potentially arise as a result of such cyclical shifts. Another reason for needing a degree of clear independence is for protection against interference by politicians, or politically connected persons, in individual supervisory decisions. Attempts at such interference are sometimes made because of the inevitable close links between financial and political influence. They tend to attract most attention when they backfire and cases where political intervention is subsequently revealed to be seriously ill-judged may remind politicians that it can be in their own interest to be able to say to those pressuring them that they are legally precluded from involvement in decisions in individual cases. It is perhaps fortunate that the letter from former Prime Minister Callaghan to the Bank of England commending the management of BCCI only came to light many years later, but much more discomfort has arisen from recent investigation of the apparently successful attempts of former Dutch ministers to cause the Dutch central bank not to exercise its powers when it should have done. Measures to help counter improper political interference may include security of tenure of the executive and a balanced composition of the governing body.

Overall, though, there is a trade-off between the insulation of regulatory authorities from the interference of their political masters and measures to ensure adequate accountability to the legitimate needs of the political process. Too much independence can leave regulators unchallenged without proper checks and balances in an exclusive institutional context dominated by the financial sector. Too little can result in a harmful and inaccurately targeted regime.

It can be seen from this analysis that supervision needs very special individuals at its head and in the key decision making positions, equipped to navigate their way through not just the technical requirements but also a permanently charged political environment. Public expectations will normally be at variance with what supervisors are able to deliver, either because their legal framework may not match what the public expects at any given point or because the very nature of the environment in which supervision operates is itself so prone to instability, whatever the nature of the legal regime. Financial supervision is a risk-taking business: it operates within an uncertain and unpredictable world with extremely limited resources on the basis of information that can often be incomplete or wrong, and uses tools whose impact depends on the behavioural response of others.

There are not many other jobs like it, and it takes a very special kind of individual to be ready to take on this challenge. Even an essentially rule-based regime will require the exercise of judgement. A principles-based one will require still more. The task of the supervisor is constantly to turn potentially conflicting mandates into politically acceptable day-to-day operational decisions in respect of every one of the individual firms and markets they supervise. They must have as complete as possible an understanding of the commercial marketplace and of the many diverse business models in it, yet their role is not to replace the management of a firm. Instead it is to pursue a legal, even if also rather imprecise public policy mandate to constrain what market practitioners would do if left to their own devices.

What are the qualities needed of a financial regulator? How much should the regulator bend to political wishes even when the formal regime points to other requirements? How much should they reform the regime through operational practice even if there has been no legislative decision that this should happen? Is supervision a profession in its own right or is it something that any market participant with the right attitude can pick up? What sorts of people are needed to make the forward-looking judgements that have always been required of the supervisor?

8.4 Who is to perform these balancing acts and who has these qualities?

Supervisory agencies everywhere, not just in the UK, face a challenge in terms of staff resources. The board of a supervisory agency must ensure that it is staffed with people with the appropriate mix of personal character and experience to withstand inappropriate pressure from the market participants whose behaviour it is required to modify. Some of these skills can indeed be brought in from the market, as is frequently called for, but many can only be cultivated on the job. The senior supervisor can never expect to have the same degree of current technical knowledge of the market environment as a market practitioner because by definition they can never be currently active participants. To counterbalance this, the supervisory agency has instead the unique capacity to know what each and every market participant is doing, to compare and contrast this against what is happening in the market as a whole and in the wider environment surrounding it, and to make a judgement as to where the market has it wrong, again within the legal constraints.

Vital though market knowledge, expertise, and experience is, the role of supervisor is not at all that of the market participant. The core job of the supervisor is rather directly to challenge the market professional and where necessary stand in the way of the risk the market is prepared to take. Experience suggests that not all those with market experience can make the transition from poacher to gamekeeper satisfactorily and indeed may well be more tempted to give former market colleagues the benefit of the doubt. They may also have future job opportunities at the back of their mind if a supervisory role is seen as just one stage in a market career, as is often recommended.

Rather, personal qualities of tenacity in the face of inevitable challenge from senior management of firms are critical and can perforce only come with a certain minimum supervisory experience in terms of both length and breadth of service. Learning on the job is critical in creating the confidence to overcome fear of lack of respect from the supervised firm, who will always have superior resources or skills in one area or another and quite possibly a dominant CEO. This confidence is also needed to withstand improper political interference in their work. Such confidence is not acquired overnight. As recent bitter experience has taught us, supervisors have to go where even experienced NEDs fear to tread.

Salaries will never come remotely close to matching those at the higher levels of the financial services sector. Supervision is a quite separate business, much in the same way that central banking is. For its practitioners to do the job that is needed they must acquire over time, not just a few years, the distinctive and wide-ranging set of skills involved. All their failures are public and their successes must usually remain untold. They need, therefore, to be the kind of people who feel inner pride in the contribution this role can play in promoting a crucial public good, take satisfaction in the almost unparalleled complexity of the vital subject in which they deal and possess deep understanding of the importance of their direct influence on the leaders of the financial world.

8.5 Conclusions

If it is accepted that the political attitude towards the nature of a good supervisory regime is prone to swings over time, partly in light of changing circumstances and partly in reaction to likely previous overshoots in regulatory approach, there are a number of measures which might help mitigate this.

8.5.1 Legislative process

- The tools of better regulation need to be deployed rigorously by legislatures to ensure that changes in supervisory regime are correctly targeted to the right market failure and are proportionate to the risks at stake.

- Legislation should be subject to periodic review, irrespective of whether a crisis or scandal has taken place and irrespective of the general health of the economy.
- Supervisory agencies need to be sufficiently independent of government as well as the regulated industries in terms of security of tenure of the executive and composition of the governing body.

8.5.2 The behaviour and staffing of supervisory agencies

- The board of a supervisory agency must ensure that the agency makes clear exactly how it interprets its legal mandate and what it intends to do to give effect to this.
- The board of a supervisory agency must ensure that it acts as it says it will act, irrespective of pressures to change regime without legislative cover, and give protection to staff that are under pressure to do otherwise.
- The board of a supervisory agency must ensure that it is staffed with people with the appropriate mix of personal character and experience to withstand inappropriate pressure from the market participants whose behaviour it is required to modify.

9.0 Regulatory Capture: A Former Regulator's Perspective

Andrew Sheng[1]

"Institutions are not necessarily or even usually created to be socially efficient; rather they, or at least the formal rules, are created to serve the interests of those with the bargaining power to create new rules."[2] Douglas C. North

9.1 Introduction

Regulatory capture applies to a situation where the regulatory agency that is supposed to act in the public interest inappropriately acts in the interest of the industry that it has responsibility for regulating. The economic concept of regulatory capture was first pointed out by Nobel Laureate George Stigler (1971).

The 2007-09 financial crisis has exposed serious regulatory failure, with many cases of alleged regulatory capture. Indeed, in the United

---

[1] Andrew Sheng is a Chartered Accountant by training, is currently the Chief Adviser to the China Banking Regulatory Commission and a Board Member of the Qatar Financial Centre Regulatory Authority and Sime Darby Berhad, Malaysia. He is Adjunct Professor at the Graduate School of Economics and Management, Tsinghua University, Beijing and the University of Malaya, Kuala Lumpur. Andrew was Chairman of the Securities and Futures Commission of Hong Kong between 1998 and 2005. Between October 1993 and September 1998, he was the Deputy Chief Executive responsible for the Reserves Management and External Affairs Departments at the Hong Kong Monetary Authority. Between 1989 and 1993, he was Senior Manager, Financial Sector Development Department at the World Bank. From 1976 to 1989, he held various positions with Bank Negara Malaysia, including Chief Economist and Assistant Governor in charge of Bank and Insurance Regulations.

[2] North, D.C. (1994). Economic Performance through Time. American Economic Review 84(3): 359-63.

States one conclusion was that 'widespread failures in financial regulation and supervision proved devastating to the stability of the nation's financial markets. The sentries were not at their posts, in no small part due to the widely accepted faith in the self-correcting nature of the markets and the ability of financial institutions to effectively police themselves.'

However, the Financial Crisis Inquiry Commission: '[does] not accept the view that regulators lacked the power to protect the financial system. They had ample power in many arenas and they chose not to use it. ... In case after case after case, regulators continued to rate the institutions they oversaw as safe and sound even in the face of mounting troubles, often downgrading them just before their collapse. And where regulators lacked authority, they could have sought it. Too often, they lacked the political will — in a political and ideological environment that constrained it — as well as the fortitude to critically challenge the institutions and the entire system they were entrusted to oversee.'

The Report showed that: 'the financial industry itself played a key role in weakening regulatory constraints on institutions, markets, and products. It did not surprise the Commission that an industry of such wealth and power would exert pressure on policymakers and regulators. From 1999 to 2008, the financial sector expended $2.7 billion in reported federal lobbying expenses; individuals and political action committees in the sector made more than $1 billion in campaign contributions. What troubled us was the extent to which the nation was deprived of the necessary strength and independence of the oversight necessary to safeguard financial stability.'[3]

Unfortunately, despite substantive efforts made to make regulatory reforms, such as the Dodd-Frank Act of 2011 and the Basel III capital and liquidity requirements, the reforms and regulatory practice to date have not appeared to deal with the difficult issue of regulatory capture that may have played a part in regulatory failure. Indeed,

---

[3] Financial Crisis Inquiry Commission (2011). Report Conclusions, pp.xvii–xviii, January, Accessed March 4, 2012 http://fcic.law.stanford.edu/report.

many eyebrows have been raised as to why almost no one has gone to jail despite the trillions of dollars of losses incurred by the public.[4]

This chapter reviews the issue from a regulatory practitioner's perspective. It examines the types of regulatory capture and incentives that drive its existence and how one should deal with this problem.

9.2 Typology

In modern regulatory theory and policy intention, the regulatory agency is supposed to be independent of the industry that it regulates. Indeed, regulatory agencies are ideally independent of the political process, in order to shield them from political interference and allow them to independently protect the rule of law.

This is easier said than done. There is one aspect of the financial industry that shows network effects – the general tendency to concentrate. Network industries tend to concentrate in key hubs, since there is a "winner-take-all" effect of several key hubs (financial institutions or centres) gaining very large proportion of the business. In most domestic banking markets, for example, the top five banks or insurance companies tend to account for half or more of the banking assets. The UK Independent Commission on Banking (Vickers Commission) noted that the total assets of the top four banks in the UK rose to 77% of total banking accounts at the end of 2010.[5] In the financial derivatives business, for example, the US Office of the Comptroller of Currency noted that the top five banks in the United States account for 96% of the total business.[6]

This high concentration means that the power between the industry and the regulators is never exactly equal, with economic and sometimes political power concentrated in the hands of the financial

---

[4] Matt Taibbi (2011). 'Why Isn't Wall Street in Jail? – Financial crooks brought down the world's economy – but the feds are doing more to protect them than to prosecute them', *Rolling Stone Magazine*, March 3, 2011.

[5] Independent Commission on Banking, Final Report and Recommendations, p.166, London, available at http://bankingcommission.independent.gov.uk/

[6] Office of the Comptroller of Currency

industry. For example, outstanding assets of the financial industry (bank assets, stock market capitalization and bond market value) amounted to $250 trillion or 397.5% of global GDP, with EU financial assets as high as 551.4% of GDP at the end of 2010.[7] Including the notional value of derivatives would increase the "leverage" of the financial system by another 16 times global GDP. Small wonder that the financial sector has become 'too big to fail' and can hold the real sector to ransom.

The concept of capture therefore has multi-party dimensions in which the regulator is never in practice independent of the industry nor the political process, since it is possible that the industry can capture the political process through lobby or political contributions and indirectly affect the regulators even though the latter tries to maintain independence. Indeed, political theorist Anthony Downs pointed out in 1957 that 'a democratic government is usually biased in favor of producer interests and against consumer interests, even though the consumers outnumber its producers.'[8]

Using game theory, Ayres and Braithwaite (1991) saw theoretically four types of capture. The first one (which the authors only discuss in a footnote and call reverse capture) involves the rare event when regulators capture the industry. This can improve social welfare if the regulators have good clear objectives, but can also reduce social welfare if the regulators push their industry towards inefficient behaviour. Reverse capture is possible under state-ownership and planning, where regulators may have more political power than the industry.

The second variety is what Ayres and Braithwaite called inefficient capture, which is clearly corrupting, when the regulators behave at the behest of the industry in their interest. The third variety of zero-sum capture has ambiguous welfare effects, but since the industry has power and informational advantages over the investors and

---

[7] International Monetary Fund (IMF) (2011). Global Financial Stability Report, Statistical Appendix, Table 1.

[8] Anthony Downs (1957), An Economic Theory of Political Action in a Democracy, *The Journal of Political Economy*, Vol. 65, No. 2, p.149.

consumers, there are distributional and inequity issues involved. The fourth variety is an "ideal environment", whereby the industry cooperates with the regulators and tries to optimize social welfare. So far, this variety is a rare form of capture, but in some epochs of financial crises, industry statesmen did stand up to take the industry to a higher moral plane and worked closely with the regulators to achieve stability and restore public confidence in the financial system.

There are, however, three types of capture that affect regulators: political or elite capture; process capture; and cognitive capture.

9.3 Political or elite capture

Here, the definition of the Indian National Council for Applied Economic Research is succinct: 'elite capture is a phenomenon where resources transferred for the benefit of the masses are usurped by a few, usually politically and/or economically powerful groups, at the expense of the less economically and/or politically influential groups.'[9] This definition can be applied more generally to political capture by an industry (such as finance), which ensures that the industry benefits from an explicit or implicit subsidy, from a deposit insurance scheme which ends up for finance as too big to fail.

Elite or political capture is more insidious than direct capture, since the industry controls the political system that oversees or controls the funding or nomination process of the regulatory bureaucracy. For example, even if tougher regulations have been passed, the political influence can be exercised in such a way, such as the tight control over expenditure of the regulatory agencies, such that it would be impossible for the regulators to enforce the new regulations due to resource constraints.

Another type of elite capture is when the leadership of the regulatory agencies is comprised of political appointees or someone who is more likely to be "friendly" to the industry, even if the regulatory institution staff are professional and independent. Sometimes, the capture is

---

[9] Dutta D. (2009). 'Elite Capture and Corruption: Concepts and Definition', National Council of Applied Economic Research, India, October 2009.

intentional, in order that the regulatory agency reflects the views of the industry. For example, it is well known that many of the board of directors of the New York Federal Reserve Bank comes from the industry itself.

Oxford University political scientist Tim Besley has a novel way of expressing the benefits of political capture in his essay on Political Selection (2006). He argues that 'a key ratio for determining who will be attracted to run for office in a political system is the attractiveness ratio, defined as:

$$A = (rents + wages) / (public service motivation + wages)$$

In other words, the attractiveness ratio is higher, for example, when available rents are higher.[10] Such rents for regulatory staff would include very well-paid jobs with the industry when they leave their official posts. Thus, even if corruption is not evidently present, the fact that the attractiveness ratio for capture can be high means that the regulators may not exercise sufficient "countervailing power" against industry behaviour relative to their customers, investors or even shareholders. Under such circumstances, the level playing field exists only in name.

9.4 Process capture

Process capture involves undue influence at different stages of policymaking such as rulemaking, supervision and enforcement. Since much rulemaking is already delegated to the regulatory agencies by the legislature, the industry can exercise considerable pressure on getting "industry-friendly" rules. The problem with the public consultation process is that the "public at large" are often not professionals and cannot devote considerable time and resources to review draft rules, relative to the legal and professional expertise

---

[10] Besley, T. (2006). 'Political Selection', World Ethics Forum Conference Proceedings. Edited by Charles Sampford and Carmel Connors Griffith University, The Joint Conference of The International Institute for Public Ethics (IIPE) and The World Bank, *Leadership, Ethics and Integrity in Public Life*, 9–11 April 2006, Keble College, University of Oxford, pp.7-24.

available to the vested interest in industry. The industry could be affected significantly in terms of profit and loss or business opportunities from the rule changes and would therefore give strong objections to such rule changes.

Capture in the area of supervision is possible when the regulated company is very large and complex compared with the skills of the regulator. For example, the AIG was supervised on a consolidated basis by the Office of Thrift Supervision (OTS), arguably the weakest of the Federal financial regulators. The FCIC Report concluded that:

> 'the OTS failed to effectively exercise its authority over AIG and its affiliates: it lacked the capability to supervise an institution of the size and complexity of AIG, did not recognize the risks inherent in AIG's sales of credit default swaps, and did not understand its responsibility to oversee the entire company, including AIG Financial Products'.[11]

Capture in the area of enforcement is most controversial in the area of settlements. Since most financial infringements are civil cases in an area of litigation, financial regulators have in recent years "settled" cases with no admission of guilt on the part of the investigated party. Very often, other than the payment of hefty sum of money, no individuals are prosecuted and the only party that is really hurt is the shareholder. A common criticism of recent financial regulation is that very often there is insufficient tough enforcement and investigations to change egregious behaviour. How different is settlement without admission of guilt from the "indulgencies" that the Church used to collect revenue from absolution of a person from sin in the fifteenth century?

In other words, if there is no personal accountability, diffused responsibility and culpability, in which egregious behaviour is not stopped by tough sanctions such as "name and shame", what chance is there to prevent the industry from slipping into another financial crisis?

---

[11] Financial Crisis Inquiry Commission (2011), p.352, op. cit. footnote n.2.

9.5 Cognitive capture

Perhaps the deepest form of capture is cognitive, sometimes called intellectual capture. Kwak defines this as the ability of special interests to 'shape policy outcomes through influences other than material incentives and rational debate'[12]. Cognitive capture was perhaps most evident in the securities markets, where the free and efficient market hypothesis imbued the regulators with zeal to liberalize competition, cut transaction costs and trading fees and resulted in the market performing in perverse ways through the law of unintended consequences. For example, the liberalization of minimum levels of broking commissions forced securities firms to cut back on research, move towards proprietary trading and in the process changed industry behaviour from fiduciary agents to become principals in their own right competing against their customers.

The free market ideology that swept markets since the 1980s, which was a period in which policymakers pushed for greater financial innovation, deregulation and driving competition through lowering transaction costs, had an underlying intellectual belief that the market knows best. Since both financial market theoreticians and regulators assumed that efficient markets were self-stabilizing and that financial innovation was good for the real economy, there was complicity in not enforcing too toughly on the industry. Indeed, in an era of globalization, there was considerable regulatory arbitrage towards offshore markets, laxity in due diligence in considering consumer protection, and systemic risks of derivative financial products and overall regulatory failure. Central bankers were relaxed about financial stability because they felt that once monetary stability was achieved, financial stability would follow, not paying sufficient attention to asset bubbles and system leverage. Financial supervisors and policymakers did not vigorously question bad behaviour, given buoyant markets and the excuse that "self-interest of the industry would take care of itself". Underpaid, under-resourced and knowing much less about complex

---

[12] Kwak (forthcoming). 'Cultural Capture and the Financial Crisis.' In: *Preventing Regulatory Capture: Special Interest Influence, and How to Limit It*, by Carpenter and Moss (forthcoming). Cambridge, Cambridge University Press

financial derivatives than the industry, many financial regulators became captured politically, process-wise or intellectually. There were few incentives to take tough action to "lean against the wind" and enforce market discipline.

Minimizing regulatory capture

The above survey and practical experience would suggest that capture is inherent in the structural nature of inter-dependency between state and markets. Ayres and Braithwaite suggest that the best countervailing power is to improve transparency and empower the consumer/investor community through 'tripartism'[13], to level the three-cornered power relationship between the bureaucracy, industry, and weaker consumer/investor community.

Recognizing that regulatory capture can be a problem and that the regulators should try to be as independent as possible, the law and rules relating to the governance of regulatory agencies should include such measures as:

- higher transparency in relationships between regulators and industry;
- rotating regulatory staff periodically to prevent familiarity and capture;
- raising pay and skill levels of regulators to reduce the pay and skill disparities;
- disqualification of regulators from working with industry or firms, with safeguards, similar to those imposed in the defence industry;
- introduction of whistle-blower regulations;
- introduction of individual and corporate liability rules so that those who engage in capture or corrupt activities will face tough sanctions; and
- empowerment of consumer groups to act as the countervailing power.[14]

---

[13] Ayres, Ian and John Braithwaite (1991). 'Tripartism: Regulatory Capture and Empowerment', *Law & Social Inquiry,* 16(3), pp. 435-96.
[14] See suggestions by Boehm, Frédéric (2007). 'Regulatory Capture Revisited – Lessons from Economics of Corruption', Research Center in Political Economy (CIEP, Universidad Externado de Colombia), Working Paper July 2007.

9.6 Conclusions

The theory and practice of effective financial regulation relates to three key elements: the written rules and laws, the tools of enforcement and regulatory authority and will to enforce.[15] Even though regulators can plead that often there are insufficient legal backing or tools to take tough regulatory action, the degree of regulatory capture in any industry will depend on the regulatory will. Those that are willing to be captured will be, despite the best rules and tools available.

It would be naive to assume that regulatory capture can be eliminated. Increasingly, there is awareness that financial failures are often governance failures. Since financial regulators are also human beings, it is not surprising that governance mistakes will be made. A weak regulator can be ignored by elements that can exploit the marketplace to their advantage, whilst a determined regulator with few resources and even backing can level the playing field.

Every economy has the power to design the regulatory structure to fit its own circumstances. Ultimately, financial markets reflect human behaviour and value systems. Regulation and enforcement are not independent of the values and incentives within that economy, but they do help shape behaviour towards sound and efficient markets, or otherwise.

---

[15] Sheng, Andrew (2009). 'The Command of Financial Regulation', in: David Mayes, Michael Taylor and Robert Pringle, *Central Banking: New Frontiers in Regulation and Official Oversight of the Financial System*, 2009.

10.0 Managing the Risks of Regulatory Capture

David Strachan[1]

10.1 Introduction

The subject of regulatory capture is one which, to resort to cliché, typically generates more heat than light. The ICFR is therefore to be congratulated on its decision to put together a series of papers on this topical subject.

My starting point, which is undoubtedly provocative to some, is that the financial services industry as a whole wants to avoid regulatory capture, and does not set out to capture its regulators.[2] However, some aspects of the relationship that industry properly seeks to have with its regulators may leave it open to criticism that capturing the regulator is indeed its aim. Concerns about capture, whether real or

---

[1] David Strachan joined Deloitte in April 2011 after a career at the UK's Financial Services Authority (1998-2011) and, before then, at the Bank of England (1985-1998). His last project at the FSA saw him lead the work on the division of the FSA into the Prudential Regulation Authority and the Financial Conduct Authority. In his role at Deloitte, David is co-head of the Deloitte Centre for Regulatory Strategy. Immediately before joining Deloitte, David's role at the FSA was as Director of Financial Stability (2008-2011). In that capacity, he worked closely with Government, the Bank of England and overseas authorities to manage the impact of the financial crisis which emerged in 2007. David's earlier international roles included representing the FSA on the Basel Committee on Banking Supervision, on a sub-committee of the Financial Stability Board and on the predecessor body to the current European Insurance and Occupational Pensions Authority. This paper reflects the personal views of the author.

[2] In its sixth survey of the FSA's regulatory performance in February 2011 the Financial Services Practitioner Panel found that 'the vast majority of firms (84%) agreed that strong regulation is for the benefit of the financial services industry as a whole'. Firms argued that strong regulation promoted both industry and public confidence and therefore resulted in a higher level of business.

perceived, which arise from this relationship can be dealt with by introducing certain safeguards. This chapter explores these concerns and the necessary safeguards in relation to rulemaking and supervision and highlights some international developments that are also conducive to reducing the risk of capture.

In order to give some context for what follows I would like to start with a definition of regulatory capture. As the opening chapter of this publication makes plain, there is no shortage of competing definitions and descriptions. However, I have chosen one as the anchor for what follows, namely that regulatory capture exists 'whenever a particular sector to the regulatory regime has acquired influence disproportionate to the balance of interests envisaged when the regulatory system was established'.[3]

The particular sector that would first come to most people's minds is that comprising the largest financial services firms. However, this definition also brings out the important point that the sources of regulatory capture extend beyond the regulated financial services industry and may include any group or body which comes to exercise an influence that knocks the regulator off its original balance. Even governments can capture regulators, as is recognized by the Basel Committee whose proposed Core Principles for Effective Banking Supervision require that 'there is no government or industry interference which compromises the operational independence of the supervisor'.[4]

It can also be argued on the basis of this definition that regulators are open to "self-capture" – pursuing their objectives in a way that distorts the outcomes they are tasked to achieve. This is one reason why the accountability mechanisms for regulators to national parliaments, which should be seen as guardians of the "balance of interests" even though in practice they may be subject to electoral considerations, are so important. Such self-capture may arise when the same regulator has two or more distinct objectives and chooses to favour one over the other(s). In the UK, the Financial Services Authority (FSA) has four

---

[3] Baxter (2011). 'Capture in Financial Regulation: Can We Channel It Toward the Common Good?' *Cornell Journal of Law and Public Policy* 21(1): 175-200, p. 187.

[4] Basel Committee on Banking Supervision (December 2011). 'Core Principles for Effective Banking Supervision', Consultative Document.

objectives and some of the motivation for moving away from integrated regulation in the UK towards a "twin peaks" regulatory structure comes from the desire to have a much clearer focus on the prudential regulation of systemically important institutions (by the Prudential Regulation Authority) and on conduct regulation (by the Financial Conduct Authority). This separation seeks to reduce the risk that an integrated regulator will be captured by one of its objectives at the expense of the other(s).

10.2 Rulemaking

When a regulator begins the process of introducing new rules, those subject to them typically want the following:

- transparency, in the form of consultation on the new requirements and their associated impacts (that is, quantitative impact studies and/or cost-benefit analyses);
- a willingness to implement the requirement in the way that generates least cost to the industry, consistent with meeting the regulator's objectives;
- access to the rule makers to understand their thinking, to give them the benefit of industry understanding of the full range of impacts that the proposals will have on their business, and to influence them on aspects of the proposed rules that they consider disproportionate or counterproductive; and
- an obligation on the rule makers to explain how they have either taken into account or rejected these points when deciding the final form of the new rules. It is essential, from an industry perspective, that the regulator is prepared to listen and, if it hears good arguments, adapt its views.

None of these wants is in any sense objectionable, but they generate three legitimate concerns. The first is that the resources available to the regulated financial services industry are vastly superior to those of the depositors, policyholders and investors whom the proposed rules are designed to protect. (There may also be a resource imbalance between the expertise available to the industry and to the regulator. This is a separate consideration dealt with below.) This in turn leads to the view that the influence of the financial services industry on the outcome of consultations is much greater than that of consumers. In other words, there is no "equality of arms".

The second, related concern is that the financial services industry has much better access to the regulators and that many of the discussions take place behind closed doors. The larger financial services firms have individual access to all levels of any regulatory body, and they also have collective access through trade associations. Individual financial services consumers do not have such access, and their representative bodies are typically under-resourced relative to their industry counterparts.

The third is that, through this process, industry and regulatory thinking gradually converge so that there is insufficient challenge to the prevailing paradigm. Intellectual capture or other forms of uniform thinking can lead to a more brittle system.

These three concerns combine to create a sense of unease which, if left unchecked, would threaten the integrity of and confidence in the rulemaking process. This is clearly an undesirable state of affairs, even if it is more perception then reality, but one which can be remedied through a series of safeguards.

10.2.1 Transparency

Transparency about which institutions and individuals have responded to consultations and access to their responses provides some safeguards. Unless these are strong reasons (such as commercial sensitivity) for not making (part of) of a response publicly available, the presumption should be for publication. This is the approach adopted by the Independent Commission on Banking in the UK, and this seems to me to be an effective model.

10.2.2 Facilitating input from consumers

Various steps have been taken by regulators around the world to reduce the inequality of arms between the financial services industry and consumer bodies. Typically these involve giving consumer groups some formal role in the rulemaking process and some financial support to facilitate this.[5]

The European Supervisory Authorities (ESAs) are required to establish stakeholder groups whose members include financial services practitioners, academics, "end users" and consumer groups. The legislation establishing the ESAs makes it clear that those members representing non-profit organizations or academia should receive adequate compensation to enable them to take full part in the debate about financial regulation. This approach unites industry and consumers in a single stakeholder group. It remains to be seen how effective these combined groups will be. The main challenge I see is that of trying to achieve a consensus within a group that contains such different interests and the possible dilution of the group's influence and effectiveness if it cannot.

This challenge is avoided in the approach currently provided for in the UK, where the legislation requires the FSA to establish practitioner and consumer panels and the proposed legislation for the Financial Conduct Authority (FCA) includes a similar requirement. The FSA's Consumer Panel has its own budget, provided by the FSA out of the funding levy it makes on regulated firms, its own small support staff and the ability to commission research into areas the Panel considers relevant. Although the resources available to the Consumer Panel remain modest relative to those of industry, the advantage of this arrangement is that it gives consumers a distinct voice within the FSA's rulemaking role (and much more besides) which can be widely heard, including by the media and Parliament.

10.2.3 A standing body of practitioners

At first sight it may seem odd to argue that a standing body of practitioners giving formal input into the rulemaking process

---

[5] The UK Government, when presenting its initial proposals for reforming the UK regulatory structure, seemed to want to go further than this by describing the conduct regulator as a 'strong consumer champion'. This raised the perception of the conduct regulator being captured by consumer interests, and the phrase has not been used since. In 'A new approach to financial regulation: judgement, focus and stability', HM Treasury, July 2010.

represents a safeguard against the risk of regulatory capture. The Joint Committee of the Houses of Commons and Lords established to scrutinize the draft legislation to create the new regulatory structure in the UK concluded that 'while we consider that it is vital for the PRA to consult with practitioners, and as far as necessary, consumers, we believe is it right that the PRA should not be obliged by legislation to establish panels on the same model as the FCA. In particular we are concerned that an obligation to create such panels could lead to regulatory capture.'[6]

The way in which the Joint Committee's conclusion is expressed suggests that, while it is unacceptable for the PRA to be "captured" by a standing panel, the same concern does not apply to the FCA. I cannot imagine that this was the Joint Committee's intention. But if it was not, the words used make it difficult to see what else was intended.

In my view there are two reasons why a standing practitioner body can help reduce concerns about regulatory capture. First, such bodies typically reflect the composition of the financial services industry as a whole and thus their views tend to be more representative and less susceptible to special pleading by individual firms and/or particular interest groups. Second, and more importantly, both their membership and their role are transparent and enshrined in legislation. These safeguards negate many of the concerns which critics voice about discussions between the regulators and regulated concerning new policy initiatives taking place behind closed doors. In the absence of such a body, the need for full transparency around which firms and trade associations the regulator has chosen to consult and engage with is much greater. Otherwise, there is a real risk of the regulator being perceived as engaging selectively with a small group of favoured firms.

In summary, even though the financial services industry wants and needs to have access to regulators during the rulemaking process, there are practical and cost-effective safeguards that can be introduced to reduce the perception and reality of capture. It is in everyone's interest that these safeguards are in place.

---

[6] House of Lords, House of Commons, Joint Committee on the draft Financial Services Bill, 19 December 2011.

10.5 Supervision

Rules set out the framework within which regulated financial firms must operate. However, the system of supervision – the assessment of firms' adherence to the rules – is equally important to the industry. As far as supervision is concerned, the industry wants:

- well-informed, expert supervisors who can understand the economics and business models of the industry and – building on this – fathom often very complex transactions and activities and interpret the rules in the light of different circumstances and commercial realities;
- a degree of continuity on the part of individual firms' supervisors so that they have some time to understand their business; and
- a means of feeding back to their supervisor concerns about the supervisory decisions or its approach more generally. This is the counterpart to the listening that is needed as part of the rulemaking process.

Again, I would argue that none of these is objectionable, yet individually and collectively they can give rise to concerns of regulatory capture. The first source of concern is that the degree of expertise needed to understand complex financial activities can often best be found in those who have worked in the financial services industry. The thought of financial services firms being regulated by "one of their own" makes some critics uneasy, as do the "revolving doors" between the regulators and regulated. Similarly, one person's continuity is another person's capture, reflecting the risks of an all too close and cosy relationship building up over time between the supervisor and the supervised firm. And opportunities for informal challenge and feedback can be perceived as enabling well-resourced firms to browbeat supervisors using clever arguments deployed by very senior people. However, there is again no shortage of safeguards.

10.5.1 Balancing the mix of supervisory staff

There is, in my view, no substitute for relevant direct industry experience and involvement in terms of understanding the real risks run by financial services firms. At the same time, direct recruitment from industry is not the only source of such experience. Secondments (both inward and outward), drawing on expertise available to professional services firms and structured training programmes for the supervisor's own staff all increase subject matter understanding. At the same time, it is important that each regulator has a cadre of "career supervisors" who identify their long-term future with its public service aims and objectives and who have a more questioning attitude towards the latest market trends and innovations.[7]

10.5.2 Funding arrangements and salary structures

If the goal is to have a balanced mix of supervisory staff, then reaching it and keeping it is far from straightforward. In general, large parts of the financial services industry will always be able to offer more attractive remuneration packages to those supervisors who are seeking to move. There is clearly a collective action problem for industry here, for as much as it wants a well and expertly resourced regulator, the self-interest of individual firms means that they will not deny themselves the opportunity to recruit a good supervisor. In order to be able to attract and retain good quality staff, the supervisor therefore needs to be able to offer competitive remuneration and prospects for career progression.

The regulator therefore needs to be properly funded. However, the means by which regulators are funded can also give rise to concerns about capture. If the regulator is funded by the government, it can be argued that this gives the government undue influence over its operations and policies. And it could enable a government to starve the regulator of resources to avoid it being able to pursue certain policies. On the other hand, if the regulator is funded by the industry

---

[7] The Financial Stability Board has noted that 'some supervisors felt that hiring specialist skills from the market was key in that they have a view "from the inside" that cannot be obtained from being a career supervisor, while others felt that internally "home grown" supervisors could do the job better and had a more questioning attitude towards market fads', In 'Intensity and Effectiveness of SIFI Supervision. Recommendations for enhanced supervision', FSB Report, November 2010, pp.5–6, available at http://www.financialstabilityboard.org/publications/r_101101.pdf

it regulates, critics will assert that the regulator cannot be relied on to bite the hand that feeds it. As a consequence, when it comes to funding, there is no easy solution. In my view, the best answer from an industry perspective consists of: giving the regulator the ability to fund itself from the industry it regulates; high transparency around how the funding is used; accountability to parliament on how it has used its budget; and periodic "value for money" audits by an external independent body.

10.5.3 Continuity

In theory the right mix of supervisory staff, the right salary structure and a sensible career path will deliver continuity in the relationship between the supervised firm and the supervisor responsible for it. However, such continuity, if achieved, could increase the risk of capture. This could be on the basis that, over a period of a number of years, a supervisor loses objectivity and begins to associate himself more with the firm's aims and less with the regulatory objectives. To the extent that this risk is real, it can be mitigated through a number of safeguards: first, a formal, structured rotation policy for supervisors; second, an internal peer and/or independent review framework to ensure that the approach being taken by individual supervisors is even-handed; and third, a decision making framework which requires that the most significant decisions be made by committees rather than individual supervisors.

The third safeguard – of having the most significant decisions (around capital, liquidity, the overall supervisory evaluation and enforcement action) taken by committee – is also important for individual supervisors. It protects them from criticism that they are subject to undue influence from the strength of arguments and seniority of people deployed by the firms, regardless of the duration of the supervisory relationship. This decision making structure has an added benefit for industry, in that it reduces the risk of an individual firm being subject to inconsistencies in the decisions taken by its own supervisor and increases the overall fairness of the process.

In summary, it is relatively straightforward for safeguards to be put in place to reduce the risk of capture arising from the relationship that exists between the individual supervisors and the firms that they supervise. This should enable industry to have the type of relationship it needs to have with its supervisors, while maintaining overall public confidence in the supervisory process.

10.6 Changes in the international approach

There are changes underway to both the global and EU approaches to rulemaking and supervision which should reassure all stakeholders that the risk of a particular form of regulatory capture at the national level is being reduced. Both the regulated and the regulators should be keen to see a level playing field which has a single set of global rules consistently applied by supervisors. If some countries were to be less zealous in their implementation of global standards for the benefit of their industry or their financial centre, this could be characterized as a form of capture affecting stakeholders in other countries.[8]

The first relevant change is the willingness on the part of global bodies, such as the Financial Stability Board (FSB), to receive complaints that individual countries are not adhering in practice to the standards they agreed to at the FSB table. One specific example relates to remuneration, where the FSB has stated that 'a bilateral complaint handling process will be established by which national supervisors work together to verify and, as needed, address specific level playing field concerns involving their respective firms'.[9]

The second relevant change relates to the introduction of the ESAs and the EU's stated ambition to achieve a single rulebook for banking, securities and insurance business across the EU. The fact that rulemaking will take place at the EU level will, on balance, neither increase nor decrease the risk of regulatory capture. However, the fact that the ESAs will pursue a series of peer reviews of how the single

---

[8] 'The United Kingdom's experiment in a strategy of "light touch" regulation to attract business to London away from New York and Frankfurt ended tragically. This should be a cautionary note for other countries deciding whether to try to take advantage of the rise in standards in the United States.' Remarks by US Treasury Secretary Timothy Geithner to the International Monetary Conference on 6 June 2011.

[9] FSB, Press Release, 10 January 2012.

rulebook is being implemented should, if done effectively, reduce the scope for a national regulator to depart from previously agreed norms. This should reduce the likelihood of this particular form of capture arising.

10.7 Conclusion

In conclusion, the financial services industry will both need and want to put itself in situations in which its engagement with its regulator opens it, and the regulator, up to criticisms of regulatory capture. There is a degree of inevitability to this. The reaction to this should not be to change the substance of industry engagement in either the rulemaking or supervisory process. Instead, the answer lies in introducing effective safeguards, of which there are plenty.

Section 3

A Stakeholder's Perspective

11.0 Addressing the Problem of Cyclical Capture

Gerry Cross[1]

11.1 Capture

The word capture has a negative intonation: indeed, it is a negative phenomenon. It skews outcomes to a greater or lesser extent than from where they would optimally be. It is, however, not necessarily rooted in negative intentions. Capture can, and does, occur despite the best intentions of all concerned – regulators, supervisors, and the regulated community. This means that in trying to address the problem it is important not to focus, solely or even mainly, on the issue of intended behaviours, but rather on the phenomenon as it occurs.

Capture is an outcropping of uncertainty. In particular, with outcomes being uncertain, there is scope for different actors to influence the process. Such influence can be benign, helping to find the right answer; or pernicious, skewing the process from its optimal results.

There are different types of uncertainty. One relates to unknowability. There are situations where there simply is not a right answer that can

[1] Gerry Cross started his career as a lecturer in Law, University of Wales, Aberystwyth. For eight years he worked for the UK Financial Services Authority, latterly as Manager, Credit Risk Policy. He spent four years at the European Commission (2001-2005) where he worked in the Internal Market Directorate General on the implementation of Basel II in Europe. Prior to his work at the AFME, Cross worked as a deputy director in the Regulatory Affairs Department at the Institute of International Finance in Washington. In June 2011 he took on a new role as a Managing Director, Advocacy with AFME. Cross is responsible for AFME's day-to-day representation with European authorities (the Parliament, Council and Commission) and will act as a bridge between AFME's business and policy divisions, which provide technical expertise, and the various stakeholder groups. The views expressed here are the contributor's own. They should not be taken to be those of the Association for Financial Markets in Europe.

be determined either ex ante or ex post. These present as questions of social and political value: what is the correct balance between equality of outcome and effective incentivization of economic actors; between security of employment and flexibility of the work force; between safety and soundness and higher costs; and so on. These are value judgements; there is no objective right answer. Only the preferences articulated and determined through an appropriate, democratically founded process can be considered the "right" answer.

Then there is the uncertainty that derives not from the inherently unknowable but from the currently unknown or difficult-to-know. For example: determining the level of capital which will deliver a high level of systemic stability while supporting good growth; identifying those assets that are likely to prove liquid in a period of crisis; establishing the constraints that should be imposed on single dealer platforms to avoid conflicts of interest while maintaining optimal capital formation. Here the situation is different. Now the aim is to have a process which allows us to approximate as closely as possible to the correct or best outcome – a result that can, sooner or later, be determined to have been attained, or not.

In both situations, it is important to make the process fair and transparent and not skewed towards particular interests. However, the second situation harbours an additional challenge. In order to get to the right outcome it is necessary to harness the expertise and insight relevant to the topic in question. This makes the process more difficult: it is needed to harness expertise and insight, without unwittingly imbibing the preferences and interests that will often, however unwittingly, accompany them.

11.2 Cyclical capture

There are different forms of capture. One that is particularly relevant to financial services regulation is what might be termed "cyclical capture". The supply of credit is critical to a growing economy.

Therefore, a difficult endogenous dynamic emerges as growth firms and the cycle enters the phase of enhancing confidence and increasing asset prices. There are a number of relevant features inherent to this stage in the cycle. These include a political imperative to maintain and enhance economic growth; a desire to avoid interfering with the (apparently) successful prevailing machinery of growth; increasingly fading memories of previous crises; self-validating belief in new paradigms; and a general optimism and confidence in progress.

These features mean that as the cycle proceeds through its phase of increasing optimism and strengthening growth there is a tendency for the view to develop that regulation and supervision have failed to keep up with progress – that they are founded in the old paradigm rather than the new. This developing perception becomes increasingly internalized and is seen to be consistent with the increased growth-orientated views of political actors. The result is that the perspective and opinions of the "expert" community, themselves vulnerable to undue optimism and technical hubris, tend to become increasingly weighty in the policy discourse. All of this has a self-reinforcing dynamic, which can easily lead to strong, effective regulation and supervision being eroded at the very time that the underlying developments are creating an increased need for precisely those things.

11.3 Supervisory capture

This concept of cyclical capture plays an important role in the post-crisis reform programme. Legislators and regulators are very aware of the type of "cyclical capture" described above. They are conscious that whatever they do now in the way of regulatory reform runs the risk of being eroded as the cycle proceeds. This leads them to a position of seeking to create a programme of regulatory reform which is as far as possible cycle resistant. In simple terms, if you believe that regulation runs the risk of being eroded and undermined during a prolonged upswing, then there is logic in developing regulation that will be tough enough to withstand such erosion. The risk is that this can easily become a belt-and-braces approach with new regulation being added to new regulation in a suboptimal way. Where it should be countercyclical, regulation becomes procyclical.

A second manifestation of this awareness of cyclical capture is equally, if not more, important. It is a significant degree of loss of confidence in that important form of public risk control which is seen as most vulnerable to cyclical capture: supervision. Supervision, involving a need for continually renewed judgement by official actors, falls subject to a degree of distrust with hard-wired regulation becoming seen as a more reliable way to seek the lasting outcomes sought.

This is, however, quite problematic. Achieving financial stability depends to a great extent on the effective management of risks within firms. This is something to which regulation can contribute significantly, but which is strongly dependent on high quality supervision. To the extent that regulation is sought to be used to replace supervision, there is a risk that the stability outcomes desired will not be achieved. Moreover, to the extent that risk-sensitive supervision is eschewed in favour of a more rules-based regulation, this is likely to result in economically suboptimal outcomes.

11.4 Better supervision

In order for supervision to be more reliably effective, there is, in many cases, a need for it to become more intensive, challenging, and action-focused than previously. Supervisors need to have strong and clear mandates and appropriate powers. They need to be focused on firms' risk profiles and how they make their money, not become side-tracked by process. They need to be adequately resourced in quantitative and qualitative terms.

However, it is a mistake to assume that the objective of cyclically reliable supervision can be achieved through the actions of supervisors alone; that somehow simply by being more intensive, more challenging, better resourced, supervisors can achieve this difficult goal. Supervision is quintessentially a relational activity. Just as the effectiveness of a law depends upon the general acceptance of its legitimacy and a widespread willingness to comply, so supervision requires a strong and considered commitment from the supervised community.

The fact is this: a great deal of responsibility for achieving good supervision falls on the industry itself. Until this responsibility is not only fulfilled, but understood to be being fulfilled, it should come as no surprise if the ultimate reliability of supervision continues to be doubted and focus placed on the need for hard-wired regulatory solutions.

There has been some recent work on this issue from the industry perspective, though there remains more to be done. In its September 2010 Report, Prevention and Cure: Securing Financial Stability After the Crisis, the Association for Financial Markets in Europe considered amongst other aspects the need for enhanced supervision as an important part of a successful regulatory reform programme. Amongst its determinations was the following:

'For enhanced supervision to be successful it must be underpinned by a culture of challenge and cooperation on both sides of the regulatory fence: firms must be willing to work with their supervisors at both the solo and consolidated level in a transparent and open fashion; supervisors must be willing to challenge and proactively influence outcomes'.[2]

In July 2011 the Institute of International Finance, drawing on a group of senior practitioners, former senior supervisors, and others, published its report Achieving Effective Supervision: An Industry Perspective, which explored this subject in further detail. A key theme in this report was need for the industry to improve the way it participates in the supervisory relationship.

The report notes that 'it is important that firms do not revert to earlier unacceptable practices that a minority was prone to and which contributed to a loss of trust between supervisors and supervised entities. Many supervisors legitimately feel that they were not given sufficient information by firms and that some firms looked to obfuscate, withhold information, or even outwit them rather than cooperate.'

---

[2] AFME (2010), 'Prevention and Cure: Securing Financial Stability After the Crisis', Association for Financial Markets in Europe, September, p. 35.

The report concludes that the industry as a whole has a responsibility to promote continually improved industry practices. The industry should establish sound practice standards which should be used as a benchmark by supervisors to judge the performance and controls of firms. The aim is to achieve a positively reinforcing dynamic between improved industry practices and an enhanced mode of supervision to contribute to more cycle-proof outcomes.

The report also considers the role of individual firms. Amongst the recommendations made are the following:

- firms should provide supervisors with all information material to high-quality effective supervision, including risk reports, internal audit reports, and exceptions reports and be willing to discuss these in an open dialogue with supervisors. Firms should proactively provide explanations and interpretations of date to maximize its value and meaning;
- board and senior management must set a strong positive tone from the top promoting openness, integrity, and constructiveness in individuals' and the firm's engagement with supervisors;
- there should be consciously and actively developed and embedded in the culture of the firm a positive and open approach to the supervisory relationship;
- firms and staff need to reconstruct their perception of supervisors from being adversaries to interlocutors who can bring significant value added. Incentives should be aligned with achieving a high-quality supervisory relationship. Approaches based on meagre "compliance" should be rejected;
- there should be a "no surprises" approach by firms involving candid discussions of the risks they face and prospective changes in their risk profiles;
- firms should be willing to bear additional supervisory costs to the extent that these translate visibly into higher quality supervision;
- boards and senior management should take an active role in working with supervisors. Firms should establish a primary point of regulatory contact designed to optimize the quality and effectiveness of the supervisory relationship.

11.5 Cycle resistance

These recommendations should play a key role in addressing the current weaknesses in the supervisory relationship. Importantly, they are designed to help do so not only on a static basis, but also in a through-the-cycle way. A key part of this is the emphasis on cultural change. Embedding beliefs and behaviour in culture is one of the most important ways of bringing about lasting change which will prove durable to significant alterations in the surrounding environment. By developing a strongly positive culture within firms towards supervision and the supervisory relationship, it is possible to go beyond changes to the superstructure that will be vulnerable to the cyclical pressure discussed above, to foundational modifications designed to resist those pressures.

The key to cycle resistance lies in the development of self-reinforcing dynamics which can act to counter the negative reflexivity that can arise in times of confidence and rising asset prices. Creating a culture of positivity and integrity towards the supervisory relationship across firms will make a significant contribution to creating the virtuous cycle whereby recalcitrant tendencies find infertile soil within the firm in question and receive no encouragement in the behaviour of other firms.

11.6 Conclusion

What has been argued above is that cyclical capture – one of the things that causes significant concern for political and regulatory authorities in developing the regulatory reform programme, and which tends to the valuation of hard-wired, suboptimal regulatory solutions over supervision – can be addressed by means of a renewed focus on the supervisory relationship. Achieving high-quality enhanced supervision is important. Improved industry practices are essential to doing this.

A nice symmetry to this – and one that underlines the value of a collection of papers such as the current one – is that an important aspect in bringing about within firms the change of culture described above will be the development of a more sophisticated understanding of regulatory and supervisory capture, together with a wider promulgation and deeper internalization of this understanding.

As said at the start, capture can take deliberate forms and be designed to achieve by means of undue influence outcomes favourable to the regulated or supervised community. But it can also be – and in the view of the author more usually is – an inadvertent phenomenon, the result more of failings than of doings. If this is the case, then a key to addressing the problem and significantly reducing the extent to which it might otherwise occur will be to ensure that all of those who are actors in the field correctly understand what capture is, how it occurs, and what steps they can take to avoid it.

12.0 Ensuring the Consumer Voice is Heard

Christine Farnish[1]

12.1 Introduction

Policymakers and regulators are expected to hold the ring in highly complex markets where regulated firms have a built-in advantage in terms of knowledge, data and resource. Financial services markets are probably the most extreme example of this imbalance of power. What can be done to remedy this and enable better policymaking? My experience of public policy in the UK leads me to believe that some relatively inexpensive steps could be taken to strengthen the consumer voice and ensure that it is heard, and this would lead to more balanced regulatory decisions that delivered better consumer outcomes.

This note sets out why effective consumer representation is important in complex regulated markets like financial services. It goes on to describe how the current regulatory system works in terms of consumer input and engagement, which elements work well and where there is scope for improvement. It then describes some approaches which have been shown to work elsewhere in other markets. It concludes with a set of recommendations for strengthening the consumer input to decision making.

---

[1] Christine Farnish was appointed to the Consumer Focus Board in December 2007 and became Chair at the end of 2010. Christine's varied career has included a number of senior roles in local government; Director of Consumer Affairs at both OFTEL and the Financial Services Authority; Chief Executive at the National Association of Pension Funds and more recently Managing Director of Public Policy at Barclays. Christine has served on the Boards of the Office of Fair Trading, the Advertising Standards Authority, ING Direct UK and Papworth NHS Trust. She currently chairs the Family and Parenting Institute and serves as a NED on the ABTA Board.

What follows is relevant to the regulation of retail financial services where products are sold to ordinary "non-expert" consumers – be they private individuals who want to save, borrow, make payments, buy insurance or invest, or other sorts of non-experts like small business users. Considering how the consumer interest is represented in other areas of financial regulation – prudential regulation and financial stability policy – is a wider issue that cannot be considered fully here. Suffice it to say that the proposals before the UK Parliament contain no provisions for factoring in the consumer interest in either of these important policy areas. The same is largely true for policymaking at the European level. That is regrettable. It is surely desirable to seek to develop more plurality of voice and perspective in policy areas which have been dominated to date by a degree of groupthink.

12.2 Why is consumer representation important?

If financial services markets worked perfectly without intervention, and there was a better balance between firms' and consumers' interests, then there would be no need for regulation in the first place. But financial services are some of the most complex markets that consumers face. They provide intangible products, where "price" is often invisible and difficult to gauge and where "quality" may not be apparent until years after the product was bought. Some products require one-off decisions that cannot be informed by prior experience. These are difficult markets for even the savviest consumer to navigate. Yet the products and services they provide are important to successful functioning in society.

Regulators therefore need to intervene to set the rules of the road and ensure that consumers end up with a fair deal. Effective regulation also delivers benefits for the industry, by promoting trust and eliminating unfair competition from firms that cut corners and break the rules. Most regulatory frameworks claim to put protecting or promoting the consumer interest at the heart of the regime. But day-to-day decisions often involve trade-offs between different interests, some very complex.

Consumers are on the ultimate receiving end of every action the regulator takes. They also pay for regulation, as costs are passed through to them by regulated firms. Consumers therefore have a very legitimate interest in ensuring that regulation is effective and delivering an appropriate balance between the commercial freedom of market participants on the one hand, and products which consumers can understand and which meet their needs on the other.

Expert consumer bodies, whilst not perfect, usually have a good handle on where the problems are, what interventions do and do not work, and how consumers behave in real life (as opposed to how the "rational man" in economic models might behave). They have a good feel for where there is likely to be most detriment. They therefore need to play in loud and clear to the regulatory process if regulators are to end up making the right decisions and interventions. This is easier said than done, as the next section will explain.

12.3 The current set-up: does it work?

The UK government's approach to establishing the FSA at the end of the last century was quite radical. For the first time the financial regulator was charged with statutory policy objectives. A Consumer Panel was established to advise the FSA Board, and a single Ombudsman Scheme was given the job of resolving deadlocked consumer complaints. Policymakers went home satisfied with a job well done.

But what actually happened in practice? I think it would be fair to say, from a consumer perspective, that it has been a mixed picture. The 2002 Financial Services and Markets Act set four statutory objectives for the FSA. It framed these around promoting market confidence, protecting consumers in an appropriate way, promoting consumer awareness and understanding, and fighting financial crime. On the face of it this looked good. However, the wide definition of consumer and the caveat emptor clause, which said that consumers should take responsibility for their own decisions, allowed the FSA to take a cautious approach to its new consumer protection role from the outset.

The wide remit given to the FSA as a single regulator covering all retail and wholesale markets made it hard to focus properly on consumer issues. The majority of the staff came from prudential or market regulators who had never been exposed to such matters. There was little internal challenge in the system and the main focus in the early years was on the bureaucratic necessity of producing a single rulebook. The leadership was understandably preoccupied with the external battle, which lasted four years, of getting primary and secondary legislation on the statute book to grant the necessary powers. The industry lobby against the FSA having adequate powers was intense. There are lessons here for the current reform agenda!

The establishment of an internal Consumer Panel with rights to be consulted and give advice to the FSA Board was positive. But the Panel was thinly resourced relative to the executive teams developing policy. And the constant stream of complex FSA consultative documents requiring consideration and review made it difficult for the Panel to set its own agenda. In theory the Panel had rights to speak out publicly if they disagreed with the FSA on an important issue. In practice it is difficult to do this whilst maintaining a relationship of trust which enables the Panel to have access to valuable internal information and intelligence. Thus, having a dedicated Consumer Panel within a regulatory regime is necessary, but not sufficient.

The focus on sales process and compliance with a set of rules in retail markets rather than consumer outcomes was not uncommon amongst the regulatory community at the time. It did however result in the FSA missing a number of major problems until very late in the day. The FSA had no real early warning system (for example, real time data on what was being sold to whom and on what terms) to highlight consumer problems at an early stage. Its tendency to be inward looking and risk averse – not perhaps surprising in view of the political and media uproar when things went wrong – meant there was little proactive engagement with consumer groups outside in order to seek insights into emerging issues.

Rather, consumers and their representatives were expected to devote their scarce resource to responding to formal consultation documents.

Though efforts have been made recently to change this culture and to be more outward looking and proactive, the FSA still seems to struggle to engage externally in ways that could help it do a better job.

The UK regime has focused significant resource on sorting out consumer problems once they have crystallized – for example through the Ombudsman scheme, which has grown from 350 to 1400 staff over a ten-year period. Repeated crises and scandals have damaged consumer confidence and resulted in many people not buying products they need. Firms have lived in the shadow of scale reviews of past sales and their inevitable drain on scarce management and systems resource to sort out problems which should never have been allowed to continue. It would surely be better for all if emerging problems could be tackled upstream and "nipped in the bud". This is probably the most serious criticism of the last 10–15 years from the consumer perspective.

How can more effective consumer engagement and representation deliver better outcomes for consumers and a more stable and effective regulatory regime for firms?

12.4 Learning from elsewhere

Some examples of where consumer representation has been designed into regulatory systems elsewhere and achieved beneficial results are summarized below.

12.4.1 A formal external consumer voice

In other markets where there is sector-specific regulation, policymakers recognize that there are special features of the market in question that make it difficult for ordinary consumers to engage in decision making. In the UK, for example, successive governments and Parliament have recognized this by setting up special consumer advocacy bodies to represent the consumer interest in complex markets such as energy, water, communications, rail and air transport, and postal services. These bodies are formalized in statute and have independence of voice and specific powers to investigate and advocate on behalf of consumers. They are funded by modest levies on regulated firms. Having such bodies which are able to engage in complex regulatory policymaking on behalf of consumers is seen as an important way of achieving more balanced regulatory decision making.

Most if not all regulated markets are characterized by powerful incumbents who have a huge interest in working the regime in a way that protects their own commercial interests. Many of these markets are former utility markets subject to economic regulation. But they have features in common with financial services in terms of complexity of regulatory process, lack of ability or willingness for ordinary consumers to engage, and powerful firms seeking to exercise significant influence over regulators.

The UK government is currently considering setting up a single regulated industry consumer body to represent the consumer interest in complex regulated markets. The body would have the skills, expertise and formal powers needed to be a respected and informed heavyweight consumer voice. The issues faced in these markets – such as product complexity, tariff structures and opaque charges, information asymmetry, difficulties in switching provider, fairness and burden sharing, effective redress, affordability and debt – are common across many sectors.

12.4.2 Super-complaints

In the UK the ability of designated consumer bodies to make "super-complaints" to the Office of Fair Trading on any issue likely to be causing material consumer detriment has been a powerful tool in the regulatory landscape. The OFT has a duty to consider the issue and respond within three months. A number of complaints about financial services have so far been made – on PPI, doorstep lending, holiday money, and ISA teaser rates – all of which have led to beneficial changes.

It has always seemed odd that there was no direct route for consumer groups to take their complaint to the financial services regulator. It looks as if the new regulatory framework in the UK will remedy this for the FCA (but not for the PRA or Financial Policy Committee).

12.4.3 Consumer Consultative Groups

In other sectors special time limited groups are often set up to examine the consumer interest on specific issues and feed into the regulatory process. For example, the main water companies in England and Wales are currently being required by OFWAT to set up and fund independent Consumer Consultative Groups to review their quality of service and make recommendations. OFGEM has established a panel of consumer representatives to advise the OFGEM Board on the current price review, and another on energy sustainability.

Such expert "task and finish" groups could add value on a wide range of issues in financial services. Effort needs to be taken in the selection and search for individuals with relevant skills and experience to do the job, and it is fair to offer a modest fee for the work.

12.4.4 Internal consumer advocates

Some US states have adopted a system whereby a formal Consumer Advocate Office is institutionalized within a regulatory body, with statutory powers for the Advocate to access relevant information and challenge policy, process and decision making. The Advocate is thus a serious player with real power within the system, able to take cases and challenge formal regulatory hearings and decisions.

This is a deliberate step to seek to redress the imbalance of power between consumers' and firms' resources and rebalance the regulatory system. It could either replace or supplement other internal mechanisms like consumer panels, and could complement rather than displace external consumer bodies in order to strengthen the aggregate consumer voice brought to bear on the system.

12.4.5 Competition remits

There is an active debate in the UK about the importance of financial services regulators having a proper competition remit. It is nearly always in the consumer interest for the regulator to be required to promote effective competition. That term – effective competition – implies taking steps to help make markets work well both for competitor firms, aspirant new entrants, and also for consumers.

Traditional thinking, particularly that emanating from central banks and career regulators, often suggests that competition is the enemy of sound prudential supervision and financial stability. As recent work by the Banking Commission and the OFT in the UK has shown, this should not be the case.

Having a strong competition remit can force regulators to consider non-regulatory measures to make markets work better, harnessing competitive forces to drive up standards and drive down costs. It can make them think twice before reaching for interventions that simply raise barriers to exit and entry or add avoidable cost to the system. And it can force them to think about how the demand side – consumers – can be more engaged and effective at rooting out good and punishing bad.

12.4.6 Regulated settlements

In some American states, utility regulators follow a deregulatory system whereby consumer and user groups negotiate within a structured process framed by the regulator to reach a binding settlement on quality of service and price. The regulator holds the ring and can intervene if the process appears to be going in the wrong direction, but the relative informality of the process means it can achieve relatively quick results. It has the added advantage of binding stakeholders into the final settlement. It would be worth considering whether such an approach could be effective in some areas of financial services regulation.

12.4.7 Internal culture

Internal culture is nearly always set by those at the top. OFCOM in the UK has a strong track record of delivering on its remit to promote the consumer interest. In part it achieves this by requiring a process internally whereby all policy proposals are assessed against a consumer checklist. This has helped embed the need to deliver good consumer outcomes across the organization.

12.5 Conclusion: recommendations to strengthen the consumer voice

Drawing on the above discussion, it is clear that there are a number of ways in which the consumer voice in the financial regulatory system could be strengthened. But five basic steps could help ensure that future decision making is more balanced and taken in the longer term interest of consumers.

12.5.1 Get the remit, powers and culture right

This means having the right statutory objectives, drafted in an unambiguous way to put consumers at the heart of the regulatory regime. It also means giving regulators a formal objective to promote effective competition, since in the vast majority of cases competition is the consumer's friend.

It means appointing the right Chairman, Board and senior leadership, with the commitment to the consumer interest that is needed and the ability to be resilient in times of stress.

It means an open culture, willing to engage proactively with those representing consumers, listening to their representations, and being prepared to change the agenda and priorities in response.

It means having enough appetite for risk, and the powers to intervene early when things look as if they are going wrong, even if there is a small possibility that they might right themselves.

It means engaging widely and publicly on difficult issues that involve public policy trade-offs at an early stage, in order to give legitimacy and cover to the difficulties that will invariably lie ahead: there will always be some things that go wrong.

12.5.2 Make best use of scarce consumer resource

Consumer bodies and consumer advocates are invariably under-resourced and have more work to do than people to do it. So regulators must design their consultations and engagement in a way that makes good use of consumer representatives' time. That generally means clear propositions and early engagement, in terms that enable that engagement to be meaningful. It also means a culture which is respectful of where non-expert or non-technical stakeholders are coming from.

12.5.3 Make smart use of the media

Too often the media are seen as the problem, whipping up stories into crises, problems and scandals. This leads to lack of trust and reluctance on the part of regulators to engage and inform media interests until it is absolutely unavoidable. It should be possible to develop a different style of working whereby there were more open public debate and engagement on some of the difficult trade-offs and regulatory decision options upstream, before a crisis hits. This may be difficult to achieve in practice, but any moves towards this objective should help to encourage a more informed, balanced and thoughtful climate of public opinion and give the regulator more room for manoeuvre in difficult times.

12.5.4 Improve consumer intelligence

This means having better knowledge and insights about what actually is happening with consumers and financial products on the ground. Designing supervisory systems that simply check a firm's records retrospectively, in compliance with a set of rules, will rarely get to the truth. But mystery shopping and other research approaches can. Regulators should invest in processes to gather real time intelligence from the market regarding what is being sold to whom. Mystery shopping is a useful tool here, as is systematic market data gathering. Consumer advice services, which see consumers with problems on a regular basis, and consumer policy bodies, carrying out research and analysis of how particular markets are working for consumers, are also useful sources. This intelligence should be used to help set the agenda, as part of a proper horizontal retail markets function. The regulator should seek out this external intelligence and value it as a vital supplement to internal analysis and research.

12.5.5 Be a learning organization

Too often bodies say they are learning organizations but act in the opposite way. Being a learning organization means admitting to mistakes, learning from them and being prepared to develop and change. It requires others – particularly governments, media and parliament – to move beyond a crude blame culture and accept that being a regulator is a difficult job. No one else has yet succeeded in getting everything right, including newspapers, Chancellors, and central bank governors.

13.0 Regulatory Capture and Financial Regulation: The Experience of Non-Financial End Users

Richard Raeburn[1]

13.1 Overview

The real economy – the end users of the financial system – would unequivocally maintain that it welcomes the post-financial crisis programme of regulatory reform. A well-regulated financial system is crucial to ensuring that business can use that system to manage liquidity, funding and risk, activities that are necessary but fundamentally subordinate to the core purpose of businesses.

Non-financial end users were slightly slow to recognize the extent of the post-2008 regulatory agenda and its impact on the real economy. However, as we began to engage, we found a huge understanding gap on the part of those driving the implementation of the agenda as to how the economy outside the financial sector would be affected by the various proposals. At the highest level the most evident example of this was arguably the sweeping and (I would

---

[1] Richard Raeburn has been Chairman of the European Association of Corporate Treasurers (EACT) since October 2008 where he has been a leading figure in the debate around the future regulation of derivatives on behalf of the corporate sector. Richard took on the EACT role after retiring from the UK's Association of Corporate Treasurers (ACT) where he was Chief Executive between 2002 and 2008. Prior to this he was the Lead Partner in KPMG's Corporate Treasury Practice where he built a successful global business advising corporate clients throughout Europe, North America, Middle East and Australasia. Before joining KPMG, Richard held a number of senior treasury and management positions in the corporate and financial sectors.

suggest) poorly thought-through G20 statement on the regulation of OTC derivatives.

Over the last three years we have seen profound real economy consequences for several areas of financial regulatory policy, not just on derivatives but also on bank capital requirements, credit rating agencies and the financial transactions tax. In each case the development of policy has neglected proper consideration of what regulation does to the real economy, the end users of the financial system.

I argue here that the reasons for this failure lie in the lack of appropriate professional backgrounds and experience on the part of those drafting the regulatory proposals, shortcomings in impact assessments by the European Commission and the dominance of financial sector lobbyists to the exclusion (by exhaustion) of access for others.

In the final section the case is made for: remedial action that emphasizes specialist experience for civil servants (especially in the European Commission); for a much stronger requirement that impact assessments fully recognize how end users are affected by regulatory change; and for something that might even need to resemble affirmative action to create the space for the more fragmented real economy representatives to engage with civil servants and regulators alongside the financial sector.

13.2 The stake of non-financial end users in good financial regulation

Prior to the financial crisis of 2008 non-financial end users (NFEUs) would probably have generalized their interest in financial regulation as semi-detached at best. The narrow view would stress that the overwhelming majority of NFEUs have not been and still are not directly subject to financial regulation. Many NFEUs are of course experienced in dealing with regulation specific to their industry or sector, although it would be hard to identify a sector where the pressure for a step-change in the scope of regulation can ever have matched the intensity of the experience of the financial sector since 2008.

NFEUs are however routinely dealing with regulated financial sector counterparties and have historically welcomed good regulation. Before the crisis most NFEUs would have argued that proportionate regulation provided a measure of reassurance about the risk of dealing with the financial system. Good practice in financial risk management by NFEUs would always emphasize a low-risk appetite, given that these risks are the product of the wider business risk profile of the organization; the corporate priority is to minimize the impact of financial risks as far as possible, leaving the core risks to be addressed more proactively as part of the underlying activity of the organization.

It has therefore always been important for NFEUs to know that the regulatory environment in which their financial counterparties operate is at least robust, clear, consistent, and properly supervised. In the more recent times before 2008 the most direct involvement NFEUs in Europe experienced with financial sector regulation would have been over MiFID. Whilst there was a range of views on how NFEUs felt they should be treated, common ground at least for the larger companies was that in the regulatory push to protect individuals and small organizations there should be a clear distinction between retail and wholesale customers. Failure to do so would have been costly and burdensome for NFEUs. There were those arguing at the time of MiFID I that companies large as well as small needed greater protection; the proponents displayed the same lack of awareness of how companies outside the financial sector operate[2] as has become a major issue for NFEUs in the post-crisis regulatory agenda.

---

[2] Although much of this chapter is concerned with precisely the issue of lack of awareness it is worth underlining the point here. In discussion about MiFID II (and MiFIR) the finance ministry of one of the key European Union Member States asked whether companies use voice trading for their transactions. This method has always been and shows every sign of remaining a fundamental aspect of how NFEUs trade with financial counterparties. The official presumption – up to that point – was that restricting voice trading was of no relevance to NFEUs as it has ceased to be central to the practices of interbank trading. This helps to focus on a core argument to be made here, which is the failure on the part of regulators to appreciate that NFEUs – as the central *users* of the financial system – operate entirely differently from the entities within the financial system.

13.3 Post-crisis regulatory change

It could be argued that there was a delayed realization on the part of NFEUs of the extent to which the impending and urgent reassessment of the financial regulatory framework would impact the real economy. For whatever reason it was only in mid-2009 that in the European Association of Corporate Treasurers (EACT) we recognized the significance of the G20 statements on derivatives and the impending scenario of serious and (we began to argue) unintended consequences. Few if any large companies on either side of the Atlantic appeared to be aware any earlier of what was starting to happen.

In September 2009 the European Commission held a public hearing on the early thinking about derivatives regulation. The EACT and large European companies mobilized to emphasize in the discussion that if the original proposals were passed into law they would have a seriously damaging impact on the real economy. The day prior to that hearing I was part of a small group meeting with Gary Gensler, Chairman of the CFTC, and argued that it was essential that a form of "exemption" from central clearing be allowed for the risk mitigation activities of corporates. Gensler emphatically insisted to me that no such exemption would ever be allowed.[3] Both Dodd-Frank and EMIR do of course now include precisely what we and many others in the real economy were arguing in 2009 was essential, if liquidity was not to be drained from productive investment and working capital into standby provision for possible future cash collateral requirements.

NFEUs understood the context in which financial regulation needed to be substantially overhauled. On behalf of the EACT I and of course many others have always been unequivocally clear that the regulatory change agenda has the support of the real economy. Where we have had a fundamental problem has been when there has been either a

---

[3] The other participants in the meeting were all EU Affairs representatives of the major international banks. In the meeting there was no support from them for the pleas I was making for the real economy. This absence of overt support is interesting in hindsight, given that the EACT and NFEUs have subsequently been accused of being the pawns of the big banks in the arguments we have been making.

lack of understanding of the agenda's impact on NFEUs or a dogmatic refusal to accept that – G20 statements notwithstanding – there could be fatal flaws in the structure of the original proposals.

The real economy – the manufacturers and service providers in the private, public and third sectors – needed to engage with civil servants, politicians and regulators on the detail of the financial regulation agenda and to do so in terms of both the first and second order impacts. At the first level "we" are the users of the financial system and need to be able to work with it on terms that ensure our liquidity, funding and risk management requirements can be met within a proportionate and known regulatory environment. If they are, then growth, employment and financial stability will be protected. At the second level the real economy has the same overwhelming expectation as individual taxpayers, which is that government should be doing its utmost to ensure that the fiscal drain of a poorly regulated (and managed) financial sector should never again fail and then make the sort of demands on public funds that resulted from the 2008 crisis.

As the process of engagement on the regulatory agenda began we realized that we faced one huge barrier – not just on derivatives regulation (the debates in the US and the EU on Dodd-Frank and EMIR) but also on the unfolding list of regulatory interventions. This barrier was the almost complete absence of understanding on the part of the cast of suspects – the civil servants, politicians and regulators – of how NFEUs use the financial system. This publication is concerned overall with the issue of regulatory capture. I am arguing in this contribution that a particularly pernicious form of regulatory capture has made the debate of the last two or three years much more challenging because wittingly or unwittingly the needs of the real economy have been at best overlooked and at worst ignored.

13.4 The impact of regulatory change on non-financial end users

To understand the extent of real economy dissatisfaction with the approach to the recent regulatory agenda it is important to document the range of areas where NFEUs have felt most concerned about the impact. The following list is not intended to be exhaustive and complete; it is significantly biased towards those areas where in the EACT we have felt it most important that we express our voice, acting where possible as a leader or at least contributor to NFEUs intervening to obtain a better regulatory outcome.

These areas include (the acronyms refer to current EU initiatives):

- regulation of derivatives (EMIR);
- bank capital requirements (Basel III, CRD IV and CRR);
- regulation of financial instruments' markets (MiFID II and MiFIR);
- regulation of credit rating agencies;
- proposals for a financial transactions tax (FTT).

The real economy impact of these regulatory initiatives can be illustrated briefly through these examples, where each is an area on which the EACT has engaged. The views documented below reflect the positions taken by the EACT and are presented here as such.

First, the need for an exemption from central clearing for NFEUs' transactions in OTC derivatives. The implementation of the original proposals would have had the effect of shifting NFEUs away from managing the credit risk of their derivative positions (risk with which they are familiar and experienced in managing), substituting for this a liquidity risk that is essentially unmanageable. As noted earlier, all but the most highly liquid companies would, without an exemption under EMIR and Dodd-Frank, find themselves having to reduce productive investment as current or future cash is husbanded for possible margin calls.

Second, the economic impact of the CVA charge in Basel III (and by extension, CRD IV and CRR) that would have the effect of forcing the real economy to make much greater use of standardized derivatives capable of being centrally cleared, thereby vitiating the value of the exemption under EMIR. If such standardized derivatives are unavailable – or if the liquidity risk burden of collateralization were considered intolerable – then the real economy would be subjected to greater volatility as NFEUs elected to hedge less of the underlying risks within the business.

Third, the proposal to require mandatory rotation of credit rating agencies after three years (when there is a single agency rating an issuer's instrument). If implemented this would undermine the quality of the rating process for NFEUs as issuers. Both agency and issuer make a substantial investment in the process and three years is simply too short to ensure that the value of this investment is fully realized. Implementation of the regulatory proposal would probably lead to a reduction in the number of ratings and be directly associated with less rather than greater fundraising capacity for the real economy – at a stage in the economic cycle when such activity is critically important.

Fourth, the likelihood that a financial transactions tax would be borne predominantly by individuals, pension funds and companies rather than by the financial institutions that the tax targets. NFEUs take the view that broadly speaking the accumulation of the proposed tax within the system would be a "cost" that customers of the financial system would in practice have to bear. If implemented in the form originally proposed by the EU – and done so in isolation from the actions of the rest of the world – a perverse and surely unintended outcome would be a dilution of the new regulatory framework. Those threatened with the economic cost of the tax would seek to move activities outside the scope of the tax, where a reasonable presumption would be that the regulatory framework would be inferior to that within the European Union.

In each of these areas of actual or planned financial regulatory initiatives the real economy has identified fundamental flaws in the approach being taken. The charitable interpretation has been to talk in terms of "unintended consequences". The reality more often seems to be that, whether or not this is due to regulatory capture, the development of financial regulatory policy takes place within a bubble defined by the financial sector. Those driving this agenda – the triumvirate of civil servants, regulators and politicians – perhaps need regular reminders that the financial sector serves the real economy and not the inverse. The investment, trade and risk management needs of NFEUs drive the financial sector's existence and the regulatory impact on the real economy should therefore be of primary concern in the development of policy.

13.5 Why is regulatory policy development failing the real economy?

I suggest here four areas where current practice is failing the real economy and change is needed. The challenge of change varies greatly as will be evident from the description of the problem.

13.5.1 Civil servants and regulators working on financial regulatory policy are not always sufficiently well qualified to consider wider, real economy impacts.

The lack of appreciation (by civil servants and regulators) of real economy impacts has already been highlighted. Other contributors to this publication will be no doubt also comment on this aspect of regulatory capture. My own experience has largely been in dealing with the European Commission and to a lesser extent with national finance ministry and regulatory officials. The reasons for these shortcomings are probably multiple. Whether professional education or prior experience are dominant concerns I would certainly argue that the financial sector has in consequence been able to use its resources (financial and people) to dominate the regulatory dialogue with institutions such as the Commission. This overwhelming attention from bankers and lobbyists has not served the real economy well in ensuring that there is the capacity to identify the implications of the regulatory actions being debated, beyond the financial sector.

A slightly ironic consequence of this is that when we as the EACT sought to talk to the Commission on CRD IV / CRR we were effectively told that the door was shut, as the Commission had been "over-lobbied". Our own investigation could find no instance of discussions between Commission staff and representatives of NFEUs but plenty of anecdotal evidence that the Commission was exhausted by pressure from the financial sector. Whilst much of CRD IV / CRR is of concern only to that sector, the Commission must surely have known that whether on CVA charges for uncleared OTC derivatives or on the treatment of trade finance there were serious implications for the real economy.

In our discussions on EMIR with the Commission it had become apparent that the staff were overstretched in setting out to meet the G20 deadline and under qualified to assess the impact on end users. In all the subsequent exposure to the Commission's other regulatory proposals we have noted the same inadequate appreciation of real economy consequences and a reluctance to engage on these.

13.5.2 European Commission impact assessments – in financial regulatory matters – appear unable to reflect dynamic implications for the real economy.

To an outsider the production of impact assessments by the Commission seems to be an academic exercise in economic dark arts, with a narrowly based (if very complex) model generating conclusions that seem remote from the experience and anticipation of end users. For example, in the development of EMIR, although we and a number of NFEUs offered to quantify the impact of collateral requirements on models of current usage of derivatives, the Commission failed to take advantage of this. If such data had been used in the impact assessment it could be argued that the protracted debate with the Commission, Parliament and Council on the need for an end user exemption would have been shorter and more immediately conclusive.

My personal view is that the reasons for the shortcomings of impact assessments are very similar to those underlying the first area of failure discussed above, combining both the narrowness of the economic modelling and the limited breadth of experience on the part of those working on financial regulatory policy (and reinforced by the time pressures). As an example of the modelling issues, the Commission's impact assessment of the FTT proposal assumed a closed economy for Europe – an apparently bizarre assumption in a world where barriers to trade and movement are supposed to be being dismantled, capital is highly mobile and NFEUs will tend to move their transactions with the financial sector to the location where they can be most effectively conducted. In the case of FTT, relaxing the closed economy assumption does of course radically reduce the claimed benefits for an EU FTT implementation.

13.5.3 The real economy is poorly organized to balance the focused representation of the financial sector in dialogue on regulatory proposals.

I have described above the inability to talk to the Commission about the implications of CRD IV / CRR for the real economy. It is difficult not to feel a degree of sympathy for the Commission staff, subject as they are to the lobbying of a well-funded and organized group of representatives of the financial sector. The real economy, in contrast, has much more fragmented representation in its dealings with the EU. Participants are significantly dispersed whether by geography, sector, trade, profession, size, degree of internationalization and so on. In contrast to the financial sector there is no homogeneity of skills and commercial interest.

If discussion of this shortcoming is focused on how Brussels works then it is difficult to identify any self-evident focal point for the real economy other than Business Europe (BE), the representative of Member State employer organizations. I suspect BE itself would agree that the organization has found it difficult to harness the resources, expertise and timely awareness of the issues to play an effective role in a sufficient number of the financial regulatory proposals that have emerged since 2008.

The combination of the inadequate recognition of the real economy impact by civil servants (the Commission) and the power of the financial sector's lobby has deepened the problem caused by the lacuna of coordinated input by NFEUs and others concerned with the evolution of financial regulation and its impact on the rest of the economy.

13.5.4 The real economy has been accused of being the pawn of the financial sector.

As I write I am increasingly hearing that the big banks have used NFEUs and organizations such as the EACT as their pawns – to argue for regulatory solutions that are more acceptable when framed by the end users but are fundamentally in the interests of the banks and other participants in the financial sector, on whose behalf the end users are said to be working. It is of course not the big banks that are making this claim but senior Commission officials and politicians in Brussels. The claim would be risible if it were not being made by responsible and influential players in the regulatory debate.

I see elements of both flattery and of despair in the argument. The serious point however is that the very ability to float the allegation underlines the weak starting position of the real economy. If there were a better understanding on the part of civil servants, regulators and politicians of the underlying issue – which is that financial regulation affects end users – then the calumny would gain no credence.

13.6 Conclusion: taking the real economy into account – what needs to change?

It will be clear from my analysis above that there are deep concerns about the way in which financial regulation has been developed since 2008. Support for regulatory change – and acceptance of the need for it – should not be in doubt. But talk of unintended consequences has been too common and with good reason; coupling this with some of the emotion generated around the malign claim that end users are the puppets of the vested interests of the financial sector makes an overwhelming case for change. A more effective approach would focus on the following:

- Specialist experience for civil servants: at national and EU level we need individuals working on financial regulation whose backgrounds qualify them to recognize impacts beyond the usual suspects of the participants in financial markets, a group too narrowly perceived as the banks, brokers, fund managers and so on.
- Impact assessments: it needs to be explicit that assessment of the impact of developing proposals must extend to a credible identification of the real economy implications and measurement of these consequences.
- Access for real economy representatives: the ability of the financial sector to allocate seemingly unlimited resources to lobbying and

other forms of influencing cannot be allowed to have the result that the fatigued drafters of regulation close their doors to the real economy. There must be a recognition that the latter's representation is much more fragmented and will continue to be so, despite the concern that many of us feel about the need for change. This means that we almost require a form of affirmative action on the part of the European Commission, to ensure in particular that access is allowed even if the requests for it are later than those made by the better funded financial sector lobby.

The real economy has undoubtedly struggled to deal with the round of financial regulation since 2008. Whilst apportionment of the responsibility for this needs to be judicious, I am in no doubt that there has been a form of regulatory capture and systemic failure on the part of those driving the regulatory agenda. What is important is that the lessons of this are understood. The regulatory framework is incomplete and the NFEUs in the real economy accept that further interventions are needed. Our hope must be that lessons are learned and future policy development is more inclusive of that part of the global economy ultimately driving the existence and need for the financial sector – the manufacturers and service providers on whom we all depend for long-term growth of employment and economic stability.

14.0 Lessons from the Experience of the UK Financial Sector

Adam Ridley[1]

14.1 Introduction

This chapter reflects over 30 years' involvement in financial regulation, first as policy adviser to the British Government, and then in the investment banking industry and other financial sectors, negotiating important legislation and regulation such as the UK's Financial Services & Markets Act (FSMA) and the EU's Financial Services Action Plan (FSAP). These experiences lead me to suggest that "capture" in general and "regulatory capture" in particular are only part of the story which should concern us. Analyses of regulatory capture have frequently built upon the US experience, where capture has been treated as one of the dominant sources of bad regulation, and in some observers' views as the major cause of the crises of 2007/2008 onwards. However, the experience of the UK, Europe and the rest of the OECD points to the importance of other kinds of capture, whether political or intellectual, to the significance of development in sectors other than those in and around banking, and to the need to seek answers to

---

[1] Sir Adam Ridley was a member of the Government Economic Service from 1964 to 1975, Economic Adviser to the Conservative Party Shadow Cabinet from 1974 to 1979, Assistant Director and Director of the Conservative Research Department from 1974 to 1979, Special Advisor to Sir Geoffrey Howe and Nigel Lawson from 1979 to 1985, and Executive Director, Hambros Bank and Plc from 1985 to 1997. He has been a Name since 1977, a member of the Committee of the Association of Lloyd's Members (ALM) since 1988, and Deputy Chairman since 1994. He represented the ALM in the 1993 settlement negotiations and chaired the Names' Committee which devised the basis for the Reconstruction and Renewal Settlement. From 1997 to 1999 he was a member of the Council of Lloyd's and various regulatory committees. In 1996 he became a trustee and Chairman of the Equitas Trust. Sir Adam was Director General and Special Adviser at London Investment Banking Association from 2000 to 2006.

regulatory capture (or capture of any kind) in a broad framework of promoting "good regulation".

In the first section of this note, I draw some lessons about regulatory capture from the experience of the regulatory process in the UK and Europe, highlighting important differences from the USA. In the second section, I discuss how best to mitigate this phenomenon, in the framework of promoting better regulation more generally. At many points I offer brief general judgements without full explanation in the interests of clarity and brevity.

14.2 Some features of regulatory capture in the UK and Europe

The study of regulatory capture has traditionally been dominated by the North American experience. Classic regulatory capture focuses on those instances when powerful monopolistic or oligopolistic firms serving large numbers of small clients induce their regulators to favour the industry's interests in ways detrimental to the public interest. This definition well reflects the experience of utilities regulation in the US, characterized by a small numbers of firms in privately owned, oligopolistic utilities (energy, telecoms etc.), and a fairly motley complex of regulators, state and Federal. But to what extent is this notion of capture applicable to the regulation of financial markets?

In wholesale financial markets, the producers are generally still relatively numerous. Typical clients and counterparties are not weak citizens, but companies and trained professionals who are usually able to look after themselves. There is a relatively small "Conduct of Business" (COB) agenda about which firms might wish to "nobble" the regulators.

Therefore, while capture in the regulation of banking is the fashionable objects of study for so many scholars today, the experience of British wholesale investment banking presents few striking examples of this phenomenon. Although it is often alleged that the investment banks have exercised excessive influence on the Basel and EU Capital Adequacy debate, there is no solid evidence of this. Each side won important arguments but not illegitimately, and recent research suggest that "the process of constructing Basel II's main risk models featured more resistance to private sector pressures than is commonly appreciated".[2] The outbreak of the crisis in 2007 has sapped the bargaining power of the banking industry. The subsequent tightening of requirements for both liquidity and capital now in prospect reflects both the change in the balance of power in financial regulation and a degree of capture by non-industry parties, even if some financial institutions clearly needed stronger capital and liquidity.

At the same time, instances of regulatory capture can be found in other areas of financial markets, in particular in retail financial services. For instance, the British experience shows how since the Financial Services Act of 1986 retail banks and the fund management sectors (personal investments, life insurance, pensions etc.) have successfully defended industry practices which are not in the public interest, such as not disclosing details of their fees, commissions and conflicts of interest. The Financial Services Market Act of 2000 left a good deal of this structure intact nearly fifteen years later. In both cases cited, capture occurred primarily through the legislative process and of the two Governments concerned, Conservative (1986) and Labour (2001). Moreover, major scandals involving retail services have also arisen under the Financial Services Authority, despite the emphasis on consumer protection in this institution's objectives (e.g. Equitable Life, pensions mis-selling, life insurance mis-selling, PPI, etc.).

Furthermore, despite the focus of much of the literature on the investment banking industry, one of the most spectacular cases of capture in Britain can be found elsewhere, in the regulation of the Lloyd's Insurance Market. Since the seventeenth century this market has operated under a special Act of Parliament, responsible for its own by-laws, supervision, enforcement and safety net for policyholders and, until 2001, regulation. However, by the 1980s the peer group pressure and the internal disciplines responsible for keeping the

---

[2] Young, K. (2012). 'Transitional Regulatory Capture? An empirical examination of the transitional lobbying of the Basel committee on Banking Supervision', *Review of International Political Economy*, February 2012.

market commercially healthy had become ineffectual. Neither the recently revised Lloyd's Act, nor rather remote surveillance by the Bank of England and the Department of Trade & Industry measured up to these challenges. Moreover, capture by producer interests of various kinds affected then not only Lloyd's regulatory machinery but also its governing Council and staff, which failed to detect, punish and deter various burgeoning malpractices.[3]

Instances of regulatory capture can also be found in the regulation of securities markets. Until the last fifteen years or so, most security markets outside the USA were de facto protected national monopolies, usually owned by some kind of mutual composed of individual brokers/traders, and largely responsible for their own regulation. The demutualizations of exchanges transferred most of the regulation (for example listing rules, COB, as in the UK) to public regulators. However, these regulators have not sought to prevent the vertical integration of exchanges and post-trade institutions, an outcome which usually restricts or eliminates competition and increases margins. In analogous network industries such as Telecoms, the EU has wisely introduced requirements for open access for all on fair terms to stop such developments.[4]

In contrast to the classic theory of regulatory capture, the regulatory process offers opportunities for many and varied interested parties (not just industry) to exercise illegitimate influence and to divert policies away from the public good and in favour of some group. So there will be many kinds of capture. Regulatory capture from the financial industry is only one of several important pathological dimensions of bad regulation.

After years of involvement in tedious but unromantic negotiations at home and abroad, and first-hand experience of a number of major

---

[3] The pathological governance of Lloyd's in the 1980s and 1990s is described in 'A view from the Room' by Ian Hay Davison, Weidenfeld & Nicolson, 1987; and in 'Ultimate Risk: the inside story of the Lloyd's catastrophe' by Adam Raphael, Four Walls & Eight Windows, 1995.

[4] For telecoms regulation in the EU, see e.g. 'The economics of Anti-Trust & Regulation in Telecommunications', Pierre A Buigues and Patrick Rey, eds., Edward Elgar, Cheltenham, 2004.

improvements in regulatory policymaking, one concludes that regulatory processes can go wrong in many ways and sectors. Legislators and officials are not usually experts in financial markets and services. Business leaders and managers often lack the patience and understanding demanded by the regulatory process. Few people anywhere are masters of the legal tangles arising from the clashes between, for example, home, EU and US jurisdictions. Lawyers are sometimes very inexperienced in administration. Compliance officers are ignored until it is too late. There is little economic research or analysis directed at regulatory issues. To cap it all, there is no generally accepted optimal institutional framework, whether for devising or monitoring regulation, or for holding the various parties involved to account.

For all these reasons it would be unwise to attempt to tackle it outside this much wider context.

14.3 Preventing and mitigating capture – in the context of the search for better regulation and strengthening the integrity of the regulatory process

Since the first major initiative to regulate the financial sector in the Financial Services Act of 1986, experience in the UK, Europe, and now worldwide has shown the many basic principles which need to be followed to ensure good regulation and to prevent damaging capture of any kind. This section briefly identifies some of the most important.

14.3.1 Full public consultation

Full public consultation is essential, particularly in the earlier stages of the regulatory process. While the UK has been a leader, experience and progress has been fitful and inadequate in the EU's financial regulatory initiatives over the last twelve or so years, despite periodic sincere promises to do better. EU politicians and officials appear to feel proper consultation is a privilege which they can grant or, particularly at times of overwork and embarrassment, legitimately withhold. Yet it is both a democratic right and a practical necessity, save in periods of extreme crisis. Many international bodies – such as IOSCO in the old days – have been even worse. White papers, technical studies, draft texts and so on must be made cheaply and widely available and realistic consultation periods provided. Regulatory staff must be available for serious public debate and cross-examination, as the FSA has generally ensured since it was created.

In the UK, the FSA is legally obliged to provide a minimum 3 months' consultation period for all new or revised rules, guidance, and so on – and presumably these procedures will still be imposed under the new Act. The same three months notice normally applies to Parliamentary Resolutions giving effect to new regulation. One must, however, always be wary of empty consultative procedures adopted simply to discharge a formal obligation. Posting obscurely drafted proposals on an obscure website is not consultation. Preventing such futile processes is one of the many tasks which should fall to institutions ensuring regulators' accountability.

The consultation process should be the starting point of a sequence which is built around a strong algorithm. In essence:

I. regulatory intervention should be initiated only where there is evidence of material market failure, plausible grounds for expecting intervention to help materially and evidence that the costs will be comfortably exceeded by expected benefits;
II. (after consultation on draft proposals, the responses from the world at large should be published in summary form, together with a preliminary impact or cost-benefit assessment, coupled with any revisions or elaboration of the proposals;
III. substantial regulatory innovations should be followed at a sensible interval by monitoring or a survey of the results, followed by a further revised impact or cost-benefit analysis to establish whether the "game is still worth the candle". Where it is not, legislation or regulation should be removed or radically changed.

Honest and thorough consultation based on careful analysis, subject to responsible reporting and publicity is an invaluable antidote to poor representation, or undue pressures from any quarter.[5]

14.3.2 Staff quality

Regulating complex activities in the financial markets self-evidently demands good staff, both in the regulator(s) themselves, and in relevant sponsor ministries and in the businesses being regulated. Achieving this requires a significant flow of talent in both directions through secondment and personnel exchanges. Also valuable is developing a multistage career pattern in both sectors on the US model. This solution has been regarded with neurotic suspicion within European institutions and individual countries. The risk of "revolving door" conflicts, or improper pursuit of industry or other interests is real. However, there are well-established procedures for "gardening leave" and quarantine periods, not dealing with former subordinates or employers and so forth, by which the risks can be managed.

14.3.4 Regulatory budgets and staff numbers

Both politicians and regulated businesses are sometimes disingenuous and irresponsible about staff and resources. Politicians create ambitious regulatory agencies, give them demanding tasks and then deny them the resources they need, and limit the fees regulators can impose on firms they supervise. This inconsistency has been particularly serious for financial regulation at the European level, which is aggravated by the little-noticed practice of requiring financially hard-pressed national regulators to fund the new EU regulatory institutions. Businesses resent large and growing regulatory fees, whether because

---

[5] The emphasis placed above on a structured consultative process is born not just of experience in the UK but of the accumulated wisdom and experience of the fourteen members of the International Council of Securities Associations (ICSA), which represent or regulate the overwhelming majority of the world's equity, bond and derivative markets. ICSA members agreed and presented a set of "Principles for better regulation" to IOSCO and others in November 2006. Regrettably, such initiatives have tended to be put on one side following the crisis of 2007 onwards. See ICSA website for 'ICSA publishes principles and best practices for market infrastructure governance, better regulations and self-regulatory organizations', 9 November 2006.

they recall paying next to no fees in the recent past, or because they fear they are being made to pay for the rescue or regulatory burden imposed by their feckless competitors. Almost everyone closes their eyes to the enormous managerial challenge involved in running a large complex regulator, or the financial policy division of a finance ministry (i.e. sponsor department). When disruptive changes and reorganization, draconian cuts (or both) are pursued, and management experience, folk memory and esprit de corps are at risk (as in the UK and USA today), scarcely anyone comments, let alone protests. Such pressures are, of course, very conducive to regulatory capture.[6]

14.3.5 Research and analysis

Effective regulation imposes material costs on and affects the behaviour of markets, firms and people, often in complex ways. Before introducing regulation, it is reasonable – as with other public policies – to expect policymakers to do some research on these issues, to publish the results and to debate them publicly. Once implemented, it is essential to establish whether the new measures do what is expected of them: that they are fair, economical, and do not have unacceptable side effects. Such procedures create a strong base from which regulatory capture (and other kinds of regulatory failure) can be identified and mitigated if need be. The UK has moved further than most countries in undertaking such research. However, all too often insufficient study time, money, and skilled researchers are made available, increasingly so in a period of austerity. Usually the world outside is unconcerned about this chronic absence of information and analysis until something goes wrong as a result, by which time it is often too late. A classic case is the universal ignorance of the nature and extent of the shadow banking sector until well after the recent crisis, ignorance which was only broken by the path breaking study of the sector by the NY FRD.[7]

---

[6] For eloquent evidence of such challenges, see 'Review of HM Treasury's management response to the financial crisis', HM Treasury, March 2012, undertaken by Sharon White following requests from the National Audit Office and Public Accounts Committee.

[7] See 'Shadow Banking', by Poszar, Adrian, Ashcroft & Boesky, Federal Reserve Bank of NY, Staff Report No. 458, July 2010.

14.3.6 Proceeding at a measured pace

Most financial regulation arises because of scandals or crises. When governments find themselves under intense public pressure, sometimes justifiably, to regulate quickly, they adopt measures that cannot be systematically considered. Laws tend to be very durable, hard to revise and susceptible to replacement only very infrequently. (Canada is uniquely wise and fortunate in having a Banking Act which is subject to compulsory review every ten years.) Other things being equal, therefore, regulatory law needs to be developed in a measured way, so that it is robustly applicable for a long period of time despite changing circumstances. This can only be achieved if it is composed mainly of relatively high-level principles with essentially timeless qualities. Swift legislation imposed before interested parties can really digest its effects or organize rational debate, is a marvellous vehicle for regulatory capture.

On the other hand, financial markets and regulatory challenges evolve quickly. So the detailed provisions of rules and regulations which apply at lower levels to specific and changing circumstances must be open to relatively frequent review and revision. In this way, the regulatory apparatus can be modified to track promptly the changing requirements of markets and their participants – and often shifts in government policy as well.

14.3.7 Handling scandals, crises and emergency measures with care

This leads to the important question of what to do about those measures which unavoidably must be introduced at great speed. Such measures are likely to be crude and in parts defective, but also to be durable as argued above. Therefore, at the least it is essential to build in an automatic, mandatory review process after a sensible period, so that the inevitable bad consequences of haste can be corrected. Better still is to follow the best practice which is normally adopted with emergency legislation in other areas of national life. As a rule, it should be strictly time-limited and only reintroduced after the full apparatus of initial proposals, consultations, cost-benefit and/or impact analysis, market testing, and so on.

14.3.8 Lawmaking and Parliament

Recent experience in the UK, both with the FSMA after 1997 and with the current bill to reform the FSMA, has underlined the importance of strong Parliamentary institutions and procedures. Major, complex, specialized bills of this kind call for unusually careful high-level examination. To examine both bills, Parliament has exceptionally and wisely constituted a joint committee of both Houses of Parliaments, which have been in a position to give the Government's proposals an especially thorough and authoritative review. Even so, at a time of much other hectic legislative activity (for example, reform of the National Health Service), the attention devoted by this important Committee recently to the revision of the FSMA was not as thorough or as closely followed outside Parliament as it should have been. These two episodes underline the much more general argument that in any country – and in the EU – parliamentary committees should be expected to take such important regulatory business more seriously and to employ more high powered, technically qualified staff support for their work. How to apply this principle internationally outside the EU is a looming challenge which needs urgent attention.

Equally important is continuing parliamentary scrutiny of the regulatory process. Given the complexity of it all, there is a strong case for having some kind of parliamentary body which devotes most or all of its time to the conduct of financial regulation. In the UK, the Joint Committee of both Houses might be an excellent candidate for such a permanent task. Unfortunately, it appears that this responsibility will return, rather, to the Treasury Select Committee (TSC). The TSC is able to do good work on regulation from time to time, but has many other urgent issues on its agenda and is not supported by a substantial specialist staff. Moreover at any given time it may not have a membership with the continuity, sectoral expertise and self-confidence required to grill the regulators or the regulated effectively. Reviewing regulators is a specialized business.

14.3.9 Representation of leading industries, firms or citizens and the country at large

This is an intrinsically difficult area. Some politicians and officials assume that the leading businesses in a private industry have or can create representative bodies which are effective counterparties to the legislative and the executive, not unlike the government departments they know from political life. They may feel "industries" should devote serious time and money to policy work. In reality businesses often do not do so, even when they have the money and resources. Moreover, some industries are very fragmented and the businesses comprising them may get on badly with each other. Top executives in leading firms may not have any natural talent for, or see the point of, public affairs or commercial policy. Politicians and regulators underestimate these realities and sometimes are inclined to be unreasonably demanding and impatient. The result is, therefore, frequently the opposite of regulatory capture – dominance of a sector or group of firms by the politicians/sponsor department/regulators.

The problems of representation are if anything more acute when one comes to the extremely important question of adequately representing more diffuse consumer and citizen interests. There is a tendency for politicians, officials (and political theorists) to seek (and critically bemoan the absence of) effective representation of consumers, shareholders and clients of particular sectors. The more one confronts this, the more puzzling it is that no one asks why parliament and its members are so feeble at representing so large a part of every nation. There is a strong case for saying that in the default case, it is parliament's task to speak for ordinary citizens and to develop procedures for ensuring a proper voice for the diffuse general public in the regulatory debate. Parliaments should be regarded as a potentially versatile if partial solution to the "collective action" problem.

14.3.10 Accountability of regulators

"Quis costodiet custodes ipsos" is as apt as ever when applied to financial regulators. In the ten years of its life (it was in effect replaced by two successor organizations on 1 April 2012), the UK's FSA has been a test-bed for methods of accountability, and one should briefly note the procedures followed. One does so against the sad reality that in most OECD countries most regulators are not systematically held accountable, do not like to draw attention to themselves, and face the obvious temptation to organize for themselves as quiet a life as possible. In other words, they may well be susceptible to industry pressures where yielding to them may sustain the quiet life.

In the case of the FSA, parliamentary review apart, accountability was ensured in at least four ways, most of which are set to be continued more or less when the revised Act comes into force:

- The FSA's Board. The FSA is a company which therefore has a board and directors, whose role may have been conceived as rather similar to that of the "Court" of the Bank of England. Neither, of course, has been given executive responsibilities. The FSA Board's effectiveness has not been the object of much academic study or public comment. Its roles included approval of the FSA rulebook – an important task. Its composition – involving substantial practitioner membership – incorporated the inevitable clash between industry expertise and regulatory capture.
- Consultative Panels for wholesale firms and small businesses were created under FSMA, and the FSA wisely created an additional panel for Consumers. These largely invisible and little appreciated panels have functioned confidentially, advising on imminent FSA initiatives or debates. They usually work without the right to seek much external advice from relevant market participants and with a micro-staff of one executive for each Panel, through the Consumer Panel had more recently. To be seriously effective, one suspects that the Panels which succeed them will need more teeth and more freedom to determine their agenda and modus operandi, and probably fewer confidentiality restrictions. However, they had a real value, not least in terrorem, since each panel could demand that the FSA explain/justify proposals in public if it had not received adequate explanations in private. The Government's intention is that the new Prudential Regulatory Authority should not work with any panel, and no good reason has been given for this retrograde move.

- Annual Report and Open Meeting. The FSA has held well attended Open Meetings each year and published a full Annual Report beforehand. Both the meetings, the reports and other published documents such as the Annual Risk Survey have been consistently well received and appreciated.
- Appeals Tribunal. Where the objects of FSA enforcement procedures wish to dispute their treatment, the FSMA provides for access to an independent appeals body, The Upper Tribunal.

14.4 Challenges of today and tomorrow

The last few decades of regulatory policymaking in the UK – and latterly the EU – provide important insights into capture of all kinds. They give us a range of lessons about how to make regulation better generally and to reduce capture. However, the challenges have become more acute recently. Since 2007, the balance of power in financial regulation has changed dramatically. Investment banks and securities houses have lost almost all public credibility, as have "the bankers". There is an overwhelming conviction in almost all quarters that much more regulation is required, as well as much more capital and liquidity. In such conditions, prominent politicians and economists have been able to put forward successfully very ambitious regulatory proposals, as have lawyers, regulators and groups representing those that have suffered in the crisis. As a result, a host of aggressive and controversial measures have been imposed by the regulators, whose capture is now from a very different quarter. Thus the possible virtues of the proposed Financial Transactions Tax, the EU's Alternative Investment Fund Directive, the Volcker Rule and some important aspects of the UK's Vickers reforms are all vitiated because they break many of the canons of good regulation.

The regulators have been captured by intellectuals, popular sentiment, politicians and those who wish to punish and extract compensation from those who they feel they are responsible for the financial crisis. It is not a very good way to run the world's economy.

Section 4

A Perspective from Outside Finance

15.0 Regulatory Capture: a Perspective from a Communications Regulator

David Currie[1]

15.1 Introduction

My aim in this note is to examine the issue of regulatory capture from a cross-industry perspective. The introductory chapter by Stefano Pagliari provides a masterly survey of the literature on regulatory capture, primarily focused on financial regulation. I am reminded that when I met with Howard Davies to discuss research when he had just been appointed founding Chairman of the FSA, he told me that he found very little of use in the academic research literature on regulation. If that was fair comment then, this chapter shows that it would not be so now. And it led me to reflect on my early period as Chairman of Ofcom, essentially doing for communications regulation what Howard was charged to do earlier for financial services regulation. We had many issues to grapple with including bringing together five hitherto separate regulatory bodies with different cultures, pay and pension structures and developing new relationships

[1] Lord Currie is currently Chairman of the ICFR and the Alacrity Foundation, and a board member of the Royal Mail, the Dubai Financial Services Authority, BDO, IG Group, and the London Philharmonic Orchestra, and a Governor of the Institute for Government. He was formerly the founding Chairman of Ofcom, the UK communications regulator (2002-9), a board member of Ofgem (1997-2002). In his academic career, he was Professor of Economics and Deputy Dean at London Business School, where he ran the Centre for Economic Forecasting (1988-1995) and then the Regulation Initiative (1995-2000); and then Dean of Cass Business School (2001-8). He has acted as an adviser to a wide range of companies and organisations, particularly in financial services. He sits on the cross benches of the House of Lords as Lord Currie of Marylebone, and serves on the Economic Affairs Select Committee.

with multiple stakeholders. But a crucially important cluster of issues concerned establishing our independence from industry and government; that is, avoiding the risk of regulatory capture whether by industry or politicians.

At the heart of the issue is the conundrum of independent regulation. Effective regulation requires a thorough understanding of the regulated industry, and sensitivity to political currents, but at the same time it needs to be independent of both the industry and government. But how then does it achieve its legitimacy? The answer in practice is that complete independence of both industry and government is not possible, because complete independence risks degenerating into a self-perpetuating and illegitimate oligarchy. One option is that the regulator derives its legitimacy from the industry in a form of self-regulation. The other is that the regulator gets its authority from some form of statutory underpinning. Or, most interestingly, it may be possible to construct a hybrid of the two.

This line of thought puts the issue of regulatory capture into context. If legitimacy can derive only from the industry or government, complete independence of either is not possible. The challenge is to design a regulatory structure which has legitimacy, but which is sufficiently distant from both regulator and government to serve the broader interests of society. From this perspective, capture is a matter of degree.

In what follows, I reflect on how, in the context of a statutory basis for regulation, one can put in place bulwarks against undue political and industry influence on regulatory decisions. (I therefore do not comment on self-regulation.) My comments reflect my practical experience of communications regulation, but also refer to and reflect experience across other industries. I have structured my comments under the following headings: marching orders; selection processes; revolving doors; internal audit; external audit and appeal; funding; and intellectual capture. Throughout, I will be concerned with two forms of capture: capture by the industry; and capture by the politicians. Where lobbying is rife, the second may well be a route to the first.

15.2 Marching orders

A key starting point about regulation is that it is based on the marching orders given to the regulator in legislation by Parliament or Congress. An essential precondition for effective regulation is a well thought-out set of duties and sufficient powers to pursue these duties effectively. Getting that right requires a well-judged policymaking process and a proper political process to see it through to final legislation. It is rare for that to be perfect, and often it can be very far from perfect, not least because of the lobbying activities of the major, often well-heeled, players. Pagliari (this publication) gives the examples of the US OCC having to promote the interests of the US over other banks; and the FSA's requirement to have regard to the competitiveness of the financial services industry. In the case of Ofcom, we had a few orphaned duties – duties without the power to enforce – which meant we could only use the soft power of the regulator to persuade some form of compliance, a rather diluted form of regulation. However, the legislators did get our primary duty right: to promote the interests of consumers and citizens, present and future. The mix of consumers and citizens meant that we could balance the commercial and cultural aspects of communications in our decisions; and the present and future meant that we had to have regard for the health of the industry, insofar it is the crucial deliverer of communications services to future consumers and citizens. The tradition in UK regulation has been to postulate a range of duties (and "have regard to") as well as to place on the regulator the onus of balancing those duties. In my experience, there is considerable advantage in having a clear primary duty, such as the Ofcom one, sitting above these.

Once the legislation is in place, then the regulator must assert its independence of politicians. My experience was pretty good in that regard. Having established one's credibility (a matter to which I return), I found that politicians were generally cognisant of our independence and respectful of it. We generally operated a "no surprises, no veto" policy: we kept government informed of what was happening and what could happen, and they expressed their views but did not seek to veto our decisions or instruct us. Indeed, although the legislation rightly specified some areas (notably spectrum issues) where ministers retained some powers to direct, they were very reluctant to use such powers: they understood the political advantage of distance from decisions. This was not always the case. I well remember having to point out to a Westminster politician that our relationship with the Scottish Government was the same as that to the Westminster Government – we were equally independent of both. But this stance requires credibility – an ineffective regulator is likely to find itself under much more sustained and effective political pressure. And I did observe that one or two heads of other regulatory bodies were in and out of No. 10 more often than certain press barons.

15.3 Selection processes

The means of selection for the chairman and board of a regulator is also critical to its independence, and Stefano's paper says rather little about this, perhaps reflecting the literature. The US model is typically that the appointment is a political one, chosen by the executive subject to approval by Congress. (I well remember a delightful dinner with my counterpart, the then Chairman of the FCC, where his conversation focused entirely on US electoral politics.) That has the problem that it places politics at the heart of regulation. And since industrial lobbying is so powerful in the US, it provides a direct mechanism for capture by well-positioned industry players.

The UK model is rather different. The relevant permanent secretary (senior civil servant) establishes a panel including an independent OCPA assessor and one or two knowledgeable experts, and therefore with industry experience. They shortlist and interview candidates obtained from both search and public advertisement, and put their rank order to ministers. Ministers often follow the judgement of the panel, but have the discretion to choose any of the candidates judged by the panel to be appointable. This process is usually, though not always, quite effective in preventing politicians appointing their chums, but it does not always ensure that the best candidate is appointed. A strong appointment as chairman is likely to result in a virtuous circle, since they will be better able to attract strong non-executives and executives to the regulatory body. But the opposite is a clear risk.

The appointment process is a key issue in the current debate around UK press regulation. Government involvement in the appointment process is widely seen as inconsistent with a press free to challenge executive power. The challenge, seen by many, therefore concerns how to devise an appointments process with sufficient independence of both the industry and government, but one that is nonetheless seen to be legitimate.

15.4 Revolving doors

The paper puts considerable emphasis on revolving doors, the movement of people to and from the regulator to the industry. My views on this are relatively straightforward. When we set up Ofcom, we were careful to set salaries above the levels that had been the norm in the legacy regulators because we wanted to be able to attract high calibre people with current knowledge of the industry (and we more than paid for this hike in salaries by a greater proportionate reduction in headcount), to be mixed with the best of those who had ploughed the regulatory furrow. We selected them on four criteria: intrinsic merit; a commitment to the public policy goals of the regulator; avoiding those with a regulatory role in the industry who would be stuck in old mind-sets; and coming from a good mix of businesses and functions. Without them, we would not have been able to do some of the radical things that we did. But we made sure that the senior executive team was led by people who had no major baggage, whether from the industry or from the regulators. That was on entry. On exit, we applied tough gardening leave arrangements, costly in terms of payroll but necessary to maintain the independence of the regulator. After a suitable gap, a few individuals did move from Ofcom to regulated businesses. My observation, contra capture, is that industry was keenest to hire those that had been most tough and rigorous in their earlier interaction with the business, not the softies. That observation, admittedly anecdotal and lacking in any statistical significance, fits uneasily with the usual academic model of capture.

Tougher criteria still applied to the Board, which was the ultimate decision making body of the regulator, allowing no conflicts and no immediate past involvement with any of the major players. Our practice was in very marked contrast to that of the FSA, which had the chief executive of a major bank on its Board and serving as its Deputy Chairman. We did inch towards the FSA after a number of years by defining a narrow range of conflicts that were deemed manageable; but the contrast remained stark. And all such conflicts were transparently declared. This regime seemed to work: I do not recall an occasion when Ofcom's decisions were challenged on grounds of lack of independence.

In addition to the question of hiring, there is the question of the revolving party door. My predecessors at Oftel, the telecoms regulator that was absorbed into Ofcom, adopted markedly different styles. Don Cruickshank adopted a policy of monkish seclusion, shunning industry gatherings and hospitality. His predecessor, the founding Director General of Oftel, adopted a very different approach, always to be found at such gatherings, glass of wine in hand, open and accessible, listening carefully to the points that people wanted to make to him. I incline to his approach, believing in open competition in access. But it needs to be managed. One must recognize that the large companies have plentiful hospitality budgets and deliberately seek out those with less time and resource to entertain: the SMEs, the consumer groups, the relevant single-issue groups, even if it means drinking poor coffee and plonk. And all such interactions should be declared immediately and openly on the website so that any biases in interactions can be highlighted by the critics and corrected. And a lot of hospitality as well as gifts should be out of bounds: we turned down innumerable invitations to F1, Wimbledon, the Six Nations and the Proms, as well as offers of free phone handsets and the like.

15.5 Internal audit

The revolving door model of regulatory capture rests on a very narrow concept of regulatory decision making – that an individual (or possibly a team) can make a decision favourable to a company and then reap the rewards in terms of subsequent lucrative employment with that same company. That presupposes that decision making rests with the individual or group. But if that is the case, it represents a profound failure of organizational structure and culture within the regulatory body.

In building Ofcom, we aimed to ensure that throughout the organization there was a good mix of people from different backgrounds and culture: one that avoided the narrow cliques that could be susceptible to industry blandishments. Believing in the power of collective, rather than individual intelligence, we also worked hard to make sure that decisions did not rest with any one individual or group but were a matter of wider interrogation. That wider consideration involved people with different backgrounds and mindsets: commercial, legal, economic, technology. All major decisions came to the Board, usually in several stages to ensure that the Board grasped the issues and was not presented with a forced decision or fait accompli.

It was of equal importance to incorporate internal checks. One of the interesting aspects of the Ofcom architecture laid down by legislation was the Consumer Panel, an advisory board to represent the interests of consumers (interpreted in the communications context to include citizen interests). But Ofcom had a primary statutory duty to look after the interests of consumers, and this duty was placed on the Ofcom Board. So what was the role of the Consumer Panel?

In the early days of Ofcom, Ofcom staff turned to the Consumer Panel to provide the consumer perspective on issues. But this had two difficulties. First, how with the best will in the world can a panel of twelve people represent the consumer perspective in the multi-ethnic, multi-cultural and regionally diverse Britain of today? To understand consumer perspectives requires consumer research, carefully designed and implemented, especially when dealing with future technologies of which individuals have limited knowledge. But that research needed to be undertaken by Ofcom, not the Consumer Panel, in pursuit of its primary duty. This left the Consumer Panel on the sidelines.

So the Chairman of the Consumer Panel, Colette Bowe, and I re-thought the role of the Consumer Panel as a body undertaking a crucial bit of internal audit. Ofcom has the statutory duty to pursue consumer and citizen interests in the communications sphere. It should embed these interests at the heart of all that it does. But does it, in fact, do so? We defined the key role of the Consumer Panel as checking, through a form of audit, whether it was indeed doing so and suggested ways in which this highlighting of the consumer and citizen interest could be enhanced. With Colette's lead, the Consumer Panel developed a Consumer Toolkit, which specified an audit process that checked whether, and how far, Ofcom regulatory decision making had placed the consumer and citizen interest at the heart of its processes from the outset. This toolkit attracted wide interest, not least at a European level.

This audit function undoubtedly provided a crucial discipline and checks on Ofcom decision making and enhanced its effectiveness. It gave the Ofcom Consumer Panel a well-defined and crucial role. By insisting on the primacy of the consumer and citizen interest (laid down by statute) in decision making, it lessened the risk of capture, whether by industry or government. I believe it provided a crucial buttress to regulatory independence. It derives its force from the clear primary duty that Ofcom was given, which the FSA was not given. But for me this reinforces the need for clear marching orders for the regulator and the benefits of a clear overarching primary duty.

15.6 External audit and appeal

As well as internal scrutiny of regulatory decisions, there is an important need for external scrutiny. I see this in two parts.

First, there is the on-going scrutiny of regulatory decision by the media, parliamentary committees, and other bodies. Such scrutiny should be welcomed by the regulator, if it is confident and well founded. To facilitate it, the regulator should be as open as possible, setting out the basis of its thinking and making available its data and analysis. Openness allows the smaller, less well-funded interests (notably consumer interests and SMEs) to engage in the issues, possibly against the deep pockets of the incumbents.

Indeed, capture is easier to avoid when there is a vibrant debate among different interests. The regulator can then rise above the debate among the multiple players, rather than being the interlocutor between the players. It is crucial to provide the basis for an informed debate. My early observation of the communications sector is that, whereas the broadcast luvvies met regularly to debate and argue interminably, the telecoms anoraks did not. We moved early to create a similar forum, both national and international, for telecoms issues. We also undertook a major annual review of the communications market, both in the UK and internationally. I am told that it was invaluable to the many consultants in the sector. More importantly, it pre-empted the fact-free debate which all too often passes for policy analysis.

Parliamentary scrutiny, though necessarily imperfect, is also important, not least because an independent regulator created under statute is ultimately answerable to Parliament (not government). With its span across broadcasting and telecoms, Ofcom answered to two House of Commons Select Committees: the Industry Committee (as was) and the Culture, Media and Sport Committee. It was too easy to play one committee off against the other. To avoid this and enhance effective parliamentary oversight I encouraged the chairmen of the two Committees to come together for consideration of Ofcom. Personality clashes between the two chairmen meant that this did not happen immediately, but persistence paid off when the individuals changed.

So far I have considered forms of oversight and challenge that, though crucial, they are somewhat soft in character. Much harder oversight is provided by the legal system. Ofcom was created after the birth of the Competition Appeals Tribunal (CAT). Parliament in its wisdom (and I mean that) made almost all regulatory decisions by Ofcom appealable to the CAT. Appeal can be not just on process failures (as in normal judicial review) but also on substance. In the early stage of the CAT, Christopher Bellamy, the first head of the CAT, had an expansionist view of the CAT's role, and inclined to substitute the view of the CAT for the reasonably grounded view of the regulator. This was problematic, because with the best will in the world the CAT's considered view could not be as well grounded in fact and analysis as that of the regulator, not least because of lack of time and resource. But the CAT position subsequently shifted to the entirely defensible and appropriate position of substituting the CAT view for that of the regulator, when the CAT's judgement was that the regulator's position could reasonably be sustained.

A disadvantage of such external legal review is that it undoubtedly slows down the regulatory process: the liberalization of spectrum for 4G has been mired in the courts interminably and has not yet reached escape velocity, to the undoubted detriment of citizens and consumers. Given the fast-moving nature of technology in communications, this is a serious problem: justice delayed is justice denied. Nevertheless, external scrutiny of this kind serves a very crucial function that in my view on balance makes it desirable. It makes the regulator much more mindful of the need to ensure that its decisions comply with its statutory duties and are well reasoned and grounded in fact. Necessarily this also limits the possibility of regulatory capture, whether by the industry or short-term political considerations: such capture could be identified by the CAT and the consequent decisions struck down.

My understanding is that regulatory decisions in the financial sector are subject to the same possibility of wide-ranging legal challenges: decisions of individual regulatory effect are filtered internally at the Regulatory Decisions Committee, but if unresolved the individual or firm can refer the case to the Upper Tribunal, with the further possibility of appeal to the Court of Appeal (rarely taken). But I also hear it said that these cases are less grounded in hard analysis and evidence, and that the Upper Tribunal tends to sympathize with the regulator, the opposite of the Bellamy strategy. My argument is that stronger challenge would enhance the quality, and its basis in hard evidence, of regulatory decision making in the financial sector. This is a case of the benefits of tough love. But since such challenge would represent a seismic shock for the Bank of England, which will shortly assume major regulatory powers alongside its existing monetary powers, I am not waiting with baited breath.

15.7 Funding

The last two issues that I want to discuss are the most difficult. The first is the funding of the regulator. This has two aspects. First, what is the source of funding for the regulator? There are two obvious sources: government and industry. The second is who decides on the level of funding: the regulator, the government, the industry, or some other body?

It is evident that, when the source of funding decides on the level of funding, the risk of capture is high. If industry both funds and decides on the level of funding, there is a real risk of funding inadequate to the legitimate regulatory task. Direct funding of regulators by government is common only for limited regulatory functions, perhaps because of the obvious problem that competition for public funds will mean that the regulator is starved of resource and unable to do its job.

For statutory regulators, a mixed model is most usual: funding mainly from the industry, though perhaps with a small element from public funds to meet special public interest objectives, but with government oversight of the level of funding. This puts in place checks and balances around funding: industry cannot emasculate regulation through lack of funding, but excessive levies can be challenged through the political process. Yet, although it is the best option, it is very imperfect as we see from the US, where Congress approval for regulatory budgets is a well-established weapon to beat the regulator into submission.

15.8 Intellectual capture

Guarding against intellectual capture is the most difficult of all. As Stefano's paper makes clear, the theory of efficient markets reached well beyond financial markets and financial regulators into many parts of society, including government and academia: almost all of us were swept up by the heady brew, including me. Resisting such pervasive groupthink is very hard indeed, and the challenge is a much wider one than regulation. It would be foolish to imagine that any regulatory bulwarks will be strong enough to withstand the kind of collective and repeated madness so well documented in Charles Kindleberger's Manias, Panics and Crashes and so consistently forgotten.

Nonetheless, some defences should be put in place against less all-penetrating inundations, not least to limit groupthink in the regulator. Perhaps reflecting my own academic research background, Ofcom put in place a number of advisory boards to challenge and think the unthinkable. Perhaps the most influential was the Ofcom Spectrum Advisory Board, which helped us to think beyond the headlights in the management of that crucial national resource spectrum. We were also careful to participate in and occasionally promote conferences on a range of issues. My view was that we should regularly put ourselves in the position where our thinking could be exposed and challenged. A risk with this was that we could be condemned as something of a think tank, and indeed we were. But if a regulator does not think, and where needed out of the box, then it is not doing its job.

15.9 Conclusion

In this note I have argued that it is very hard to find a basis for legitimacy of independent regulation that does not have its root in either government or the industry, so that total independence of government and industry, and hence lack of capture, is not possible to achieve. Capture is therefore a matter of degree. But I have described a variety of mechanisms that minimize, though not eliminate, the degree of capture. I would make two concluding remarks about these mechanisms. First, they are difficult to incorporate in the types of models that economists and political scientists use to analyse the issue of capture. Second, they are rather culturally specific: what may work in the context of UK regulation and politics may not work in the rather different context of the US, let alone Asian and Middle Eastern polities. But in my view that does not diminish their importance in helping to ensure that regulation is independent and has legitimacy.

16.0 Lessons from the Regulation of the Energy Sector

John Mogg[1]

16.1 The risk of regulatory capture

As the Chairman of GEMA, the body supervising Ofgem's activities as gas and electricity regulator in Great Britain, I find that the topic of regulatory capture (or, rather, how to avoid it) is of central relevance in my day-to-day work. As the Chair of two European regulatory bodies – for the Board of Regulators of the Agency for the Cooperation of Energy Regulators (ACER) and the Council of European Energy Regulators (CEER) – I also have the opportunity to see how other energy regulatory bodies across the European Union (EU) are sensitive to the issue of regulatory capture, and how they are setting about tackling it.

As a general definition, I would describe regulatory capture as meaning that a regulator has become unduly or inappropriately

---

[1] In 2008, Lord Mogg was appointed for a second five year term as the non-executive Chairman of the Gas and Electricity Markets Authority which oversees the work of Ofgem (the energy regulator for Great Britain). In the same year he was also elected for a second term as Chairman of the Board of Regulators of the new European Agency for energy (ACER) and as President of the Council of European Energy Regulators (CEER). He is also Chair of the International Confederation of Energy Regulators (ICER). His other positions include the Chair of Governors of the University of Brighton, and special Adviser to the Office for Harmonization in the Internal Market in Alicante Spain. From 1990 to 2003, he worked in the EU Commission initially for three years as Deputy Director General, Industry and thereafter for nearly a decade as Director General, Internal Market and Financial Services. Before then Lord Mogg held a number of positions in the UK Civil Service including the Deputy Head, European Secretariat in the Cabinet Office; and Principal Private Secretary to three Secretaries of State at the former DTI. He held other senior posts in the Department of Trade and Industry having spent 8 years in the private sector after graduating from the University of Birmingham. Lord Mogg was knighted in 2003 and was awarded a peerage in 2008.

influenced by an interest group. When we speak about regulatory capture, we normally see the main risk as coming from those commercial enterprises which are regulated. In the world of gas and electricity, this includes the network companies, gas shippers, power generators, suppliers and others. The scope of regulatory capture is, in my view, wider than that. I would include governments and, perhaps controversially, consumers – notably large consumers. I will explain later why I see risks of regulatory capture, paradoxically, from the very group that regulators are duty-bound to protect.

16.2 The importance of independent energy regulation

A central requirement of any regulatory authority is that it is independent. Certainly, it must be independent of commercial interests, and it should also be independent of political influence – at arm's-length from government or a similar central authority (including any relevant regional arrangements).

The risk of regulatory capture comes from two main sources. First, in our day-to-day business of regulation, there is a structural source: the huge information imbalance between the regulator and the regulated companies. Energy regulators set the rules on how competitive businesses can access and use the monopoly networks and also control the costs and revenues of the monopoly network companies. The functions of individual national regulatory authorities across the EU may vary somewhat, depending mainly on the stage of development which Member States' energy markets have reached. But there remain core activities for regulators. Secondly, regulatory capture may also arise as a result of human failings where individual members of staff fail to adhere to the professional standards expected. Such failures cannot simply be categorized as fraudulent acts; they may be legal but wholly inappropriate.

To undertake their duties, regulators need detailed information on costs, expenditure, contracts, and operational matters which relate to the networks. We need to understand about future innovation, accounting policies and corporate structures. In more recent years we have increasingly sought to understand how companies are managing the new changes they face in the market – for example, policies which are aimed at tackling climate change (such as carbon pricing) or enhancing security of supply for energy (such as through systems of capacity payments).

Thus, information is the "fuel" that regulators need in order to manage and regulate in this complex environment. Yet the holders of such information are the regulated companies themselves. Moreover, the companies have expertise and the ability to develop and present a powerful case in favour of their preferred outcome. How can we ensure, against this background of information asymmetry, that the decisions we take are truly independent and balances the overall interests of society? How do we ensure that the risk of intellectual capture has been avoided?

A further concern is that the sheer number of people within the regulatory community who are engaged in jobs requiring close working relationships with regulated companies is very large. Regulators must work closely with the industry to gather information and to understand industry practices. The individuals responsible for regulating must form professional relationships with individuals from the regulated companies. How can we be sure that each individual is conducting himself or herself with the level of professional probity and detachment we expect? How can we ensure that professional engagement does not turn into friendship, or misguided "favours", or perhaps worse?

I mentioned that I consider consumers to be a potential source of risk in relation to regulatory capture. The energy market has quite different types of consumer. Domestic consumers are among the millions of energy customers who pay their bills, and maybe, sometimes, try to switch suppliers to get a better deal. (Incidentally, our information to date suggests that some half of all households have not switched and declare that they will not. The huge number and complexity of tariffs is no incentive and we are tackling this head-on in our current retail market review.) Customers do not engage in the debate on energy market design, on tariff structures or price controls. However, decisions on these matters, notably tariffs and payment methods, can make a fundamental difference to energy costs and are of high impact for the growing number of households deemed to be in fuel poverty. Such issues are really challenging even for those well-informed, representative organizations who are championing these consumers' interests.

On the other hand, large energy consumers – for example in our industrial base - are very well organized. They can be quick to engage and resist proposals or decisions which may adversely impact their interests. Regulators therefore have to be aware that certain decisions can impact differentially on consumer groups – and even on consumers in different geographic regions. Decisions may have to be taken against a background of both information asymmetry and where intellectual capture by those with the best information may present a real risk.

It may seem strange to those whose focus is on the different world of financial regulation (although, set against recent events, perhaps less strange than formerly!) that governments themselves should be considered a risk. One of the major advantages of independent energy regulation is that it provides a stable regulatory climate for investors making long-term (sometimes forty-year) investments in energy infrastructure – generation and the so-called "pipes and wires" of transmission and distribution systems Independence from government means that regulatory decisions are taken against known and established economic criteria and thus are relatively predictable. This predictability – so inevitably different from short-term political demands – has resulted in lower investment risk, lower borrowing costs and lower relative prices to consumers.

However, governments have a growing interest in energy regulation because energy is central to the achievement of political goals relating to sustainable development, the response to climate change, security of energy supply – and perhaps also aspects of economic growth and development. In these circumstances national regulatory authorities can become the delivery arm of government and be drawn into the business of achieving policy goals – putting at risk their prime responsibility for protecting consumers. This intellectual (and, in fairness, political) capture could, in the extreme case, undermine the role of independent regulation. This potential operational erosion of independence must be set against the underlying intention of government that regulators should be independent from undue government influence – something all of the 27 EU member states agreed to in the clear legal obligations set out in the EU's third energy package.

Therefore, what is increasingly needed is a balanced judgement from government, as it sets its broader policy goals, about the context and constraints of independent regulatory arrangements and of the need to protect the interests of consumers, present and future.

16.3 Tackling the risk of regulatory capture

This short description of the sources of risk of regulatory capture and the scope of areas upon which it can impact demonstrates, I hope, that regulatory capture is not only a deceivingly complex topic, but is also a very real issue for regulators. Regulatory capture puts at risk the central concept of independent regulation, and independent regulation is the central foundation upon which our system of economic regulation is built. We must therefore be constantly vigilant in countering this risk. We must also devise systems and processes which give confidence that regulatory capture can be avoided, and should it occur can be detected and dealt with.

But even that is not enough. The term "independent" is as much about perception and confidence as it is reality. Investors in energy have a perception of whether any particular regulator is independent and if that perception is negative, then the consequences can be very serious for energy consumers. A key reason for this is that energy infrastructure is highly capital intensive and where investment needs are commonly expressed in multiple billions, not millions of pounds. Lack of confidence in the regulatory regime will increase investor risk and will result in higher costs of capital. This translates directly into higher prices for consumers. Lack of confidence in the regulatory framework will also undermine the faith of participants in a competitive energy market and the scope for fair playing fields. In turn, this will undermine the operation of markets themselves. The stakes are very high.

I should be clear that it is not possible to eliminate completely all risks of regulatory capture. Consequently, the processes that regulators adopt are aimed at understanding risks fully and managing them as far as possible, reducing the risks that it may occur. I note here, and in general terms, the ways in which energy regulators seek to reduce these risks and specifically about the way in which my regulatory authority – OFGEM – does so.

Foremost among the mechanisms used to address the risk of regulatory capture – and to demonstrate that it is not occurring – is transparency. Transparency, carried forward through substantial consultation with stakeholders in the decision making of energy regulators, is also central. Used properly, it can effectively illustrate how individual decisions have been reached and how the views of stakeholders have been taken into account in reaching those proposals and final conclusions. Consultation is, most obviously, a tool to ensure that regulators get their proposals right. But it is also a central mechanism to ensure that regulators have not succumbed to the undue influence of any one (generally powerful) lobby. Well-designed consultation mechanisms require regulators to stand before the all-seeing court of transparency. Equally, the rights of stakeholders to mount legal challenges (and in the UK that can mean appeal to the courts, including judicial review, and to the Competition Commission) mean that undue and inappropriate influence is open to detection.

The specific mechanisms for achieving that vary, but the Council of European Energy Regulators and OFGEM use similar approaches. For any significant decision, a consultation of stakeholders is undertaken and reasonable times for responses are allowed (up to twelve weeks). This is followed by a "conclusions" document which contains the decision, setting out the evidence to support it. A further document is also prepared which summarizes individual responses by stakeholders (unless the respondent has indicated that their views need to be treated as confidential); and for each response the regulator provides a commentary on how the response has been treated in respect of the conclusions reached. This process may seem relatively heavyweight in terms of regulatory resources. However, it does reflect the wishes of stakeholders. It also provides a clear linkage between responses received to a consultation and the final decision. In the context of regulatory capture, it limits the scope for one or a group of stakeholders to have disproportionate influence over the regulator and the decisions taken.

In our complex work of setting price controls for the regulated industries – now for forward periods of eight years – we engage very fully with the industry, challenging them in individual meetings, and scrutinizing their business plans. The range of factors embraces just about every aspect of their approach to investment, operations, financing through debt and equity and their costs, network repairs, safety, reducing the environmental inputs of generation and transmission, system losses, and more. Incentives are provided, accordingly. And there are measures also for the extent to which regulated companies seek to engage effectively with their customers. In these ways, we aim to redress asymmetry of information, reduce the risks of "gaming", and so reach the best conclusions to protect consumers' interests.

As the Chair of three regulatory bodies, I find that I am classed as a "Senior Regulator". As such it is my misfortune to be called by political and other public bodies to account for the operation of the regulatory bodies I chair. This provides an opportunity to account for how important decisions have been reached, and importantly, for my authorities to demonstrate that their decisions have been reached on firm policy grounds rather than favouritism. This form of senior level accountability is not, in my view, well suited to rooting out the source of regulatory capture when it is buried deep within the staff of a regulatory body where many policies are first formed. However, I believe it can be quite an effective mechanism for detecting intellectual capture where one policy approach has been adopted over another and where the reasons may not be entirely in line with the underlying primary duty of the regulator. I have yet to experience this personally, but I can see the danger. The mere fact that a process of political and public challenge exists does help to reduce the risk of intellectual capture; all the senior staff in a regulator will know very well that they will have to justify the policy under scrutiny.

One of the challenges we must face is to try to ensure that the staff of a regulatory authority are wholly professional in their dealings with the regulated industry. They must avoid the risk that the personal relationships they build might interfere with the professional decisions they must take. Many regulatory bodies, including OFGEM, have rules to which their staff must adhere. Unfortunately, these rules sound like a charter for the avoidance of enjoyment. We see them as an essential requirement if regulators are to reduce the actual risk of regulatory capture as well as the perception of it. The rules amount to a relatively long list. The more important ones include such things as: declaring to their employer any hospitality, such as lunches, offered by a regulated company, and refusing if it is other than modest; refusing all gifts; restrictions on the holding shares in regulated companies, requirements which also extend to immediate family members; and declaring any other relevant interests.

Breaches of these rules do have direct consequences for the employee, from a reprimand to dismissal. The experience in OFGEM is that the reasons for the existence of these rules is profoundly understood by staff and is supported by them. There is a culture of "good regulatory practice", which results in staff supporting one another to ensure that the risk of regulatory capture is avoided to the greatest degree. In addition, there is a whistle-blowing policy. Collectively, we believe these measures to be effective, with incidents of departure a very rare thing indeed.

In many ways, the challenge of avoiding regulatory capture in relation to consumer groups is greater than that with industry. Fundamentally regulators want to listen to and help consumers. Large consumers are well organized and well informed. They argue their case coherently and persuasively. In contrast, small consumers are not well organized, are (inevitably) ill-informed of the complexities of energy markets, and have no strong organized voice. As a consequence, the regulator is placed in the position of making decisions in the interests of consumers where the case is presented more effectively by one group of consumers than another.

To avoid the risk of intellectual capture it is important that the voice of small consumers is heard. OFGEM operates against a background of a government policy aimed at empowering consumers. There is an organized consumer body – Consumer Focus – which is the national consumer advocate. To enhance further the ability of consumers to present their views, OFGEM has established its own mechanism called Consumer First. The Consumer First initiative has established a series of consumer panels, each of which is focused on a specific topic. The panels are constituted of a cross section of typical small consumers. In these ways, OFGEM can demonstrate that it is able to balance the views of all consumers. This is an on-going process and we continue to examine ways in which small consumers can be included in the policymaking process in a more direct ways.

In the wider European context, we are seeing major changes to the development of wholesale markets as a result of EU legislation. Well-organized groups from the industry and large consumers are heavily involved in the debate. Through CEER, we are developing policies aimed at building the capability of small consumers to participate effectively in these complex discussions. Part of the approach is likely to be based on enhancing the accessibility of information to consumer organizations, and part may be aimed at enhancing the capability of the organizations themselves. The outcome, we hope, is that the consumer view, on which regulatory decisions will be based, will be truly representative of all consumers.

The last area of potential regulatory capture is the most difficult of all – and in today's policy environment, perhaps the one where the risks are greatest. Governments of many persuasions have adopted the philosophy of independent energy regulation as the model which can best deliver efficient investment and competitive markets with the aim of improving first the UK's and subsequently Europe's economic competitiveness. This model has been very successful and has since been adopted in many countries around the world.

However, in the intervening years, energy policy has evolved and the current focus is on tackling climate change and ensuring security of energy supply. Energy regulation has come to be seen by policymakers as a tool for delivering government policies on climate and security, with regulators as facilitators (or, conversely, can sometimes be seen as obstacles!). Of course, elected governments are quite correctly determining energy policy objectives in these areas. Where the delivery of these policies works with the grain of the market, then these policies can work alongside independent regulation. Increasingly, we see governments wanting to determine outcomes rather than relying on markets to deliver. Where the outcome of the market is determined centrally by government rather than by the market, there is a potential for conflict with independent regulation. Even in these circumstances, clarity and a sound understanding of the respective roles (and constraints) of government and the regulator can help to ensure that regulatory duties can operate in an independent way within their proper scope. However – and here is the risk – governments may use regulators as mechanisms to deliver deterministic energy policy goals. That risks mixing independent regulation, where decisions are based on defined duties and clear economic principles, with a requirement to distort the market to achieve predetermined policy objectives. In these circumstances, the advantages of independent regulation are lost.

17.0 Regulatory Capture in Finance: Lessons from the Automobile Industry

Tony Porter[1]

Like finance, the automobile industry is highly globalized, with a relatively small number of powerful multinational firms playing a leading role. Also like finance, the automobile industry has played a key part in some countries' economic growth, and has a systemic significance that extends far beyond its own boundaries, with implications for the geopolitics of oil, climate change, and the restructuring of local and national infrastructures. The glamour, speed, and mobility associated with each industry have at different times amplified their prestige. It is therefore useful to consider whether the automobile industry can provide insights into the problem of regulatory capture that are relevant for the financial industry.

The automobile industry involves two main regulatory concerns. The first is vehicle safety. This is not a trivial concern. Every year vehicle crashes kill more than a million people and injure as many as 50 million, rivalling casualties from war (WHO 2004). The second is

---

[1] Tony Porter is Professor in the Department of Political Science at McMaster University. Dr. Porter conducts research on business regulation and global governance, including especially financial regulation, private and hybrid public/private rulemaking, the organizational effects in governance of technologies, and safety and environmental standards in the automobile industry. He is the author of *Globalization and Finance* (Polity Press, 2005), *Technology, Governance and Political Conflict in International Industries*, (Routledge, 2002), and *States, Markets, and Regimes in Global Finance*, (Macmillan, 1993), and coeditor, with Karsten Ronit, of *The Challenges of Global Business Authority: Democratic Renewal, Stalemate or Decay?* (SUNY Press, 2010), and with A. Claire Cutler and Virginia Haufler, of *Private Authority in International Affairs*, (SUNY Press, 1999).

sustainability. Cars and trucks are estimated to contribute to between 15 and 20 percent of worldwide CO_2 emissions[2]. If all countries moved towards the per capita vehicle ownership rates of the United States, the impact on the climate and the quality of urban life would be disastrous. Moreover, it is almost certain that affordable oil will be exhausted over the next few decades, and the development of alternatives to the internal combustion engine involves massive changes (such as fueling infrastructures for alternative fuels) that are impossible for individual firms to manage. These sustainability challenges pose an existential systemic risk for the industry.

Despite the industry's initial negligence and aggressive opposition to regulation, there have been dramatic improvements in vehicle safety since the 1960s, when vehicle safety regulation began to be taken seriously by governments. For example, between 1975 and 1998 per capita road traffic fatalities dropped by 27% in the US, 63% in Canada, and 43% in France[3]. These safety improvements are not evenly distributed across countries. Road fatality rates in Europe are 11 per 100,000 people as compared to 28 in Africa[4]. In part this is due to shortcomings in the quality of regulation in developing countries, and in part to a greater reliance on cheaper products and poorer infrastructure because of lower living standards. Despite these shortcomings, the regulatory successes are impressive, and it is useful to see if these offer lessons for finance.

What accounts for the successes in vehicle safety regulation? One factor is the entrepreneurial energy of one critic, Ralph Nader, whose 1965 book Unsafe at Any Speed made the problem visible and helped create a consumer movement concerned with safety issues. US legislation enacted in 1966 resulted in a regulatory agency, the National Highway Traffic Safety Administration, and the consumer movement continued to actively lobby for improved vehicle safety, accumulating knowledge and experience as it did so. Other NGOs focused on complementary campaigns, such as the highly successful

[2] International Energy Agency (IEA) (2009). *Transport, Energy and CO2: Moving Toward Sustainability*. Paris: IEA/OECD pp. 29
[3] World Health Organization (WHO) (2004). *World Report on Road Traffic Injury Prevention* Geneva: WHO, p. 37.
[4] Ibid p.34.

Mothers against Drunk Driving efforts to have drunk driving laws enacted[5].

Today automobile crashes, which are tangible, dramatic, and involve the destruction of human bodies, seem easier to bring to the public's attention than the more intangible damage that financial regulation seeks to mitigate. However, before 1966 road "accidents" were not widely recognized as a problem requiring regulatory action. Crashes were attributed to the "nut behind the wheel" and were widely dispersed in their effects. The engineering involved in vehicle safety was obscure, and auto makers successfully claimed that safety innovation was not feasible[6]. Crashes only came to be linked to industry irresponsibility through a political process in which consumer groups and the NHTSA played a key role. A mark of the success of the consumer movement launched by Nader was the appointment of his long-time colleague, Joan Claybrook, as Administrator of the NHTSA from 1977-81. Subsequently, as president of Public Citizen, Claybrook brought a wealth of knowledge to enhance the technical knowledge and lobbying capacities of that NGO[7]. This is an interesting case of a revolving door between a regulator and a public interest group critical of the regulated industry.

Two other countervailing forces to industry are important in US vehicle safety regulation. The first is the insurance industry, which is well resourced and participates very actively in advocacy and research on vehicle safety issues. A second is the legal industry. US vehicle safety regulation relies to a significant degree on manufacturers' self-certification, backed up by requirements to recall defective products and the threat of private litigation. US "adversarial legalism" is extraordinarily costly, inconsistent, and often harshly punitive[8], but it

---

[5] Ibid p. 18.

[6] Claybrook, Joan and David Bollier (1985). 'The Hidden Benefits of Regulation: Disclosing the Auto Safety Payoff', *Yale Journal on Regulation* 3, Fall, pp. 87-131.

[7] See Claybrook, Joan (2000). 'Statement of Joan Claybrook on Firestone Tire Defect and Ford Explorer Rollovers', United States Senate Committee on Commerce, Science and Transportation, Washington DC, September 12, at http://www.citizen.org/autosafety/article_redirect.cfm?ID=5414, accessed March 27, 2012.

[8] Kagan, Robert A. (2003). *Adversarial Legalism: The American Way of Law.* Cambridge: Harvard University Press.

can create serious risks for non-compliance with safety standards. Moreover, class actions can generate sizable revenues for the law firms, creating well-financed allies for the consumer groups that expose safety problems. Therefore US consumer groups, lawyers, and the insurance industry complement one another in countervailing the influence of the industry over regulators.

Another important feature of vehicle safety regulation is the quite different form it takes in countries outside North America[9]. The main global regulatory body is the World Forum for Harmonization of Vehicle Regulations, also known as WP.29, located at the UN Economic Commission on Europe. WP.29 was created in 1952 in response to European concerns about harmonizing headlamp and other safety standards for vehicles crossing European borders. The European form of regulation is a "type approval" model, in contrast to the US "self-certification" model, and relies much more heavily on testing of products by government or third party laboratories before products are released on the market. Until 1998 WP.29 primarily reflected European concerns, codified in a 1958 Agreement, although the US, Canada, Japan and Australia also attended meetings.

In 1998 WP.29 adopted the World Forum for Harmonization of Vehicle Regulations name, and, with strong US support, created a new Agreement that aimed to produce "Global Technical Regulations" that would be incorporated into national regulations around the world, including in North America, but progress on these GTRs has been extremely slow. With the exception of partial acceptance of the US model of regulation by a few countries (South Korea, Australia, Brunei, and Singapore) the rest of the world has moved towards the European style type approval system. The public/private Japan Automobile Standards Internationalization Center (JASIC), established in 1987, has played a leadership role in Asia in promoting convergence with World Forum regulations, especially with the 1958 Agreement[10]. Europe and

---

[9] Porter, Tony (2011). 'Transnational Policy Paradigm Change and Conflict in the Harmonization of Vehicle Safety and Accounting Standards', in Grace Skogstad, ed., *Internationalization and Policy Paradigm Change*, Toronto: University of Toronto Press: 64-90.

[10] Ibid.

Japan therefore are a very strong countervailing force to any attempt US firms and regulators might make to globalize US regulations. The creation of government and third party laboratories creates expert capacities and constituencies with a commitment to vehicle safety that have some independence from the industry. The type approval model of regulation is a better match with countries that lack US adversarial legalism and strong consumer groups.

In the automobile industry, regulations focused on sustainability have a much more mixed record than those on vehicle safety[11]. Beginning in the 1970s, stimulated by the 1973 oil price shock, a primary concern has been fuel efficiency, to reduce reliance on oil imports. Over time the impact of CO_2 emissions on climate change has also become a concern. The main US regulatory instrument, dating back to 1975, has been the Corporate Average Fuel Economy (CAFE) standard governing a manufacturer's sales-weighted model years. When introduced, the goal of the CAFE standards was to double new car fuel economy to 27.5 miles per gallon by 1985. The standards for light trucks, which came to include sport utility vehicles (SUVs), were set much lower. In its first decade the CAFE standards enjoyed some success: the average fuel economy of passenger cars and of light trucks each improved more than 60%[12]. Unfortunately the average of both together declined significantly over time because of a massive shift of car buyers from passenger cars to SUVs and other light trucks[13]. After a hiatus during the Bush administration, the Obama administration has moved to aggressively increase CAFE standards, aiming for 35.5 miles per gallon by 2016 and 54.5 miles per gallon for cars and light trucks by 2025[14].

---

[11] Porter, Tony (2012). 'The Automobile and Climate Change: The Embeddedness of Private Regulation', in Karsten Ronit, ed. *Private Voluntary Programs in Global Climate Policy: Pitfalls and Potentials*, Tokyo: UNU Press: 179-281.

[12] Onoda, Takao (2008). 'Review of International Policies for Vehicle Fuel Efficiency.' IEA Information Paper in Support of G8 Plan of Action. Paris: IEA pp.28

[13] An, Feng, and Amanda Sauer (2004). *Comparison of Passenger Vehicle Fuel Economy and Greenhouse Gas Emission Standards around the World*. Pew Center on Global Climate Change. Arlington VA pp.9

[14] White House (2011). 'President Obama Announces Historic 54.5 mpg Fuel Efficiency Standard', Office of the Press Secretary, July 29, available at http://www.whitehouse.gov/the-press-office/2011/07/29/president-obama-announces-historic-545-mpg-fuel-efficiency-standard, accessed March 27, 2012.

This shift was facilitated by the weakening of the industry during the 2007-08 crisis, the smaller part that the oil industry plays in the Democratic Party as compared to the Republican Party, the greater enthusiasm of the former for environmental issues, and the geo-strategic case for reducing dependence on Middle East oil supplies. A lesson from this experience is that the strengthening of regulations is more likely during periods where industry opposition is weakened and the regulation can be linked to geo-strategic or other issues that extend beyond the industry.

There are lessons from other jurisdictions as well. In the 1990s the EU experimented with a voluntary agreement on CO_2 reductions with industry, and while average emissions from new cars had dropped by 12.4 percent between 1995 and 2004, it had become clear by 2007 that the EU was not going to meet its climate change objectives with voluntary agreements, in part because of the industry's difficulty in devising a coordinated plan, and they were replaced by mandatory targets[15]. Mikler has convincingly demonstrated the superior fuel efficiency and emissions performance of the Japanese "Top Runner" system of "co-regulation", as compared to the more simple rigid system in the US and EU[16]. In the less adversarial Japanese system the industry is very actively involved in devising solutions, as best industry practices become the regulatory standard[17]. However, this success relies on distinctive characteristics of Japanese-style capitalism and an active role for the state that may not be easily transferable elsewhere.

Governments have also put a significant amount of effort into trying to shift the automobile industry entirely beyond its dependence on oil, by developing alternatives such as biofuels, hydrogen or electric cars.

[15] Porter, Tony (2012). 'The Automobile and Climate Change: The Embeddedness of Private Regulation', in Karsten Ronit, ed. *Private Voluntary Programs in Global Climate Policy: Pitfalls and Potentials*, Tokyo: UNU Press: 179-281.

[16] Mikler, John (2009). *Greening the Car Industry: Varieties of Capitalism and Climate Change*. Cheltenham, UK; Northampton, MA: Edward Elgar; Mikler, John (2007). 'Varieties of Capitalism and the Auto Industry's Environmental Initiatives: National Institutional Explanations for Firms' Motivations.' *Business and Politics*, 9(1): Article 4.

[17] Mikler, John (2005) 'Institutional reasons for the effect of environmental regulations: Passenger car CO2 emissions in the European Union, United States and Japan', *Global Society*, 19:4, October, 409 — 444.

Biofuels were initially attractive because they were also beneficial to the agricultural industry, a powerful political constituency, and because they could be phased in without huge changes in engine or fueling technologies; but, enthusiasm has been reduced as negative effects of biofuels on ecosystems and food prices have been recognized. Progress on other fuels has been slow. There is strong recognition from the industry that sustainability issues will need to be addressed by very significant technological transformations if the industry is to survive over the long run, but also that the industry by itself is incapable of making this transition. For instance, a major industry report noted that 'we believe it is essential to our companies' long-term interests that mobility becomes sustainable' but also that if greenhouse gases are to be significantly reduced 'incentives will probably be needed, and only governments have the resources and authority to create them'[18]. This confirms the difficulty of regulating long-range systemic risk even when it threatens the existence of the regulated industry.

What lessons can be drawn from the regulation of the automobile industry for the regulation of financial industries? First, consistent with Pagliari's analysis of the literature (this publication), avoidance of regulatory capture is greatly facilitated by actively countervailing non-governmental organizations. This involved graphically linking the damage from unregulated conduct to the regulated firms. Following the 2007 financial crisis there has been some strengthening of NGO efforts to monitor and criticize the financial industry and its regulators; this publication is one example. Others examples include the FSB Watch project, the European Commission's creation of a Financial Services User Group[19], and the European Parliament's sponsoring of Finance Watch as a counterweight to industry lobbying. In the US, Americans for Financial Reform, a coalition of over 250 NGOs, has

---

[18] Sustainable Mobility Project (2004). *Mobility 2030: Meeting the Challenges to Sustainability*. Geneva: World Business Council for Sustainable Development pp. 12, 105
[19] European Union (2010). 'Commission Decision of 20 July 2010 setting up a Financial Services User Group', *Official Journal of the European Union* C 199/12, 21.7.210, http://eur-lex.europa.eu/LexUriServ/LexUriServ.do?uri=OJ:C:2010:199:0012:0014: EN:PDF, accessed March 18, 2012.

been very actively monitoring and lobbying on reform developments since 2009, and Occupy the SEC produced an impressively detailed 325-page formal response to the proposed rulemaking on the Volcker Rule. However, overall these NGOs are too dispersed and small to act as an effective counterweight to industry. Despite the graphic quality of some regulatory failures, such as home foreclosures, their links to industry conduct have not been drawn as strongly in finance as in vehicle safety. It would be useful for official bodies to encourage interactions with finance-oriented NGOs to become more like the technical, sustained interactions of Public Citizen with the NHTSA rulemaking process.

Second, it is important to integrate into the rulemaking process, where possible, industries or firms that have an interest in preventing capture of regulators by the financial industry. Greater exposure of negligent financial firms to private litigation can create incentives for regulatory compliance, but also create a constituency of law firms to act as a counterweight to the regulated industry. Providing whistleblowers generous rewards for uncovering regulatory violations, such as the 10-30% share of monetary sanctions over $1 million that Dodd-Frank rulemaking has mandated[20], and extending this to outside regulatory "bounty hunters", could create a set of firms with a strong interest in effective regulation[21]. Expansion of contingent capital – bonds that convert into equity in time of crisis – may create a constituency for strong prudential regulation. In general, it is useful when designing regulatory mechanisms to strengthen the role of firms that will act as a counterweight to the influence of the regulated industry over regulators, as has happened with insurance and law firms in vehicle safety regulation.

A third lesson is the importance of considering the benefits of some level of regional diversity, while taking into account the interaction of

---

[20] Securities and Exchange Commission (SEC) (2011). 'Implementation of the Whistleblower Provisions of Section 21F of the Securities Exchange Act of 1934' Final Rule, available at http://www.sec.gov/rules/final/2011/34-64545.pdf, accessed March 28, 2012.
[21] Braithwaite, John (2008). *Regulatory Capitalism: How it works, ideas for making it work better*. Cheltenham: Edward Elgar.

regulation with the varying cultures and institutions in different jurisdictions. In finance there has been a tendency for US or UK regulatory practices favourable to the industry to be exported to all other jurisdictions. In contrast, in vehicle safety two different models have coexisted, with most countries following the European type approval model, relying less on industry self-certification. For fuel efficiency regulation the Japanese top runner system outperforms the US and European approaches. Permitting such variation can stimulate the search for best practices and reveal deficient regulatory mechanisms, as suggested by research on experimentalist governance (Sabel and Zeitlin 2010), as well as creating countervailing political pressures to a dominant model. This type of experimentation is likely to occur where global agreement on a single harmonized standard is less important, as with European efforts to strengthen regulation of credit rating agencies.

A fourth lesson is that complex systemic risk regulation is more prone than product regulation to being undermined by private interests, even if there is a strong incentive for the industry as a whole to address such risks. This is evident in the difficulty for the industry and governments to shift vehicles away from reliance on increasingly uncertain oil supplies. The biofuels example shows that if a powerful industry can be recruited and if changes require only incremental adjustments, some forward movement can occur, but overall neither the automobile industry nor governments have yet been able to bring about the scale of change that is most likely needed to avoid longer-range catastrophic systemic problems.

Bibliography

Acemoglu D. & S. Johnson (2012), 'Who captured the Fed?', Economix Blog, The New York Times, March 29, 2012, available at http://economix.blogs.nytimes.com/2012/03/29/who-captured-the-fed/.

Adams, R. B. (2011), 'Who Directs the Fed?', ECGI - Finance Working Paper, No. 293/2011.

Admati, A. R., P. M. DeMarzo, M.F. Hellwig, and P. Pfleiderer (2010), 'Fallacies, Irrelevant Facts, and Myths in the Discussion of Capital Regulation: Why Bank Equity is Not Expensive', Rock Center for Corporate Governance at Stanford University Working Paper No. 86, Stanford Graduate School of Business Research Paper No. 2065, August.

AFME (2010), Prevention and Cure: Securing Financial Stability After the Crisis, Association for Financial Markets in Europe, September, p. 35.

AIMA (2009), European Directive Could Cost European Pension Industry 25 Billion Euros Annually, Alternative Investment Management Association, London, 4 August.

Americans for Financial Reform (2010), Wall Street Influence, By the Numbers', 14 May 2010, available at http://ourfinancialsecurity.org/.

An, F., and A. Sauer (2004), Comparison of Passenger Vehicle Fuel Economy and Greenhouse Gas Emission Standards around the World, Pew Center on Global Climate Change, Arlington VA.

Arculus D. (2005), Chairman of the Better Regulation Task Force, Speech to staff of the Financial Services Authority, 29 June, available at: http://www.fsa.gov.uk/library/communication/speeches/2005/0705_sda.shtml.

Ayres, I. and J. Braithwaite (1991), 'Tripartism: Regulatory Capture and Empowerment', Law & Social Inquiry, 16(3): 435-96.

Ayres, I. and J. Braithwaite (1992), Responsive Regulation: Transcending the Deregulation Debate, New York, Oxford University Press.

Baker, A. (2010), 'Restraining regulatory capture? Anglo- America, crisis politics and trajectories of change in global financial governance', International Affairs, 86(3): 647-663.

Balleisen, E. (2011), 'The Global Financial Crisis and Responsive Regulation: Some Avenues for Historical Inquiry', University of British Columbia Law Review, 44(3): 557-8

Barker, A. and B. Masters (2012), 'Paris and Berlin seek to dilute bank rules', Financial Times, 22 January.

Barkow, R. E. (2010), 'Insulating Agencies: Avoiding Capture Through Institutional Design', Texas Law Review 89(1): 15-79.

Barth, J. R., G. Caprio Jr., R. Levine (2012), Guardians of Finance. Making Regulators Work for Us, Cambridge, MA, MIT Press.

BCBS (2004), Basel II: International Convergence of Capital Measurement and Capital Standards: a Revised Framework, Basel Committee on Banking Supervision, Bank for International Settlements, June .

BCBS (2011), Core Principles for Effective Banking Supervision, Consultative Document, Basel Committee on Banking Supervision, Bank for International Settlements, December.

Baxter, L. G. (2011), 'Capture in Financial Regulation: Can We Channel It Toward the Common Good?', Cornell Journal of Law and Public Policy, 21(1): 175-200.

Baxter, L.G. (2012), 'Betting Big: Value, Caution and Accountability in an Era of Large Banks and Complex Finance', Review of Banking and Finance Law, 31 (Fall, forthcoming).

Bebchuk, L. A. and H. Spamann (2010), 'Regulating Bankers' Pay.' Georgetown Law Journal, 98(2): 247-287.

Beck U. (2006), 'Living in the world risk society', Economy and Society, 35(3), August.

Beck U. (2008), 'This free-market farce proves the state is crucial', Guardian blog 'Comment is free', April.

Becker G. (2011), Capture' of Regulators by Fannie Mae and Freddie Mac, available at http://www.becker-posner-blog.com/2011/06/capture-of-regulators-by-fannie-mae-and-freddie-mac-becker.html (accessed July 21, 2011).

Berkshire Hathaway (2002), Annual Report, available at: http://www.berkshire hathaway.com/2002ar/2002ar.pdf.

Besley, T. (2006), 'Political Selection', World Ethics Forum Conference Proceedings. Edited by Charles Sampford and Carmel Connors, The Joint Conference of The International Institute for Public Ethics (IIPE) and The World Bank, Leadership, Ethics and Integrity in Public Life, 9–11 April 2006, Keble College, University of Oxford, pp.7-24.

Blair T. (2005), Risk and the State, Speech at The Institute for Public Policy Research, 26 May.

Boehm, F. (2007). 'Regulatory Capture Revisited – Lessons from Economics of Corruption', Research Center in Political Economy (CIEP, Universidad Externado de Colombia), Working Paper, July .

Braithwaite, J. (2008), Regulatory Capitalism: How it works, ideas for making it work better, Cheltenham, Edward Elgar.

Brandeis, L. (1913), 'What Publicity Can Do', Harper's Weekly, Dec. 20, 1913, available at: http://www.law.louisville.edu/library/collections/brandeis/node/196.

Briault C. (1999), 'The rationale for a single national financial services regulator', Financial Services Authority Occasional Paper 2, May.

Briault C. (2010), 'Risk Society and Financial Risk', in B. Hutter (ed.), Anticipating Risks and Organising Risk Regulation, Cambridge University Press, August.

Briault C. (2012), 'Incentive Structures', Paper presented at the ICFR/SUERF Conference on Future Risks and Fragilities for Financial Stability, London, 8 March.

Buigues, P. A., and P. Rey, eds (2004), The economics of Anti-Trust & Regulation in Telecommunications, Cheltenham, Edward Elgar.

Buiter, W. (2009), 'Central Banks and Financial Crises', Maintaining Stability in a Changing Financial System, Federal Reserve Bank of Kansas City.

Carpenter, D. (2004), 'Protection without Capture: Product Approval by a politically Responsive, Learning Regulator', American Political Science Review, 98(4): 613-31.

Carpenter D. & D. Moss (Forthcoming), Preventing Regulatory Capture: Special Interest Influence, and How to Limit It, Cambridge, Cambridge University Press.

Centre for the Study of Financial Innovation (2012), Banking Banana Skins 2012, February.

Che, Y.-K. (1995), 'Revolving Doors and the Optimal Tolerance for Agency Collusion', RAND Journal of Economics, 26(3): 378-97.

Christensen, J. G. (2010), 'Public interest regulation reconsidered: From capture to credible commitment', Paper presented to the 'Regulation at the Age of Crisis' ECPR Regulatory Governance Standing Group, 3ʳᵈ Biennial Conference, University College, Dublin, June 17-19, 2010, available at http://regulation.upf.edu/dublin-10-papers/1J1.pdf.

Chwieroth, J. M. (2009), Capital Ideas: The IMF and the Rise of Financial Liberalization, Princeton, NJ, Princeton University Press.

Claybrook, J. (2000), Statement of Joan Claybrook on Firestone Tire Defect and Ford Explorer Rollovers, United States Senate Committee on Commerce, Science and Transportation, Washington DC, September 12, at http://www.citizen.org/autosafety/article_redirect.cfm?ID=5414, accessed March 27, 2012.

Claybrook, J. and D. Bollier (1985), 'The Hidden Benefits of Regulation: Disclosing the Auto Safety Payoff', Yale Journal on Regulation, 3 Fall: 87-131.

Croley S.P. (2008), Regulation and Public Interests: The Possibility of Good Regulatory Government, Princeton, Princeton University Press, pp. 143-44.

Culpepper, P. (2011), Quiet Politics and Business Power: Corporate Control in Europe and Japan. Cambridge, Cambridge University Press.

Dal Bó, E. (2006), 'Regulatory Capture: A Review', Oxford Review of Economic Policy, 22(2): 203-225.

Davies, H. (2010), 'Comments on Ross Levine's paper 'The governance of financial regulation: reform lessons from the recent crisis'', BIS Working Paper 329.

Davison, I. H. (1987), A View from the Room. Lloyd's Change and Disclosure, London, Weidenfeld & Nicolson.

DeHaan, E., K. Koh, et al. (2011), Does the Revolving Door Affect the SEC's Enforcement Outcomes?, Unpublished manuscript.

Dorn, N. (2010), 'The Governance of Securities. Ponzi Finance, Regulatory Convergence, Credit Crunch', British Journal of Criminology, 50(1): 23-45.

Downs, A. (1957), An Economic Theory of Democracy, Cambridge, Cambridge University Press.

Duchin, R. and D. Sosyura (2010), 'TARP Investments: Financial and Politics', Ross School of Business Working Papers.

Dutta D. (2009), Elite Capture and Corruption: Concepts and Definition, National Council of Applied Economic Research, India, October .

Dyck, A., D. Moss, and L. Zingales (2008), 'Media versus Special Interests ' NBER Working Paper Series, No. 14360.

European Union (2010), 'Commission Decision of 20 July 2010 setting up a Financial Services User Group', Official Journal of the European Union C 199/12, 21.7.210, available at: http://eur-lex.europa.eu/LexUriServ/LexUriServ.do?uri=OJ:C:2010:199:0012:0014:EN:PDF, (Accessed March 18, 2012).

FCIC (2011), The Financial Crisis Inquiry Report: Final Report of the National Commission on the Causes of the Financial and Economic Crisis in the United States, Washington, DC, The Financial Crisis Inquiry Commission, January 2011.

FHFA Office of the Inspector General (2012), 'FHFA-OIG's Current Assessment of FHFA's Conservatorships of Fannie Mae and Freddie Mac', White Paper WPR-2012-001, US Federal Housing Finance Agency, March 28.

Frisell, L., K. Roszbach, et al. (2008), 'Governing the Governors: A Clinical Study of Central Banks', Sveriges Rikbank Working Paper Series, 221.

FSA (2009), Turner Review: A regulatory response to the global banking crisis, London, Financial Services Authority, March.

FSA (2011), The Failure of the Royal Bank of Scotland. Financial Services Authority Board Report, London, Financial Services Authority, December.

FSB (2010), Intensity and Effectiveness of SIFI Supervision. Recommendations for enhanced supervision, Financial Stability Board, November 2010, available at http://www.financialstabilityboard.org/publications/r_101101.pdf

FSB (2012), Meeting of the Financial Stability Board in Basel on 10 January. Press Release, Financial Stability Board, 10 January 2012, available at: http://www.financialstabilityboard.org/press/pr_100112.pdf

Financial Services Practitioner Panel (2003), Annual Report, available at http://www.fs-pp.org.uk/.

Fullenkamp, C. and S. Sharma (2012), 'Good Financial Regulation: Changing the Process is Crucial.' ICFR-Financial Times Research Prize.

GAO (2011a), Federal Reserve Bank Governance. Opportunities Exist to Broaden Director Recruitment Efforts and Increase Transparency, United States Government Accountability Office, October.

GAO (2011b), Securities and Exchange Commission. Existing Post-Employment Controls Could be Further Strengthened, United States Government Accountability Office. Report to Congressional Committees, July.

Geithner T. (2011), Remarks to the International Monetary Conference, 6 June.

Grabosky, P. and J. Braithwaite (1986), Of Manners Gentle: Enforcement Strategies of Australian Business Regulatory Agencies, Melbourne, Oxford University Press.

Greenspan A (2002), Remarks on International Financial Risk Management, Council on Foreign Relations, Washington, D.C., 19 November, available at: http://www.federalreserve.gov/boarddocs/speeches/2002/20021119/default.htm.

Grocer, S. (2010), 'Want to Fix SEC's Revolving Door? Give the Agency More Money', Wall Street Journal, 16 June.

Hall, R. and A. Deardorff (2006), 'Lobbying as Legislative Subsidy.' American Political Science Review, 100(1): 69-84.

Hampton Report (2005), Reducing administrative burdens: effective inspection and enforcement, HM Treasury, March.

Hardy, D. C. (2006), 'Regulatory Capture in Banking', IMF Working Paper WP/06/34, January.

Helleiner, E. (2010), 'What Role for the New Financial Stability Board? The Politics of International Standards After the Crisis', Global Policy October 2010.

Helleiner, E. and S. Pagliari (2011), 'The End of an Era in International Financial Regulation? A Post-Crisis Research Agenda', International Organization, Vol. 65, No.1, pp. 169-200.

Helleiner, E. and T. Porter (2010), 'Making Transnational Networks More Accountable', Economics, Management and Financial Markets 52.

HM Treasury (2010), A new approach to financial regulation: judgement, focus and stability, July.

HM Treasury (2012), Review of HM Treasury's management response to the financial crisis, March.

Hutter B (2005), 'The Attractions of Risk-based Regulation: accounting for the emergence of risk ideas in regulation', Centre for Analysis of Risk and Regulation Discussion Paper 33, March.

ICSA (2006), ICSA publishes principles and best practices for market infrastructure governance, better regulations and self-regulatory organizations, International Council of Securities Associations, 9 November.

IEA (2009), Transport, Energy and CO_2: Moving Toward Sustainability, International Energy Agency, Paris, IEA/OECD.

IEO (2011), IMF Performance in the Run-Up to the Financial and Economic Crisis: IMF Surveillance in 2004–07, Independent Evaluation Office of the International Monetary Fund.

Igan, D., P. Mishra, et al. (2009), A Fistful of Dollars: Lobbying and the Financial Crisis, Washington, DC, IMF.

IIF (2010), Interim Report on the Cumulative Impact on the Global Economy of Proposed Changes in the Banking Regulatory Framework, Institute of International Finance, June.

IIF (2011), Achieving Effective Supervision: An Industry Perspective, Institute of International Finance, July.

IMF (2002), Transcript of an Economic Forum: Governing the IMF, International Monetary Fund, 17 September.

ISDA (2010), US Companies May Face US $1 Trillion in Additional Capital and Liquidity Requirements As a Result of Financial Regulatory Reform, According to ISDA Research, International Swaps and Derivatives Associations, 29 June.

Kagan, R. A. (2003), Adversarial Legalism: The American Way of Law, Cambridge, Harvard University Press.

Johnson, S. (2009), 'The Quiet Coup', The Atlantic, May.

Johnson, S. and J. Kwak (2010), 13 Bankers: The Wall Street Takeover and the Next Financial Meltdown, New York, Pantheon Books.

Johnson, S. (2011), 'Deceptive Lobbying on Derivatives', Economix Blog, The New York Times, 17 February .

Kane, E. J. (2010), 'The Importance of Monitoring and Mitigating the Safety-Net Consequences of Regulation Induced Innovation', Review of Social Economy, 58.

Kauffman D. (2009), 'Corruption and the Global Financial Crisis', Forbes, January 27.

Krawiec, K. (2011), 'Don't "Screw Joe The Plummer": The Sausage-Making of Financial Reform', Working Paper, 09/2011, available at: http://scholarship.law.duke.edu/faculty_scholarship/2445/.

Kroszner, R. S. and P. E. Strahan (2000), 'Obstacles to optimal policy: the interplay of politics and economics in shaping bank supervision and regulation reforms', Center for Research in Security Prices Working Paper, 512, February.

Kwak, J. (forthcoming), 'Cultural Capture and the Financial Crisis', Draft Chapter in D. Carpenter and D. Moss, eds (forthcoming), Preventing Regulatory Capture: Special Interest Influence, and How to Limit It. Cambridge, Cambridge University Press.

Kwak, J. (2012), 'Americans Like Regulation', The Baseline Scenario, 13March, available online at http://baselinescenario.com/2012/03/13/americans-like-regulation/.

Laffont J. and D. Martimort (1999), 'Separation of Regulators Against Collusive Behavior', RAND Journal of Economics, 30(2), pp. 233, 257.

Laffont, J. J. and J. Tirole (1991), 'The politics of government decision making. A theory of regulatory capture', Quarterly Journal of Economics, (106): 4.

Lall, R. (2011), 'From failure to failure: The politics of international banking regulation', Review of International Political Economy.

Leonard, D. (2011), 'Dick Parsons, Captain Emergency', Bloomberg Businessweek, 24 March, available online at http://www.businessweek.com/magazine/content/11_14/b4222084044889.htm.

Levine, R. (2010), 'The Governance of Financial Regulation: Reform Lessons from the Recent Crisis', BIS Working Paper 329.

Lin, C. (2010), 'SEC's 'revolving door' under scrutiny', MarketWatch, 16 June.

Magill, E. M. (2012), 'Courts and Regulatory Capture', Draft Chapter in Carpenter, D. and D. Moss, eds (forthcoming), Preventing Regulatory Capture: Special Interest Influence, and How to Limit It, Cambridge, Cambridge University Press.

Masciandaro, D., M. Quintyn, et al. (2008), Financial Supervisory Independence and Accountability – Exploring the Determinants, Washington, DC, International Monetary Fund.

Maskell, J. (2010), Post-Employment, 'Revolving Door', Laws for Federal Personnel, Congressional Research Service, 12 May.

Masters, B. (2011), 'King calls for discretionary powers', Financial Times, London, 3 November.

Masters, B. (2012), 'Enter the revolving regulators', Financial Times, London, 23 April.

Mattli, W. and N. Woods (2009), 'In Whose Benefit? Explaining Regulatory Change in Global Politics' in W. Mattli and N. Woods eds., The Politics of Global Regulation,. Princeton, NJ, Princeton University Press.

Mayo, M. (2012), Exile on Wall Street: One Analysts Fight to Save the Big Banks From Themselves, Hoboken, N.J. Wiley.

McCarthy, C. (2006), Is the present business model bust?, Speech at the Gleneagles Saving and Pension Industry Leaders' Summit, Gleneagles, 16 September.

McCarty, N. (2012), 'Complexity, Capacity and Capture', Draft chapter in Carpenter, D. and D. Moss, eds (forthcoming), Preventing Regulatory Capture: Special Interest Influence, and How to Limit It, Cambridge, Cambridge University Press.

McCubbins M.D., Noll R.G. and Weingast B.R. (1987), 'Administrative Procedures as Instruments of Political Control', Journal of Law, Economics, & Organization, 3(2), p. 247.

Mikler, J. (2009), Greening the Car Industry: Varieties of Capitalism and Climate Change, Cheltenham, UK; Northampton, MA, Edward Elgar.

Mikler, J. (2007), 'Varieties of Capitalism and the Auto Industry's Environmental Initiatives: National Institutional Explanations for Firms' Motivations', Business and Politics, 9(1): Article 4.

Moe T. M. (1995), 'The Politics of Structural Choice: Toward a Theory of Public Bureaucracy', in O. Williamson, ed., Organization Theory: From Chester Barnard to the Present and Beyond, expanded edition, New York, Oxford University Press.

Momani, B. (2005), 'Recruiting and Diversifying IMF Technocrats', Global Society, 19(2): 167-187.

Moss D and Oey M. (2010), 'The Paranoid Style in the Study of American Politics', in Balleisen E. and Moss D. eds, Government and Markets: Toward a New Theory of Regulation, Cambridge, Cambridge University Press.

Mügge, D. (2010), Widen the Market, Narrow the Competition, Colchester, ECPR Press.

Nader, R. (1965), Unsafe at any Speed: The Designed-In Dangers of the American Automobile, New York, Grossman.

North, D.C. (1994), 'Economic Performance through Time', American Economic Review, 84(3): 359-63.

Nugent J D. (2009), Safeguarding Federalism: How States Protect their Interests in National Policymaking, Norman, OK, University of Oklahoma Press.

Nyberg P (2011), 'Misjudging Risks: the Causes of the Systemic Banking Crisis in Ireland', Department of Finance, Ireland, 19 April.

O'Driscoll, Jr G.P. (2010), 'The Gulf Spill, the Financial Crisis and Government Failure', Wall Street Journal, June 12.

Olson, M. (1965), The Logic of Collective Action: Public Goods and the Theory of Groups, Harvard University Press.

Omarova, S. T. (2012), 'Bankers, Bureaucrats, and Guardians: Toward Tripartism in Financial Services Regulation', Journal of Corporation Law, 37(3).

Onoda, T. (2008), Review of International Policies for Vehicle Fuel Efficiency, IEA Information Paper in Support of G8 Plan of Action. Paris, IEA.

Paletta D. (2010), 'Late Change Sparks Outcry Over Finance-Overhaul Bill', Wall Street Journal, 1 July.

Pagliari, S. and K. Young (2012), 'Leveraged Interests: Financial Industry Power and the Role of Private Sector Coalitions', Currently Under Review, Draft available from www.stefanopagliari.net.

Peltzman, S. (1976), 'Towards a More General Theory of Regulation', Journal of Law and Economics, 19: 211-48.

Philippon, T. and A. Reshef (2008), 'Wages and Human Capital in the U.S. Financial Industry: 1909-2006', NBER Working Paper, No. 13405.

POGO (2011), Revolving Regulators: SEC Faces Ethics Challenges with Revolving Door, Project on Government Oversight, 13 May.

Porter, T. (2005), Globalization and Finance, Cambridge, MA, Polity.

Porter, T. (2011), 'Transnational Policy Paradigm Change and Conflict in the Harmonization of Vehicle Safety and Accounting Standards', in Grace Skogstad, ed., Internationalization and Policy Paradigm Change, Toronto, University of Toronto Press, 64-90.

Porter, T. (2012), 'The Automobile and Climate Change: The Embeddedness of Private Regulation', in Karsten Ronit, ed., Private Voluntary Programs in Global Climate Policy: Pitfalls and Potentials, Tokyo, UNU Press, 179-281.

Pozsar, Z., T. Adrian, A. Ashscraft, and H.Boesky (2012), 'Shadow Banking', Staff Reports No. 458, Federal Reserve Bank of New York, February.

Raphael, A. (1995), Ultimate Risk: the inside story of the Lloyd's catastrophe, New York, Four Walls & Eight Windows.

Sabel, C. F. and J. Zeitlin (2010), Experimentalist Governance in the European Union: Towards a New Architecture, Oxford, Oxford University Press.

Scholte, J. A. and A. Schnabel, Eds. (2002), Civil society and global finance. London, Routledge.

Schwarcz, D. (forthcoming), 'Preventing Capture Through Consumer Empowerment Programs: Some Evidence from Insurance Regulation', Draft Chapter in D. Carpenter and D. Moss, eds (forthcoming), Preventing Regulatory Capture: Special Interest Influence, and How to Limit It, Cambridge, Cambridge University Press.

Seabrooke, L. and E. Tsingou (2009), 'Revolving Doors and Linked Ecologies in the World Economy: Policy Locations and the Practice of International Financial Reform', CSGR Working Paper 260/09.

Securities and Exchange Commission (2011), Study on Investment Advisers and Broker-Dealers, available at: http://www.sec.gov/news/studies/2011/913 studyfinal.pdf

Securities and Exchange Commission (2011), Implementation of the Whistleblower Provisions of Section 21F of the Securities Exchange Act of 1934, Final Rule, available at http://www.sec.gov/rules/final/2011/34-64545.pdf, accessed March 28, 2012.

Sheng, A. (2009), 'The Command of Financial Regulation', in Mayes D., Taylor M and Pringle R. eds, Central Banking: New Frontiers in Regulation and Official Oversight of the Financial System, London, Central Banking Publications.

Spiller, P. T. (1990), 'Politicians, Interest Groups, and Regulators: A Multiple-Principals Agency Theory of Regulation, or "Let Them be Bribed"', Journal of Law & Economics, 33(1): 65-101.

Stigler, G. (1971), 'The Theory of Economic Regulation', Bell Journal of Economics and Management Science, 2: 3-21.

Sustainable Mobility Project (2004), Mobility 2030: Meeting the Challenges to Sustainability, Geneva, World Business Council for Sustainable Development.

Tsingou, E. (2008), 'Transnational private governance and the Basel process: banking regulation, private interests and Basel II', in Nolke A and Graz J.C. eds, Transnational Private Governance and its Limits, London, Routledge.

Trumbull G. (Forthcoming), Strength in Numbers: The Political Power of Weak Interests, Cambridge, Harvard University Press.

Turner, A. (2009), 'Roundtable: How to tame global finance', Prospect (162 - August 27).

Underhill, G. and X. Zhang (2008), 'Setting the rules: private power, political underpinnings, and legitimacy in global monetary and financial governance', International Affairs, 84(3): 535-554.

Valencia, F. and K. Ueda (2012), Central Bank Independence and Macro-prudential Regulation, International Monetary Fund, April.

Vibert F. (2010), 'When experts fail', Central Banking, 20(3), February.

Viñals, J. and J. Fiechter (2010), 'The Making of Good Supervision: Learning to Say "No" ', IMF Staff Position Note, SPN/10/08.

Walter, A. (2006), 'From Developmental to Regulatory State? Japan's New Financial Regulatory System', The Pacific Review, 19(4), pp. 405-28.

Walter, A. (2008), Governing Finance: East Asia's Adoption of International Standards, Ithaca, Cornell University Press.

Warwick Commission on International Financial Reform (2009), In Praise of Unlevel Playing Fields, The Report of the Second Warwick Commission, Coventry, University of Warwick, December 2009.

Wheatley M. (2012), 'My vision for the FCA', Speech at the British Bankers' Association, 25 January.

White House (2011), President Obama Announces Historic 54.5 mpg Fuel Efficiency Standard, Office of the Press Secretary, July 29, available at: http://www.whitehouse.gov/the-press-office/2011/07/29/president-obama-announces-historic-545-mpg-fuel-efficiency-standard, accessed on March 27, 2012.

Wilson, J. (1980), The Politics of Regulation, New York, Basic Books.

Woodward, S. E. (2001), 'Regulatory Capture at the U.S. Securities and Exchange Commission', in Barth J. R., Brumbaugh D. and G. Yago eds., Restructuring Regulation and Financial Institutions, Milken Institute Press.

WHO (2004), World Report on Road Traffic Injury Prevention, Geneva, World Health Organization.

Yackee, J. & Yackee, S. (2006), 'A Bias Toward Business? Group Influence on the U.S. Bureaucracy', Journal of Politics, 68(1): 128-139.

Yackee, S. (2012), 'Reconsidering Agency Capture During Regulatory Policymaking', Draft Chapter in Carpenter D. and Moss D. eds (forthcoming), Preventing Regulatory Capture: Special Interest Influence, and How to Limit It, Cambridge, Cambridge University Press.

Young, K. (2012), 'Transnational regulatory capture? An empirical examination of the transnational lobbying of the Basel Committee on Banking Supervision', Review of International Political Economy.

Lightning Source UK Ltd.
Milton Keynes UK
UKOW041716161012

200689UK00001B/161/P